The Chromosomes of the Algae

Edited by

MAUD B. E. GODWARD

M.Sc., Ph.D.

Professor, Department of Botany
Queen Mary College, University of London

LONDON

EDWARD ARNOLD (Publishers) LTD.

First published in 1966

To

KATHLEEN DREW BAKER

Printed in Great Britain by
William Clowes and Sons, Limited, London and Beccles

CONTRIBUTORS

MAUD B. E. GODWARD, M.Sc., Ph.D., Professor, Department of Botany, Queen Mary College, University of London

SIMONE PUISEUX-DAO, Maître de Conférences, Laboratoire de Biologie Cellulaire Végétale, Université de Paris

GORDON F. LEEDALE, B.Sc., Ph.D., Lecturer, Department of Botany, University of Leeds

JOHN D. DODGE, B.Sc., Ph.D., Lecturer, Department of Botany, Birkbeck College, University of London

MARGARET ROBERTS, B.Sc., Ph.D., Lately Lecturer, Department of Botany, University of Hull

LEONARD V. EVANS, M.Sc., Ph.D., Department of Botany, University of Leeds

PETER S. DIXON, M.Sc., Ph.D., Senior Lecturer, Department of Botany, University of Liverpool

Preface

There are many standard textbooks which provide the main facts about nuclear cytology in higher plants and animals, but hitherto there has been no similar book relating to the algae. The present volume provides at least some of the knowledge of algal cytology which has been accumulated over the last ten or 15 years, in addition, it is hoped, to the most important data which was available earlier. It includes hitherto unpublished work and photographs, reference lists and lists of chromosome numbers, together with such information on culture and cytological methods as may encourage others in further study. The chromosomes of algae are, in the present state of our knowledge, of more interest than those of the well studied higher plants. Unfamiliar chromosome structure and behaviour may be found, for example, in the Conjugales, Dinophyceae and Englenophyceae. More familiar chromosome structures are found in the Oedogoniales, and apparently, in those members of Phaeophyceae and Rhodophyceae which have been studied so far. Xanthophyceae, Chrysophyceae, Bacillariophyceae, Vacuolaria and its relatives, among others, are in need of further investigation. Inspiration will be found in those classic works, 'Der Formwechsel der Protistenkunde' by Karl Belar, and the Handbuch der Protophytenkunde by Bruno Schussnig.

The pioneer work of myself and colleagues (G. F. Leedale, J. D. Dodge, B. N. Prasad, J. Nizam, D. Rayns, M. Thakur to mention some names) on the cytological effects of radiation on algae, has opened up a field which will I am sure prove rewarding (see M. B. E. Godward, 'Invisible Radiation' in *The Physiology and Biochemistry of Algae*, ed. R. Lewin (1962), London and New York: Academic Press); previous work being mainly concerned with survival data or genetic mutation, takes no account of the effects on chromosomes. A section on the effects of radiation mainly on Chlorophyceae is included.

Work on electron microscopy of chromosomes (see especially J. D. Dodge) and of nucleoli and nucleolar-organising chromosomes (M. B. E. Godward, P. E. Brandham, R. E. Newnham, E. J. Jordan) has shown how much can be seen in the algae—for example, the spiral arrangement of fine fibrils in the chromosomes of Dinophyceae, and the relationship between nucleolus and chromosome and the re-distribution of nucleolar substance at mitosis, in the Conjugales—which may well help the general interpretation of chromosome and nucleolus in other organisms.

The colleagues who have written the chapters on the algal groups other than Chlorophyceae, have, I know, each made a distinctive contribution in their field and I have not attempted any modification of their personal views, with which I do not necessarily agree.

It is hoped that the detailed instructions on practical methods which they have provided will help teachers and students, both at the University and at the more advanced levels in schools, to grow the algae and look at their cell-division. At the same time it is hoped that there are enough challenging data, with references, to stimulate and assist research workers.

The latter are further referred to the books or reviews in the German or French languages of Lothar Geitler, Elisabeth Tschermak and Francis Magne.

Queen Mary College, London
1966

M. B. E. GODWARD

Editorial Introduction

The Myxophyceae have been omitted as clearly unrelated to other algae and similar to bacteria. The Xanthophyceae, Chrysophyceae and Bacillariophyceae have also been omitted for lack of sufficient chromosome counts although there are some (Abbas 1963, Rayns 1962, Geitler (in Schussnig) 1953).

It would seem that the relatively non-committal classification of Fritsch fits the basic divergences in algal nuclear organisation better than systems which imply relationships between groups on the basis of their pigmentation and other features of metabolism often not completely investigated. Ultrastructural morphology is also increasingly relevant. There is not, among the algae, that uniformity of nuclear organisation which would justify a term such as Eucaryota, as clearly shown by Dodge; whether the institution of another term for some of the non-conforming 'Eucaryota' will be helpful, when there is so much variety and so much is unknown, cannot be foreseen.

Discontinuous staining of chromosomes at prophase is common in the algae, and is not always related to Feulgen positive and negative regions in the way that would fit in with use of the terms 'euchromatin' and 'heterochromatin'. In *Euglena* there is a rare but apparently definite form of meiosis, with a long pachytene-like prophase. Although no chiasmata have been seen, some kind of recombination might be possible. In my view the so-called endosome of Euglenoids is obviously a nucleolus and its organising chromosome probably contained within it.

There is a need for genetic studies in the algae where progress has been made only with the sexually reproducing *Chlamydomonas*, in which the chromosomes have been mapped and linkage of non-chromosomal genes demonstrated by Sager. This would seem particularly desirable in such algae as *Acetabularia* where there is a highly peculiar vegetative nucleus and elusive meiosis; *Chlorella* and other asexually reproducing algae where there must be a genetic structure susceptible at least of mutation, although it is generally assumed that *Chlorella* cultures, however long maintained, are uniform.

The lists of chromosome numbers show that it should be possible to come within sight of a chromosome Atlas for Algae. Although there is less rigid polyploidy than in the higher plants, irregular high chromosome numbers suggest a high degree of chromosomal duplication. The relationships of chromosome numbers to taxonomy seem to be not very different from those of higher plants.

Contents

1 The Chlorophyceae

MAUD B. E. GODWARD
M.Sc., Ph.D.,
Professor, Department of Botany, Queen Mary College,
University of London

Simone Puiseux-Dao [Siphonales]
Laboratoire de Biologie Cellulaire Végétale, Paris

CULTURE METHODS

Standard works on algal culture generally include a large number of methods for the culture of green algae (Pringsheim 1946, 1951; Burlew 1953; Myers 1946, 1953, 1962; Rodhe 1948; Goltermann 1960) among which are the defined media and continuous culture methods used by Myers (1946) and Tamiya (1957) for *Chlorella*. While material of green algae collected in the wild often shows mitosis (*Spirogyra*) or even meiosis, as is the case with marine *Cladophora* (Sinha 1958; J. Patel 1961, and Fig. 1.7) and *Ulva* (Sarma 1958), culture is necessary in order to see enough stages for a proper interpretation of nuclear division or enough polar views of metaphase for a chromosome count. Most fresh-water green algae will grow when merely collected and placed in a dish with some of the water of the habitat. They will grow better if a few mineral salts are added to the water. Quite often, however, they will not continue to grow in a solution of mineral salts unless soil extract, peat extract or leaf extract is added. This is an old problem, despite the efforts of the water analysts at the Freshwater Biological Station, Lake Windermere, and devisers of defined media (Provasoli 1957–64; Droop 1957–59) as yet not solved for more than a few species. For these (e.g. *Chlorella pyrenoidosa*) addition of trace elements and vitamins, sometimes chelating agents, seem adequate. Addition of amino acids and DNA precursors frequently increase the growth rate. While a rapid growth rate is desirable for cytological investigation, synchronisation of mitosis is necessary in order to provide the highest possible percentages of mitotic stages. Such synchronisation is most easily provided by the use of an artificial light photoperiod, e.g. of 18 hr., and a dark period, e.g. of 6 hr., in a controlled culture chamber, the dark period being conveniently located during the normal day. Under these conditions mitosis occurs mainly in the dark period. Experimental manipulation of the length of the photoperiod can produce restriction of mitosis to the dark period (James & Cook 1960; Tamiya 1963; Nizam 1960; Leedale 1957; Newnham 1962; Brandham 1964; Abbas 1963; Adams & Godward in press) and raise the percentage of cells in mitosis from less than 1% to 14% or more. Green algae (and probably most algae) will grow rapidly in continuous light, but without synchronisation of mitosis few stages will be found however rapid the growth rate. Quite possibly synchronisation by temperature control in continuous light with bubbled air enriched with 4% CO_2 and in continuous culture with constantly renewed medium would give the most rapid growth and highest mitotic index during the peak period, but to the writer's knowledge this has not been tried out to any significant extent.

While much time has already been expended by various workers on the effort to evolve optimum media for different algae (Hutner 1950, 1951; Provasoli 1958–64) success has been limited and the task is a never-ending one (see, however, Nizam 1960; Patel 1961; Abbas 1963). When all has been done to facilitate the growth of algae in culture and they are in fact rapidly growing, it is still not certain that they have remained cytologically or genetically like the wild species originally collected. Chromosome races evolve fairly rapidly in cultures of green algae (*Desmids*, King 1954; Brandham 1964; *Tribonema*, Abbas 1963) by mitotic irregularities, giving polyploids and aneuploids. It seems very probable that where, as frequently happens, a culture suddenly begins to grow rapidly in an artificial medium, genetically mutant cells have been selected and the rest lost. Personally I fear that 'type cultures' are subject to continual change, and probably after being maintained for many years they may show many differences from the original organisms. A few simple calculations, based on the known spontaneous mutation rates of organisms such as bacteria, will show the probable present state of an algal unicell culture, subcultured once a month and maintained for 30 years. If there were 10,000 cells per cubic centimetre, and the mutation rate were 0·01%, this centimetre would contain one mutant: 25 cm. of culture would contain 25 mutants, none of which need be lost when 25 subcultures are made. Preferential survival of only one of these mutants could, at a conservative estimate, certainly lead to the production of a new strain every year. When we add to this the higher proportion of variants, mainly cytological, normally arising in one culture (certainly 0·1% if not 0·5%), the 'normality' of the culture after some years appears unlikely (cf. for example, Bendix 1964). However, it is possible that certain algae might remain 'normal' if all genetic mutants or cytological variants were at a selective disadvantage. We do not know enough about this.

CYTOLOGICAL METHODS

The iron alum acetocarmine method (Godward 1948) is a very successful one with most green algae, although its best use needs a little practice and care. The method has been modified since its first publication to suit individual species (Sarma 1958; Sinha 1958; Patel 1961; Nizam 1960; King 1954; Brandham 1964; Dodge 1960; Leedale 1957; Thakur 1965). Modifications are frequently concerned mainly with prior fixation, whether in 3 parts 95% alcohol: 1 part glacial acetic acid, or in 2:1, or 1:1, or with prior fixation by osmic acid vapour or nitric acid vapour; or in 2% osmic acid solution, or in Bellings Navashin plus osmic acid solution; or in ethyl alcohol or methyl alcohol alone, or in iodine water, or bromine water, or chromic acid solution, or some other fixing solution. All the above methods I have found satisfactory for different green algae. Osmic acid alone is the most difficult to follow up unless fixation has been brief and the osmium can be washed out before appearing as a black deposit. Fixations including $HgCl_2$ or formalin I have found to be a nuisance in one way or another. A mixture of 95% alcohol and concentrated nitric acid can produce good fixation but is unfortunately explosive due to the production of fulminates—a warning to anyone who might feel inclined to experiment, since the mixture of concentrated HCl and 95% alcohol appears to be safe.

Whatever the fixation, it can be followed by mordanting in aqueous iron alum and the concentration best suited to the species can be found only by experiment. It is not worth while trying to be accurate since if an excess has been used it is easily removed with 45% acetic acid. Trial and error within the range: (i) saturated solution; (ii) diluted 1:1; (iii) diluted 1:10; (iv) 1:100; (v) 1:1,000 approximately, are good enough to start with. The time involved should be as short as possible, say 30 sec. or less in the solution. Subsequent repeated washing out is essential to get a clean preparation. Supersaturated carmine solution in 45% acetic acid is added and the preparation boiled to dissolve up the starch. If this proves damaging, the starch will have to be left undissolved but this is seldom necessary. If overstained, 45% acetic acid solution will destain. When filamentous forms are being fixed and stained, handle them with stainless steel forceps and pass them through the solutions in dishes. When epiphytes or sporelings settled on slides are used, again handle the slides with stainless steel forceps and pass through Coplin jars or china staining dishes. When unicellular cultures are used, everything must be done in the centrifuge tube, using just enough revolutions to bring down the cells, and the supernatants continually poured off. Even the mordanting, washing, boiling in carmine, passing through 3:1, 95% and absolute are done in this way and the final residue pipetted up from the bottom of the tube on to the slide with its drop of Euparal. Feulgen staining is carried out similarly. These are the only two stains really worth bothering about, although chromium or aluminium alum can be used instead of iron but are less effective; acetic orcein unmordanted gives a clear transparent, although faint, stain often useful with a dense nucleus; other dyes such as haemotoxylin in acetic acid stain but are not permanent. The iron alum aceto-carmine stain is permanent and unchanged after 18 years in Euparal. The iron mordant can of course also be introduced as ferric acetate. In this method, a supersaturated solution of ferric acetate in 45% acetic acid is made using a reflux condenser. A few drops of this are added to the 3:1 fixing fluid. Excess staining does not occur when the carmine is added, there is no need for washing in water; the material goes from 3:1 to carmine and then to 3:1 again, followed by 95% Euparal essence and Euparal. The method is that of Thomas (1940). It appears possible that glutaraldehyde fixation, carefully applied, may have some advantages for ordinary staining as well as for electron microscopy.

The methyl-green pyronin staining test can readily be carried out, using the B.D.H. dye mixture, dissolving a pin-head amount in a few ml. of water and *immediately* mounting the acetic-fixed material in it. A perfect result will not be obtained in all the cells but some will give the required differentiation.

Fixation times, washing times and staining times should always be kept as short as possible. Routine following up of old lengthy methods adopted for the multicellular tissues of higher plants or animals are quite unnecessary and usually damaging. Just how short the times can be for individual species only trial and error can show. A unicell or filamentous alga with a thin wall needs only minutes for penetration, although the original fixation is often better in vacuo. Thick or complicated walls, such as those of *Cladophora* or *Euglena*, may require much longer. Delicate algae with the thinnest of bounding membranes may be tried in osmic acid vapour followed by ethanol. The walls of *Cladophora* may need pretreatment, e.g. with nitric acid vapour. The standard method for keeping fixed material is in 70% alcohol at −15°C (deep freeze). No method is very satisfactory: I have used the esterified 3:1, or 95% alcohol, successfully with some material.

THE CYTOLOGY OF THE CHLOROPHYCEAE

There are two main points which stand out clearly as a result of the recent investigations by the author and co-workers, A. Abbas 1963; M. A. Allen 1958; P. E. Brandham 1964; G. C. King 1954; R. E. Newnham 1962; J. Nizam 1960; J. Patel 1961; B. N. Prasad 1958; D. Rayns 1961; Y. R. S. K. Sarma 1958; M. Serajuddin unpub.; J. P. Sinha 1958; and of M. Cave & M. A. Pocock, R. Starr & Melvin Goldstein, Janet Stein & co-workers, L. Hoffman, E. Tschermak; and the classic work of L. Geitler.

1 Chromosome centromeric organisation is predominantly like that of the higher plants, most green algae having localised centromeres as do most

higher plants; the Conjugales having predominantly no localised centromere as in the families Cyperaceae and Juncaceae.

The more extreme differences of chromosome organisaton from the higher plant type, such as those found in Dinophyceae and Euglenineae, do not occur in the Chlorophyceae, so far as known.

2 Polyploidy as a basis of species formation as it is understood in higher plants, is rarer in the Chlorophyceae than aneuploidy. The search for a basic chromosome number is not profitable except in a few series such as Cladophorales. A glance down the lists of chromosome numbers will show that in most series polyploidy may well have occurred once or twice but aneuploidy has occurred far more frequently, diversifying both diploid and polyploid chromosome numbers by additions and subtractions, into an almost continuous range. In Conjugales, fusion of chromosomes is also a possibility.

THE EFFECTS OF RADIATION ON THE CHROMOSOMES

The general effects of radiation as known up to 1961 have been reviewed (Godward 1962), although the effects of radiation on chromosomes were only touched on. The first studies of radiation on the chromosomes of Conjugales were made by the author in 1954 (abstracts of papers read, Int. Biol. Cong. 1954, and Heredity 1954b) but not published in full. The photographs (Fig. 1.1) show the mitotic chromosomes of *Spirogyra crassa*, untreated, and following different doses of X-rays. There is tolerance of a high dose. The long chromosomes, which are without a localised centromere, fragment and the fragments survive, to give a new karyotype as in *Luzula* (La Cour 1953). With moderate breakage (2–10 Kr), these karyotypes would apparently survive indefinitely; after extensive breakage (10–15 Kr) (Fig. 1.1 C) or shattering (20 Kr) (Fig. 1.1 D) although mitosis occurs and all or nearly all fragments separate at anaphase and are included in the daughter-nuclei, it is not certain that an equitable partition of the fragments often occurs. Indeed it is certain that the fragments are not equally distributed to the daughter-nuclei in some cases and it would seem that mitosis does not long continue under these circumstances. The presence of the nucleolar substance at metaphase, often it seems in bigger amounts after irradiation, seems partly responsible for carrying away unequal numbers of fragments to opposite poles.

Similar effects are seen in other species of *Spirogyra* (Godward & Bellamy unpublished) and in *Zygnema* and *Mougeotia* (B. N. Prasad & Godward unpublished), although in *Mougeotia* some chromosomes do seem to produce large fragments which get left behind at mitosis. This may point to some centromeric organisation in these chromosomes.

There is some indication although not, as yet, proof, that after long-term cultivation of new karyotypes with moderately damaged chromosomes, in Conjugales, there may be eventual repair and reconstruction of the original karyotype.

The cytological effects of radiation on *Oedogonium* (Howard & Horsley 1960) where the chromosomes are of the usual type with localised centromere, appear no different from those found in higher plants, i.e. breakage (at 500 Kr or less) with loss of acentric fragments at mitosis. *Chlorella pyrenoidosa* is

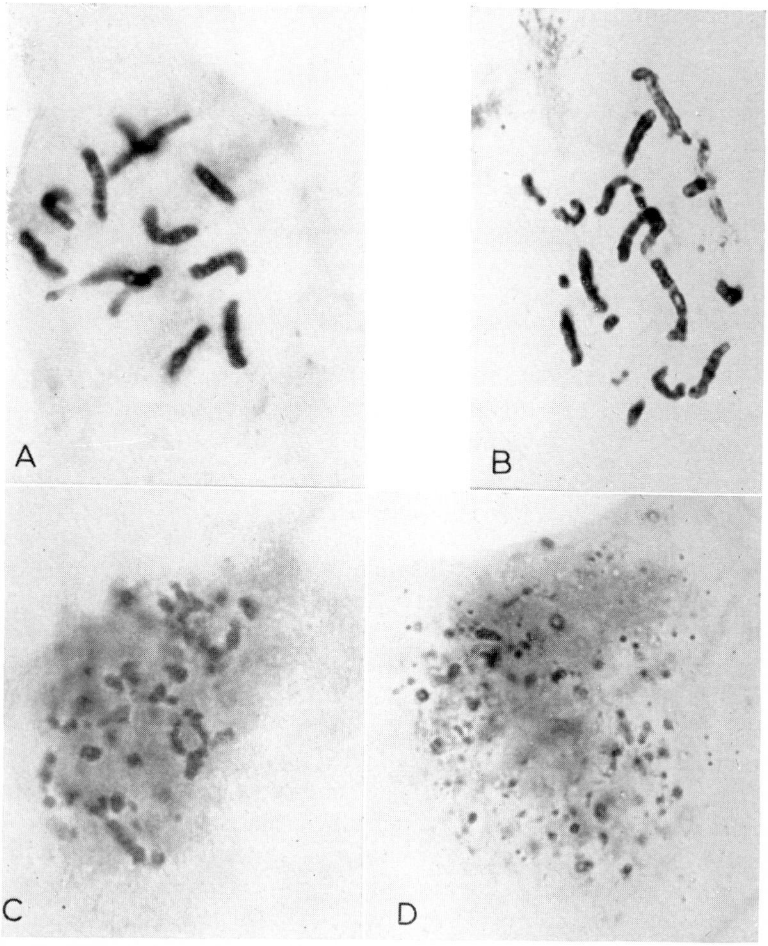

Fig. 1.1 *Spirogyra crassa.* Mitotic metaphases; **A** normal; **B**, **C**, and **D**, following irradiation: **B**, 6 Kr., **C**, 15 Kr., **D**, 20 Kr.

perhaps worthy of special mention. This species, to which a dose of 2 megarads was given (Nizam & Godward unpublished), although heavily damaged produced a small percentage of survivors which after three weeks grew at the original rate. They were bigger however. Chromosomes can just be discerned in this species and the implication of the bigger size of the surviving cells is that of polyploidy or at least polysomy. The fact that all cells are not killed off even after such a massive dose may be related to the extremely small size of the chromosomes and perhaps to a tendency on the part of the original material to become multinucleate (Fritsch 1948) which would make development of polyploids or polysomics easy.

Other green algae have been irradiated—*Cladophora* (Patel and Godward unpublished) has a low tolerance of chromosome damage; the chromosomes here are relatively large and have a normal centromere.

EFFECTS OF COLCHICINE AND GIBBERELLINS ON ALGAE

(The effects recorded are predominantly those on *Chlorophyceae*.)

COLCHICINE

Typical c-mitosis with cross-shaped arrangement of chromatids does not appear. Polyploids are however formed, predominantly in steps which are at first insufficient to give complete doubling. There is a high threshold for the effects of colchicine on green algae (Wetherell & Krauss 1956; Sarma 1958; Sinha 1958; Rayns 1961; Patel 1961) as compared with that in the higher plants (Levan 1938). Four hours in 0·005 to 0·001% colchicine is enough to produce c-mitosis in *Allium cepa*: but the algae are seldom affected by less than 0·5%.

Stigeoclonium, *Draparnaldia* and *Chaetophora* show different tolerances; diploid nuclei are produced in 1% colchicine after 48 hr. in *Stigeoclonium* and 2% colchicine after 96 hr. in *Draparnaldia*; not at all in *Chaetophora*. Saturated solution of colchicine killed *Stigeoclonium* in three days, *Draparnaldia* in five days and *Chaetophora* in two weeks (Abbas 1963). Resistance or immunity to colchicine has been reported for *Spirogyra* (Godward unpublished), *Colchicum* (Levan 1940), *Euglena* (King & Beams 1940; Levan & Sandwall 1943; Leedale unpublished). According to Abbas (1963), in *Stigeoclonium amoenum*, the chromosome number changes from 12 to 20 after 72 hr. in 0·5% colchicine, to 24 to 32 after 48 hr. in 1%, to 36 after 2 hr. in saturated solution. For *Draparnaldia plumosa* where the chromosome number is normally 14, after 24 hr. in a saturated solution the number 22 is found and after 72 hr. to 96 hr. in 2%, chromosome numbers 24, 27, 30, 36 and 50 were recorded. According to Sarma (1958), *Sphaeroplea*, *Hydrodictyon* and *Microspora* became diploid in 1% solution after a few hours, three days and a week respectively. Typical c-mitosis with a cross-shaped arrangement of chromatids was not seen. According to Wetherell & Krauss (1956), *Chlamydomonas reinhardii* becomes polyploid in 1% solution with inhibition of cell division and cell enlargement. Tschermak (1943) found *Oedogonium* to become diploid; Sinha (1958) found *Cladophora* to become diploid in 1% solution. There was little effect on the Desmid *Micrasterias* (Kallio 1951).

GIBBERELLINS

Enhanced cell division leading to increased cell numbers was found in *Porphyra* (Kinoshita & Termoto 1958) using 0·01 to 100 mg. per litre of G.A.; in *Ulothrix subtilissima* by 50 μg. per litre (Conard *et al.* 1959); in *Chlamydomonas moewusii* by 1 to 70 parts per million (Burdett & Turnbull 1960); in *Chlorella pyrenoidosa* by 1 to 20 parts per million (Kim & Greulach 1961). Inhibition of mitosis was produced in *Zygnema* at one part per million (Prasad 1958) in *U. subtilissima* by concentrations above 50 μg. per litre (Conard *et al.* 1959); in *Chlamydomonas moewusii* at 1 to 70 parts per million for nine days or more (Burdett & Turnbull 1960); in *Draparnaldia plumosa* at 20 to 50 parts per million (Abbas 1963).

Increased cell size is definitely associated with depression of mitosis in *D. plumosa* (Abbas 1963), probably associated with it in *Euglena* at 1,000 mg. per litre (Griffin 1958); *Ulva lactuca* at 100 μg. per litre (Provasoli 1958); *C. moewusii* after nine days in solution (Burdett & Turnbull 1960); *Oedogonium cardiacum* at 5 to 20 parts per million (Kim & Greulach 1961); in *Vaucheria sessilis* at 10 parts per million (Kim & Greulach 1961). The only cytological study is that of Abbas (1963) where the increase of chromosome number in *D. plumosa* from 14 to 22, 26 and 28, at 20 to 50 parts per million, with reversion on removal from gibberellic acid, has been observed.

Most of the facts in the above review were collected by Abbas (1963).

CYTOLOGY OF THE GREEN ALGAE

CHLAMYDOMONADALES

The chromosomes of *Chlamydomonas*, almost the only alga in which any significant genetic work has as yet been done, are not big enough for any details to be observable in the ordinary stained preparation, in which they appear as small dots. The genetic chromosome maps indicate that a centromere is present and eleven linkage groups have been described in *Ch. reinhardii* (Levine 1961–65), but more recently the number has apparently reached 15 (verbal communication). I do not have access to any recent published or unpublished account of meiosis although a number of workers have claimed to have found this. The account published by Moewus (1939) is not convincing from lack of photographic evidence, but in my view a final judgement on both the cytological and genetic work of Moewus should as yet be reserved.

Under intensive culture conditions, nuclear division is often not followed by cytoplasmic cleavage (Abbas 1963). Squash preparations may present overlap of two or more metaphase plates. This circumstance may have given rise to the accounts of polyploidy reported in the genus (Buffaloe 1958). Genetically, the organism is of great interest, showing chromosomal genes

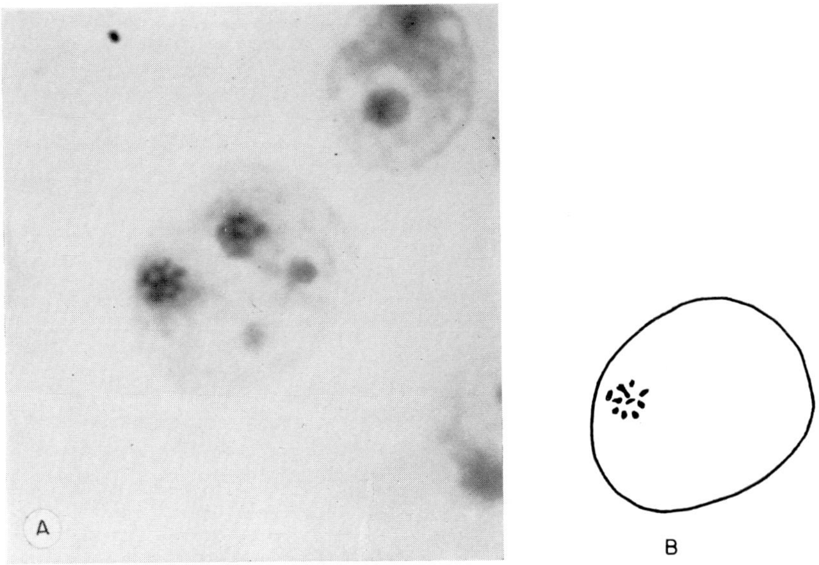

Fig. 1.2 *Chlamydomonas Reinhardii.* **A** Metaphase showing about 11 chromosomes (x 3,600). **B** Drawing of **A** showing 11 chromosomes. (Photograph by A. Abbas)

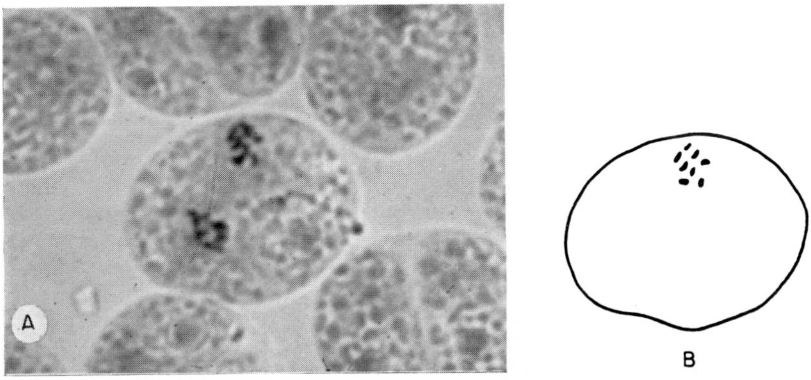

Fig. 1.3 *Chlamydomonas eugametos.* **A** Late prophase showing about eight chromosomes (x 3,600). **B** Drawing of **A**. (Photograph by A. Abbas)

affecting the same phenotype distributed over all or most of the chromosomes and non-chromosomal genes affecting this phenotype also: for example, streptomycin resistance, streptomycin sensitivity, streptomycin requirement (Sager 1962, 1963). Furthermore, it is the only organism in which evidence exists for linkage of non-chromosomal genes and recombination between them (Sager 1963).

Table 1.1 Chromosome numbers in the Chlamydomonadales

Alga	Chromosome number	Author
Chlamydomonas eugametos	10	Moewus: 10 linkage groups, 1936–48
	38 ± 4	Shaecter & De Lamater 1954, 1955
	16	Wetherall & Krauss 1957
	8	Buffaloe 1958
C. moewusii	36 ± 2	Shaecter & De Lamater
	16	Wetherell & Krauss
	8	Buffaloe
*C. reinhardii**	18 ± 2	Shaecter & De Lamater
	16	Wetherell & Krauss 1957
	8	Buffaloe
	8	Levine & Folsome 1959
	11 ± 1	Abbas 1964: 11 linkage groups, Levine 1965
C. dysosmos	16 ± 1	Shaecter & De Lamater
C. chlamydogama	8	Buffaloe
C. monadina	30	Dangeard 1899
C. variabilis	10	,, ,,
C. dilli	10	,, ,,
C. sp.	8	Belar 1926
C. nasuta	8	Kater 1929

* Fifteen linkage groups have now been reported.

VOLVOCALES

A careful study of chromosome morphology in *Eudorina* (Rayns 1961) shows that median or submedian centromeres are present, and that chromosome sizes, long, medium and short, are readily distinguished. Similar features appear in *Volvox* (Cave & Pocock 1951, 1956) and other genera. Low haploid chromosome numbers are found in *Volvox* together with higher numbers indicating approximately polyploid derivations. Polyploids have been produced by hybridisation between *Eudorina elegans* and *E. illinoisensis* (Goldstein 1964). Chromosome numbers generally show aneuploidy, a feature especially demonstrated in *Astrephomene gubernaculifera* (Cave & Pocock 1956) where variants with four, six, seven and eight chromosomes have been found. Table 1.2 shows the extent to which chromosome lengths are constant features of the genus or species. A curious feature is the changed

Table 1.2 Chromosome numbers in Volvocales (chromosome lengths are also included)

Species	Chromosome number (*n*)	Chromosome length Long	Medium	Short	Author
Gonium pectorale	17	4	9	4	Cave & Pocock 1951
G. sociale	10 ± 1				
Eudorina elegans	12	3	6	3	,, ,, ,,
	10				Hartmann 1921
	16	4	10	2	Rayns 1962
E. illinoisensis	14				Goldstein 1964
E. illinoisensis	10				Hovasse 1937
E. illinoisensis	12				Merton 1908
E. elegans x illinoisensis	24–28				Goldstein 1964
E. charkowiensis	17				Cave & Pocock 1951
E. unicocca	7	0	7	0	
Volvulina steinii	7	4	2	1	
Pandorina morum	10 ± 1				Dangeard 1900
Pleodorina californica	14	4	4	6	
Platydorina caudata	15 ± 1				
Clonal populations:					
Astrephomene gubernaculifera	4	1	?	?	Cave & Pocock 1956
A. gubernaculifera	6	1	?	?	
A. gubernaculifera	7	1	?	?	
A. gubernaculifera	8	1	?	?	
Volvox. Section Merillosphaera					
V. Powersii	15	3	5	7	Cave & Pocock 1956
V. Weismannia	14	1	8	5	,, ,, ,,
V. spermatosphaera	13	5	4	4	,, ,, ,,
Section Janetosphaera					
V. aureus	14	4	5	5	Rayns 1961
V. aureus	14	2	10	2	Cave & Pocock 1956
Section Euvolvox					
V. globator	5	11	1	3	Rayns 1961
V. globator	5	3	1	1	Cave & Pocock 1956
V. Barberi	5	3	1	1	,, ,, ,,
V. Rousseletii	5	3	1	1	,, ,, ,,
V. Merilli	5	2	2	1	,, ,, ,,

chromosome length in variants of the same species; two variants of *Volvox globator* both with five chromosomes but different proportions of short and long ones; similarly in *V. aureus*. Loss of part of a chromosome could account

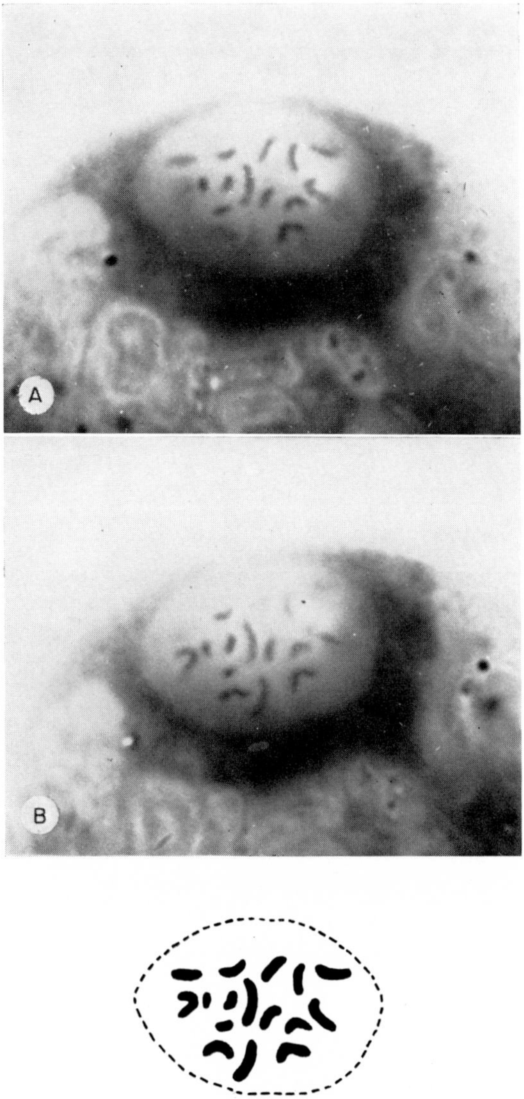

C

Fig. 1.4 *Eudorina elegans.* **A** and **B** Metaphase showing 16 chromosomes at two focal levels. **C** Drawing of **A** and **B**. (Photograph by D. Rayns) for the reduction in the number of long chromosomes and increase in the number of medium or short chromosomes, as in *V. globator*: the situation in *V. aureus* could also be explained in this way if in one variant some of the medium chromosomes were reduced to short ones, and in the other, some of the long ones reduced to medium length. Goldstein (1964) has shown that the species *E. elegans* and *E. illinoisensis* are both dioecious and heterothallic with $n = 14$. The hybrid forms have chromosome numbers between 24 and 28, and include male, female, and 'selfing male' (i.e. predominantly male

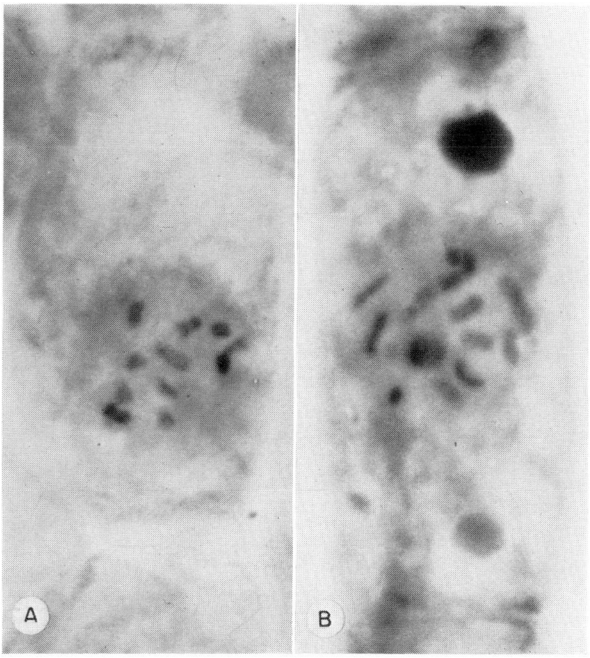

Fig. 1.5 *Draparnaldia plumosa.* Prophase showing 14 chromosomes. (Photograph by A. Abbas)

with occasional self-fertilised oogonia) strains. It appears likely that mating-type genes are among those duplicated in polysomics or polyploids, with various consequences to sexuality. Such polyploids and polysomics clearly arise with ease, and taxonomy must be a matter of convenience only. Rayns (1961) found 16 chromosomes (Fig. 1.4).

It has been shown (Rayns 1961; Cave & Pocock 1956) that the mitoses leading to colony production take 10 minutes. During these five successive mitoses reduction in metaphase chromosome size is as follows (Rayns 1961): 1·2 μ, 1·05 μ, 1·05 μ, 0·75 μ, 0·6 μ.

Table 1.3 Chromosome numbers in Ulotrichales

Alga	Chromosome number	Author
Ulothrix zonata	10	Sarma 1958
	4(?)	Schussnig 1953
U. subtillisima	14	Sarma 1958
U. rorida	5	Lind 1932
U. variabilis	7–8	Cholnoky 1932
Uronema terrestre	16	Sarma 1958
U. confervicolum	16	„ „
U. gigas	18	„ „
U. barlowi	18	„ „
Hormidium crenulatum	44–48	„ „
H. barlowi	22–24	„ „
Hormidium sp.	22	„ „
Cylindrocapsa involuta	16	„ „
Microspora amoena 'A'	32	„ „
	8–12	Neuenstein 1914
M. amoena 'B'	20	Sarma 1958
M. Loefgrenii	18	„ „
	14–16	Kostrun 1944
M. aequabilis	24	Sarma 1958
M. stagnorum	16	„ „
	8–10	Cholnoky 1932
M. tumidula	16	Sarma 1958
Sphaeroplea annulina var. *crassisepta*	16	„ „
S. annulina	16	„ „
	10	Palik 1950
Prasiola stipitata	(?2n) 12–14	Sarma 1958
P. japonica	$n = 3$	Fujiyama 1955
P. ?	$n = 7$ or 8	Friedemann 1959
Enteromorpha compressa 'A'	10 bivalents ($n-10$. $2n-20$ in *E. compressa* var. *lingulata* Ramanathan 1939)	Sarma 1958
E. compressa 'B'	9 bivalents	„ „
E. ramulosa	$n =$ c. 12	„ „
E. intermedia	$n =$ c. 16	„ „
Ulva lactuca	10 bivalents	
	10 ($=n$)	„ „
	$n = 13$, $2n = 26$	Foyn 1934
	& $n = 10$	Carter 1926
U. linza	(?2n) c. 24–25	Levan & Levring 1942

ULOTRICHALES

The chromosomes, seen at mitosis, are frequently of different sizes; although all are small (0·25–2 μ long), one or two larger ones are often present and at metaphase these are usually seen at the periphery of the plate. There is some indication in these of a median centromere. At meiosis, the longer bivalents have two or three chiasmata whereas the smaller ones have only one. The haploid chromosome number may be quite low. Of interest is the occurrence of $n = 10-16$ rather commonly in forms with a haploid life cycle such as *Ulothrix*, *Uronema*, *Microspora* and *Sphaeroplea*, and also in those with an alternation of haploid and diploid phases as *Ulva* and *Enteromorpha*. The chromosome numbers of some species are approximate tetraploids of these haploid numbers, but aneuploidy is clearly widespread and provides a range of recorded chromosome counts from 4 or 5 to 44–48. An interesting example is that of the two strains, A and B, of *Enteromorpha compressa* (Sarma 1958), as below:

Strain A	1 long chromosome pair,		3 chiasmata/bivalent		
	2 medium	,,	,,	2	,,
	7 short	,,	,,	1	,,
Strain B	1 long	,,	,,	2	,,
	2 medium	,,	,,	2	,,
	6 short	,,	,,	1	,,

CHAETOPHORALES

The chromosomes are quite similar in appearance and size to those of Ulotrichales, the haploid chromosome numbers being also similar; numbers about the 12–14 mark being common and the range from 8 to 42. Presumed aneuploidy gives many intermediate counts. Some of these may be for aneuploid asexual clones, as 477/3, 477/4 from the Cambridge Culture Collection, or indeed many of the named species where no sexual reproduction has ever been recorded. There is no reason why they should not have specific names. Meiosis has been observed only in *Coleochaete pulvinata* (Selby & Godward unpublished; Selby 1956); few details of interest are available since diakinesis was not observed. Only *Coleochaete* has relatively large chromosomes (up to 1.5 μ long), all being longer than broad, with probably more or less median centromeres.

A list of chromosome numbers, largely due to A. Abbas (Fig. 1.5A & B) (Abbas & Godward 1964; Abbas 1963).

It is possible to make a joint list of chromosome numbers for Ulotrichales and Chaetophorales, including nearly every number between 8 and 20 in which both groups are entirely intermixed. This supports the view of Fott, Christensen and Silva, that the Ulotrichales and Chaetophorales are only artificially

Table 1.4 Chromosome numbers in Chaetophorales

Alga	Chromosome number n	Author
Caespitella pascheri	9	Abbas & Godward 1964
Stigeoclonium amoenum (including *S. helveticum* var. *minus*)	12	,, ,, ,,
S. tenue (including *S. nanum*)	13	,, ,, ,,
S. farctum	8	,, ,, ,,
S. helveticum var. *majus*	20	
S. variabile	16	
S. flagelliferum	11	
S. 477/3 (Cambridge Culture Collection)	13	
S. 477/4 (Cambridge Culture Collection)	14	
Draparnaldia plumosa	14	
D. acuta	13	
Chaetophora incrassata	11	
C. elegans	12	
Microthamnion Kützingianum	8	
Trentepohlia aurea	18	
Coleochaete scutata	36, 42	Abbas & Godward 1964; Selby 1956
C. nitellarum	42	Selby 1956
Chaetopeltis orbicularis	21	,, ,,

separated. *Coleochaete* seems isolated from the others, with a count of 36 or more, although if chromosome counts were available for *Aphanochaete* and other oogamous Chaetophorales, it might not be so.

OEDOGONIALES

Sinha's (1958) study of the chromosomes of *Oedogonium cardiacum* shows that most of them have a subterminal or median centromere. They are long and easy to observe. For this reason the alga was selected by Alma Howard (Howard & Horsley 1960) for irradiation studies. Its chromosomes are essentially like those of the most favourable of the higher plants. Many other *Oedogonia* have similar chromosomes.

Details of meiosis are available from the work of Hoffman, whose figures are reproduced in Fig. 1.6. Bivalents with up to five or more chiasmata are seen.

Table 1.5 (quoted from L. Hoffman 1965) gives a list of chromosome numbers for *Oedogonium*: J. P. Sinha (1958) found $n = 20$ in *Bulbochaete basipora*. One count is recorded for *Oedocladium* sp. ($n = 24 \pm 2$: Hoffman 1965).

It is of interest that so many of the chromosome numbers are odd, although there are some even numbers. The predominance of odd numbers occurs regardless of the sex category of the species. Claims for the existence of a sex chromosome have been made from time to time.

Polyploids can be artificially obtained, as was first shown in the classic paper of Mainx (1931) by germination of an unreduced zygotic nucleus. Male and female genes were both present and female predominated. Similar polyploids were obtained by Hoffman (1965), and colchicine-produced polyploids by Tschermak (1942, 1943).

Table 1.5 Chromosome numbers in Oedogonium

	Chromosome number *n*	Author
MACRANDROUS SPECIES		
I. With bisexual filaments:		
Oedogonium vaucheri	16	Henningsen 1963
O. foveolatum	16	Hoffman
O. geniculatum	32	,,
O. terrestris	17	Chowdary 1962
II. With unisexual filaments:		
Oedogonium capillare	16	Henningsen 1963
O. capilliforme (male and female strains)	17	Hoffman
O. cardiacum (male and female strains)	19	Howard and Horsley 1958 Hasitschka-Jenschke 1960; Sinha 1958; Hoffman
O. grande	13	Ohashi 1930
O. pachyandrium	15	Kretschmer 1930
	17	Tschermak 1943a
O. plagiostomum	16	Henningsen 1963
O. princeps (male and female strains)	17	Hoffman
O. pringsheimii	18	Henningsen 1963
Oedogonium sp. (strains #4 and #5, female and male)	17	Hoffman
Oedogonium sp. (strains #8 and #9, female and male)	17	,,

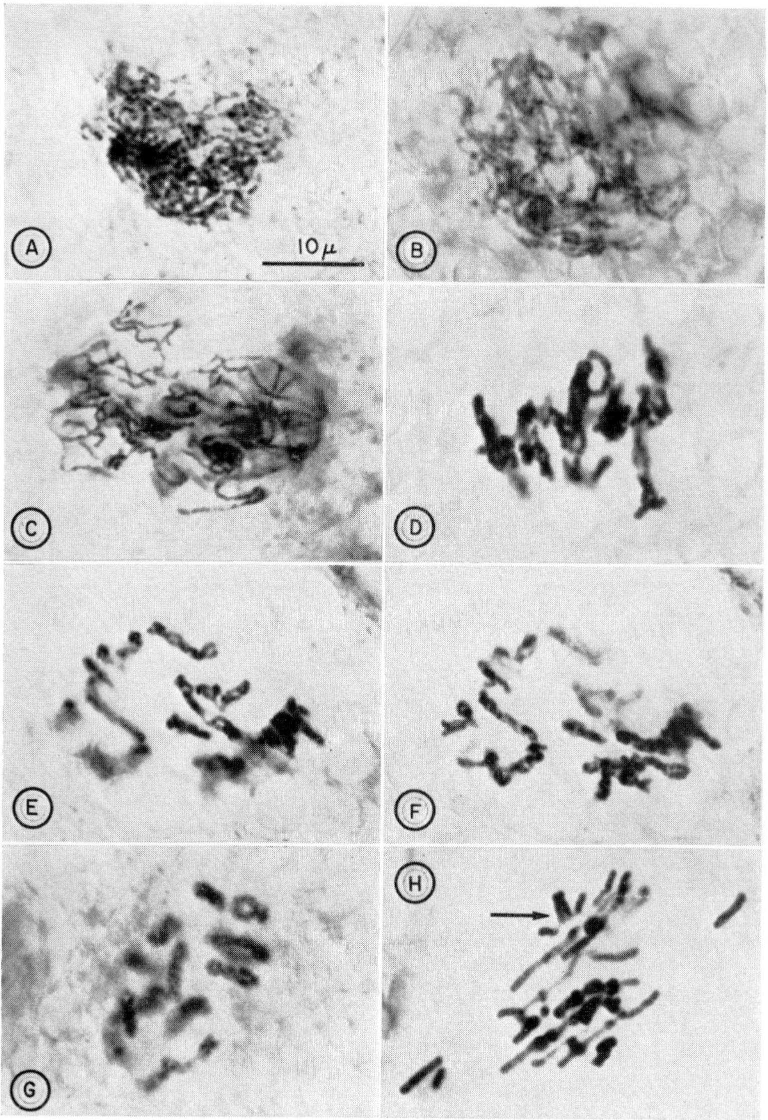

Fig. 1.6 *Oedogonium foreolatum.* Meiosis; bivalents with at least four chiasmata can be seen in **E** and **G**. (Photographs by L. Hoffman)

Table 1.5 (*continued*)

	Chromosome number *n*	Author
NANNANDROUS SPECIES		
I. Gynandrosporous:		
Oedogonium sp. (strain #12)	16 (17 ?)	Hoffman
O. sp. (strain #13)	38 ± 1	"
O. sp. (strain #14)	17	"
II. Idioandrosporous:		
Oedogonium cyathigerum	19	van Wisselingh 1908
O. echinospermum (oogonial and androsporangial strains)	13	Hoffman
O. idioandrosporum (oogonial and androsporangial strains)	13	"
O. pluviale	19	Tschermak 1934a
O. spectabile	16	Henningsen 1963
UNIDENTIFIED SPECIES (No indication of sexual type)		
1 species	19	van Wisselingh 1921
1 "	19	Tschermak 1943a
5 "	13	" "
3 "	17	" "
3 "	18	" "
1 "	19	" "
1 "	c. 41	Sinha 1958

CLADOPHORALES

In this group, distinguished by the multinucleate nature of the cells, the chromosomes are relatively large (Fig. 1.6A–D) and although it is not very easy to see the position of the centromere at mitosis, at meiosis (Fig. 1.7A and B and J. P. Sinha 1958; R. J. Patel 1961) the median, submedian or subterminal position of the centromeres is clear. Meiosis in *Cladophora flexuosa* is very like that of *Lilium*. The only detailed study is that of Patel (1961): but it would be possible in the group to undertake an investigation into chromosome morphology, chiasma frequency and comparative chromosome morphology comparable with what is done in the higher plants. Hybridisation may well be possible. A considerable amount of pioneer work was done by Geitler (1936) and Schussnig (1928–54). Polyploids have been recorded in nature, one (Schussnig 1954) a triploid or hexaploid with inviable gametes. Exactly the same form was recorded from Britain (Sinha 1958). At mitosis, chromatids are frequently although not always clearly visible. Chromosome lengths are often from 3 μ to 1·5 μ in some species, reaching 6·7 μ.

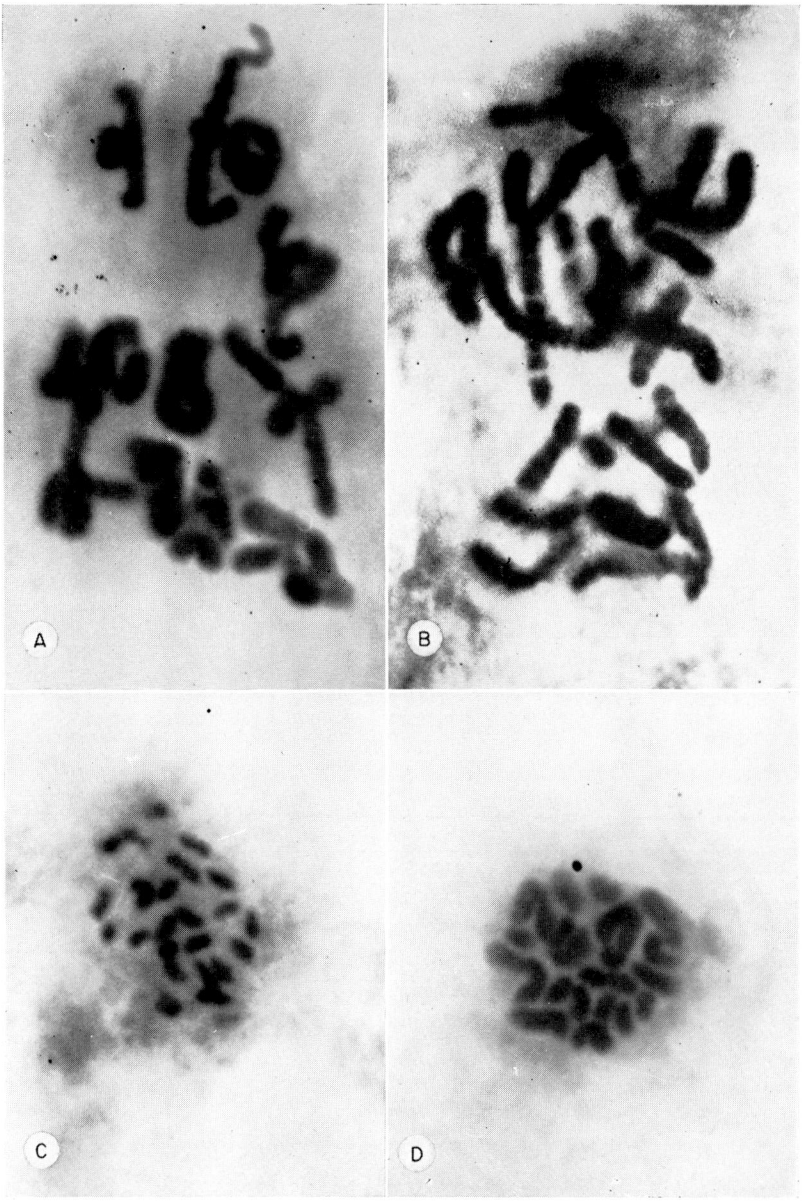

Fig. 1.7 **A** *Cladophora flexuosa* (Griff) Harv.; meiosis showing 12 bivalents. **B** *Cl. rupestris* (L) Kütz. var. *distorta* Harv.; mitosis showing 24 large chromosomes. **C** *Chaetomorpha melagonium* (Web & Mohr) Kütz.: mitosis showing 24 chromosomes. **D** *Rhizoclonium implexum* (Dillw.) Kutz.; mitosis showing 24 chromosomes in compact plate. (x 3,600) (Photographs by J. Patel)

Alone among the groups of Chlorophyceae investigated, the Cladophorales would seem to have an undoubted basic chromosome number (6); a haploid number frequently 12, and polyploid series in certain species (*Cl. glomerata*; Sinha 1958).

Table 1.6 Chromosome numbers in Cladophorales

Cladophora Kütz	Mitosis $2n$	Meiosis n	Author	Previous counts Mitosis
FRESHWATER SPECIES				
Cladophora glomerata				
(L) Kütz	48	—	J. P. Sinha 1958	$n = 48$ (Schussnig
	96	—	,,	$2n = 96$ 1954)
C. glomerata forma				$2n = \pm 72$ (Geitler
genuina	72	—	,,	1936)
C. glomerata forma				
Callicoma	48	—	,,	— —
C. glomerata subforma				
Kutzingiana	48	—	,,	— —
C. crispata	24	—	,,	— —
C. fracta var. *normalis*	24	—	,,	$n = 12$ (Geitler 1956)
MARINE SPECIES				
Cladophora flexuosa				
Harv.	24	12	Sinha 1958	
	12, 24	12	Patel 1961	
Cl. sericea Kütz.	12, 24	—	,, ,,	
Cl. gracilis Kütz.	24	12	,, ,,	
	24	13	Foyn 1929	
Cl. pellucida Kütz.	36		Patel 1961	
		±18	Sinha 1958	
	33 ?	16 ?	Foyn 1929	
Cl. rupestris Kütz.	12, 24		Patel 1961	
	24		Sinha 1958	
Cl. repestris var.				
distorta Harv.	24	12	Patel 1961	
Cl. Hutchinsiae var.				
distans Kütz.	24		,, ,,	
Cl. hirta Kütz.	24		,, ,,	
Cl. albida Kütz.	24		,, ,,	
Cl. albida Kütz.	24		,, ,,	
(refracted form)				
Cl. espansa Kütz.	24	12	,, ,,	
Cl. Macallana Harv.	12		,, ,,	
Cl. Neesiorum Kütz.	18		,, ,,	
Spongomorpha lanosa				
Kütz.	12		,, ,,	

Table 1.6. *(continued)*

Cladophora Kütz	Mitosis 2*n*	Meiosis *n*	Author	Previous counts Mitosis
MARINE SPECIES *(continued)*				
S. lanosa (sp. *uncialis* Kütz.)	30 ?		Foyn 1929	
Acrosiphonia Traillii Batt.	12	—	Patel 1961	
Chaetomorpha linum Kütz (loose form)	36		Sinha 1958 Patel 1961	
Ch. linum Kütz (attached form)	36 18		,, ,, Sinha 1958	
Ch. aerea Kütz.	12 20 18	10	Patel 1961 Hartmann 1929 Sinha 1958	
Ch. melagonium Kütz.	12, 24	12 18	Patel 1961 Sinha 1958	
Rhizoclonium riparium Harv.	36	18	,, ,, Patel 1961	
Rh. implexum Kütz.	24	—	Sinha 1958 Patel 1961	
Rh. tortuosum Kütz.	22	11	,, ,,	
Rh. (*validum* Kister 1955)	24		Sinha 1958	
FRESHWATER SPECIES				
Rhizoclonium hieroglyphicum	24, 48 24	—	Patel 1961 Geitler 1936 Sinha 1958	
Pithophora Kewensis Wittr.	24	—	Patel 1961	
P. oedogonia Wittr.	24	—	,, ,,	

The haploid numbers found are predominantly 12 or 18; counted at mitosis in the haploid plant or as bivalents at meiosis in the diploid plant, where at mitosis 24 or 36 chromosomes are seen. The two haploid numbers 12 and 18 are both found in the genera (*Cladophora*, *Chaetomorpha* and *Rhizoclonium*, 18 however being rarer and apparently of sporadic occurrence in each genus. The occurrence of the two chromosome numbers in all three genera would seem to indicate a close relationship and perhaps that they are somewhat artificially separated. In *Rhizoclonium* a tetraploid species (*Rh. hieroglyphicum*) has a haploid number of 24; and an aneuploid (*Rh. tortuosum* sensu; R. J. Patel 1961) the haploid number of 11. This is the sole aneuploid recorded for Cladophorales in which the chromosome count has been established both at mitosis and meiosis; aneuploidy is not characteristic of the group as a whole. *Spongomorpha lanosa* and *Acrosiphonia Traillii* have given mitotic

Table 1.7 Dimensions of the chromosomes

Key: Size-group: S—small (thickness 0·4–0·2 μ)
M—medium (thickness 0·7–0·4 μ)
L—large (thickness 1·4–0·7 μ)

Name of the species	Size-group S.M.L.	Chromosomes in haploid plants: Length	Chromosomes in haploid plants: Breadth	Chromosomes in diploid plants: Length	Chromosomes in diploid plants: Breadth
MARINE SPECIES					
I. *Cladophora Kütz.*					
Cl. flexuosa Harv.	L	4·1–2·1 μ	0·8–0·7 μ	—	—
Cl. sericea Kütz.	L	5·9–3·1 μ	1·4–0·8 μ	5·1–2·9 μ	1·3–0·8 μ
Cl. gracilis Kütz.	L	—	—	3·8–1·7 μ	0·8–0·7 μ
Cl. pellucida Kütz.	L	—	—	2·5–1·5 μ	1·3–0·7 μ
Cl. rupestris Kütz.	L	—	—	2·6–1·5 μ	1·6–0·9 μ
Cl. rupestris var. *distorta* Harv.	L	—	—	6·7–3·7 μ	0·9–0·6 μ
Cl. Hutchinsiae var. *distans* Kütz.	L	—	—	2·5–2·1 μ	1·3–1·0 μ
Cl. hirta Kütz.	L	—	—	5·0–3·2 μ	0·8–0·6 μ
Cl. albida Kütz.	M	—	—	1·4–0·8 μ	0·7–0·4 μ
Cl. expansa Kütz.	M	—	—	1·8–1·0 μ	0·7–0·5 μ
Cl. Macallana Harv.	L	2·0–1·5 μ	0·9–0·6 μ	—	—
Cl. Neesiorum Kütz.	S	1·5–0·7 μ	0·4–0·3 μ		
II. *Spongomorpha Kütz.*					
S. lanosa Kütz. (sp. *uncialis* Kütz.)	S	1·6–0·7 μ	0·4–0·27 μ		
III. *Acrosiphonia Ag.*					
A. Traillii Batt.	S	1·4–0·4 μ	0·35–0·28 μ	—	—
IV. *Chaetomorpha Kütz.*					
Ch. linum Kütz. (loose and attached forms)	M	—	—	1·5–0·7 μ	0·7–0·4 μ
Ch. aerea Kütz.	L	1·5–1·2 μ	1·3–0·9 μ	—	—
Ch. melagonium Kütz.	M	—	—	1·8–0·7 μ	0·6–0·4 μ
V. *Rhizoclonium Kütz.*					
Rh. riparium Harv.	L	—	—	2·5–1·3 μ	0·9–0·7 μ
Rh. implexum Kütz.	L	—	—	2·8–1·1 μ	0·9–0·7 μ
Rh. tortuosum Kütz.	M	—	—	3·0–1·0 μ	0·5–0·4 μ
FRESH WATER SPECIES					
I. *Pithophora Wittr.*					
P. kewensis Wittr.	L	1·6–1·0 μ	1·0–0·6 μ	—	—
P. oedogonia Wittr.	L	3·0–1·2 μ	1·1–0·7 μ	—	—
II. *Rhizoclonium Kütz.*					
Rh. hieroglyphicum Kütz.		4·0–2·4 μ	1·3–1·1 μ	3·9–1·9 μ	1·1–0·9 μ

counts of 12, and two species of *Pithophora* 24, meiosis not having been observed in either genus. On the basis of chromosome counts therefore the whole of Cladophorales are closely knit together and one feels that reduction in the numbers of generic names, rather than an increase of them (cf. Chapman 1954, 1956) would give a more natural classification.

Certain species seem to be characterised by their chromosome numbers, for example *Chaetomorpha linum*, 36: *Ch. aerea*, 12. These two species should not apparently be combined as was recently done by Christensen (1962, 1964). *Rh. riparium* (18, 36), *Rh. implexum* (24) and *Rh. tortuosum* (11, 12) appear to be distinct (Patel 1961).

A careful study of chromosome dimensions (Patel 1961) shows that these have some taxonomic value. The chromosomes of *Cladophora rupestris* var. *distorta* are longer (6·7 μ–3·7 μ) than those of *Cl. rupestris* (2·6 μ–1·5 μ). *Cl. sericea* (5·9 μ–3·1 μ in haploid, 5·1 μ–2·9 μ in diploid plants) *Cl. rupestris* var. *distorta* and *Cl. hirta* (5·0 μ–3·2 μ) have the longest chromosomes of those measured: *S. lanosa* (1·6 μ–0·7 μ) the shortest.

The genus is sensitive to radiation, a dose which produces more than a few fragments, prevents further nuclear division. Abnormal zoospores and gametes do not appear to be viable (Patel 1961).

The chromosome counts in Table 1.6 are very largely due to J. P. Sinha (1958) and R. J. Patel (1961); the dimensions (Table 1.7) to the latter.

CONJUGALES

Particular attention has been paid to the cytology of this group since 1950 (Godward 1950–1965; Godward & Newnham 1965; King 1954; Prasad 1958; Nizam 1960; Brandham 1964; Brandham & Godward in press).

The most significant features are the common (but not invariable) absence of a localised centromere from the chromosome, and the presence during mitosis of stainable material derived from the nucleolus (Geitler's nucleolar substance), often around the metaphase plate and distributed with the anaphase chromatids. Hand in hand with this goes the complex interphase nucleolus with internal differentiation caused by the presence of the nucleolar organising chromosome regions. All these special features, first observed although not interpreted as can now be done, are described in the classic papers of Van Wisselingh (1900) and Geitler (1930, 1936). Recent work with the electron microscope (Godward & Jordan 1965) has fully confirmed Geitler's term 'nucleolar substance' for the stainable material (other than the chromosomes) which is involved in mitosis, and the interpretation of the nucleolus (Godward 1950) made in 1950. Fig. 1.8 illustrates the relationship of the interphase nucleolus and nucleolar-organising chromosomes of *Spirogyra crassa* from interphase to metaphase. Figs. 1.14 and 1.15 show interphase nucleoli of species of *Spirogyra*; Fig. 1.24A and B nucleoli and

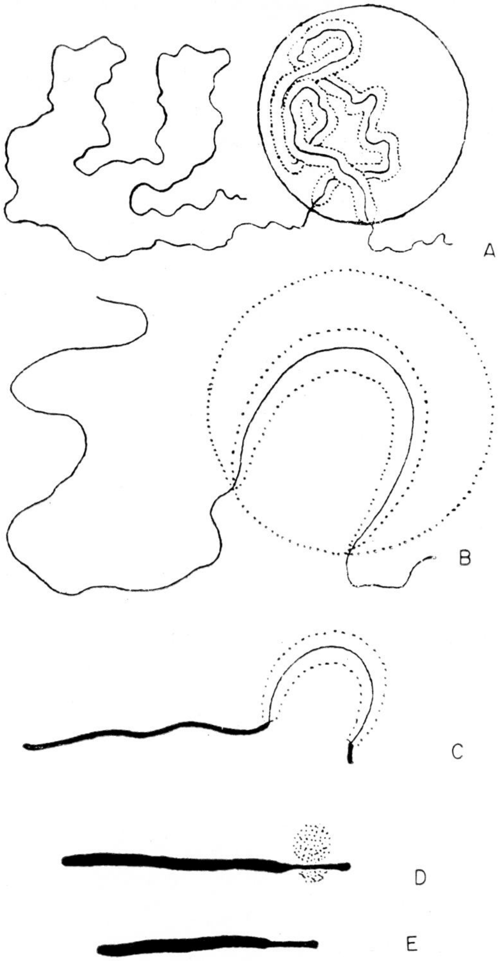

Fig. 1.8 Diagrammatic representation of nucleolar-organising or N.O. chromosome such as that of *Spirogyra crassa.* **A** At resting stage, the N.O. region coiled up inside the nucleolus; the region consists of a fine chromonema, embedded in a thick coating of deeply staining material, the organiser track. **B** At early prophase, the N.O. region contracted and no longer coiled, the organizer track broadened and the nucleolus as a whole expanded. **C** At mid-prophase, the further contraction of all parts of the chromosome; the nucleolus has become dispersed; the N.O. region has a characteristic shape and appearance. The chromonema passing through the track material is thick enough to stain distinctly at this stage. **D** At later prophase, nearly maximum contraction; the N.O. region is now much thickened and the last remains of the track material lie round it loosely. **E** At metaphase; no sign of the nucleolus remains. All to the same scale except the satellite in **A** and **B** and the long chromosome arm in **A** which are arbitrarily represented. (From Godward (1950), *Ann. Bot.*)

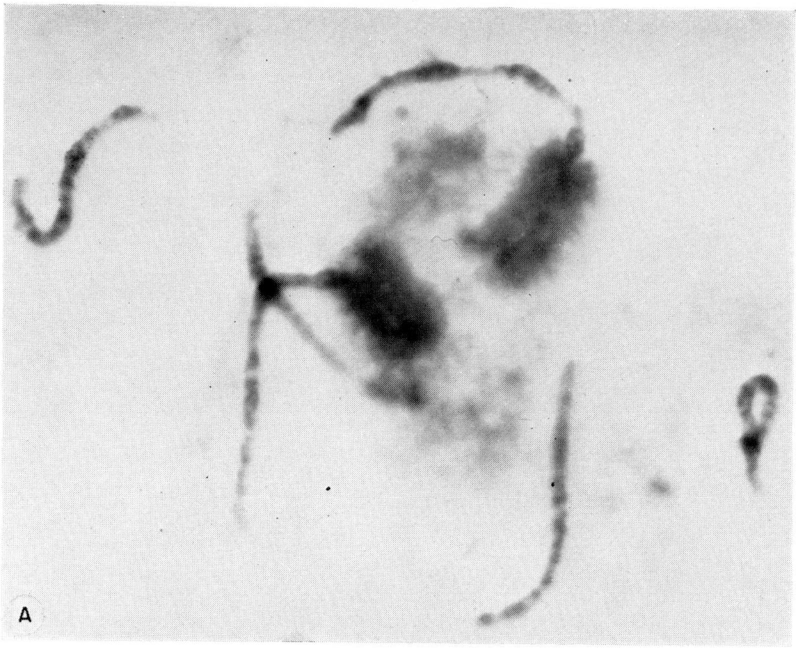

B

Fig. 1.9 *Spirogyra triformis* (Van W.). **A** Prophase, showing six chromosomes; two long, two short, two N.O. **B** Drawing of the two N.O. chromosomes showing the N.O. regions still surrounded by remains of the nucleolus.

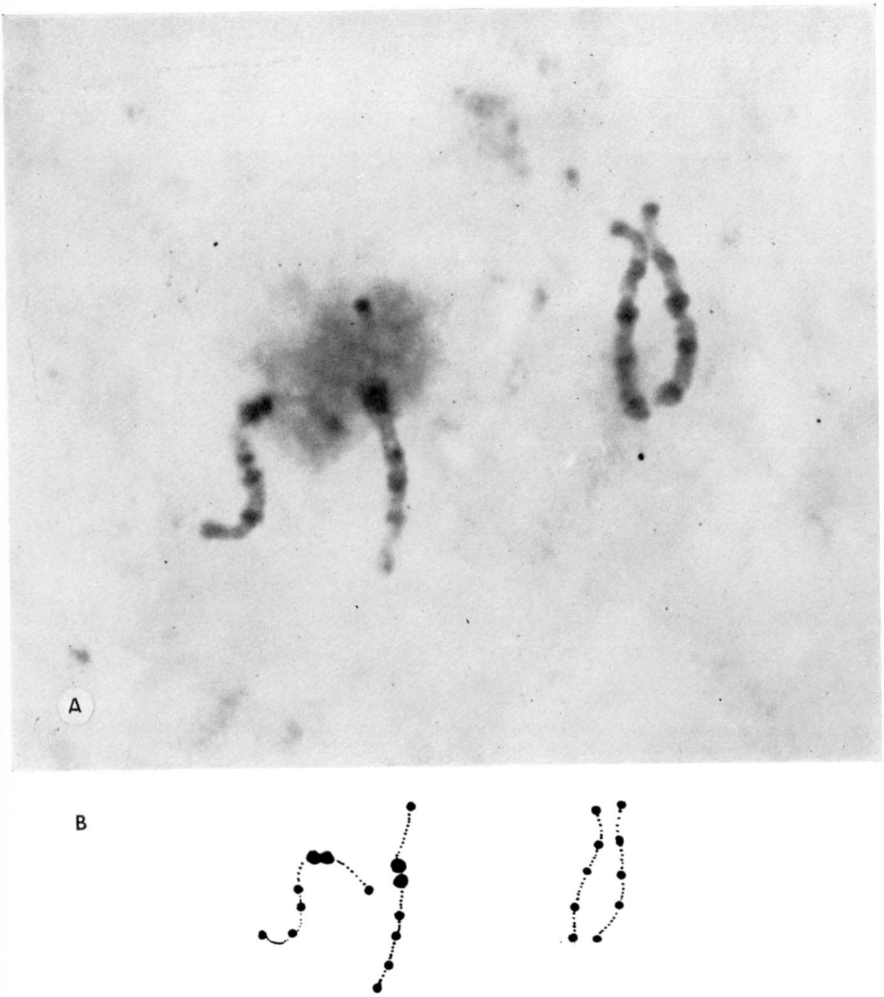

Fig. 1.10 *Spirogyra subechinata* (Godw.). **A** Prophase, showing four chromosomes; two of which are N.O. and have seven bands, the other two, five bands. The N.O. regions are still surrounded by remains of the nucleolus. **B** Drawing of **A**.

N.O. chromosomes of desmid species (Brandham 1964). Nucleolar-organising chromosomes of *Spirogyra* species are seen in Figs. 1.9, 1.10, 1.16, 1.17 and 1.18. Figs. 1.17 and 1.18 show the nucleolus and N.O. chromosome of *S. ellipsospora* in longitudinal section seen under the electron microscope.

The accumulation of nucleolar substance around the metaphase plate is seen in Fig. 1.19 and by electron microscopy in Fig. 1.20. The essential similarity of the fine structure of this N.S. at metaphase to that of the nucleolus itself is clear (for further details see Godward & Jordan 1965).

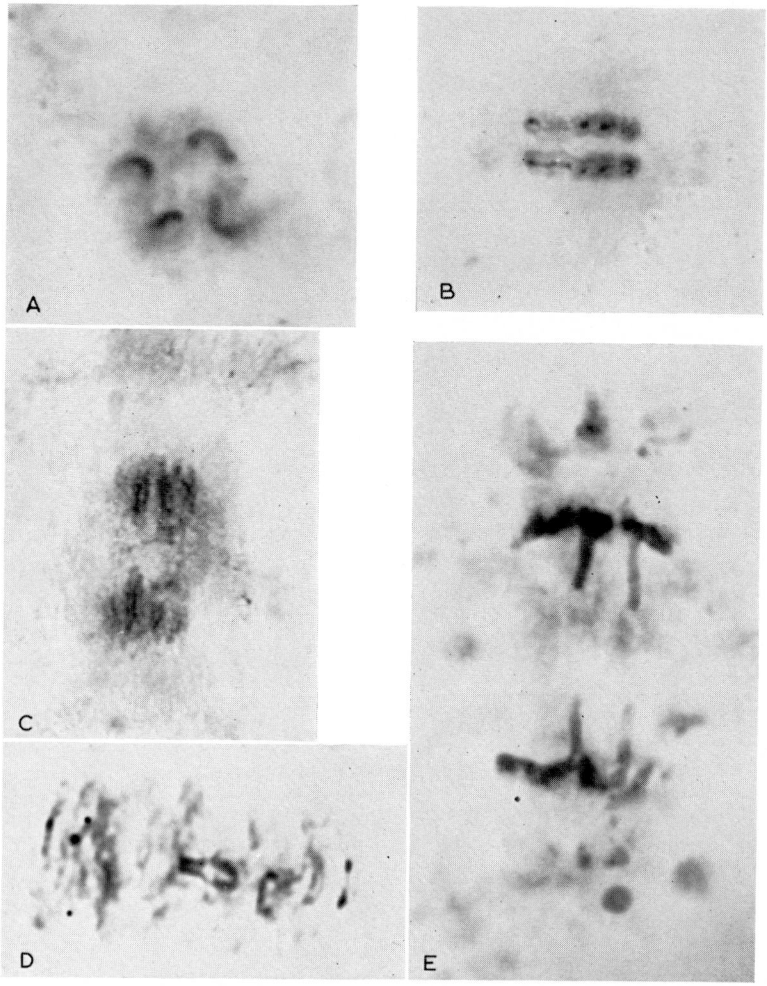

Fig. 1.11 (1) *Spirogyra subechinata*, metaphase with four chromosomes, diffuse N.S. (nucleolar substance). (2) *S. subechinata*, parallel anaphase separation of chromatids, thickly covered with N.S. (3) *S. brittannica*, anaphase, chromatids concealed by dense covering of N.S. (4) *S. oblata*, metaphase with chromosomes surrounded by N.S. (5) *S. oblata*, anaphase, chromatids covered completely by N.S., blobs of N.S. at spindle poles. (From Godward (1953), *Ann. Bot.*)

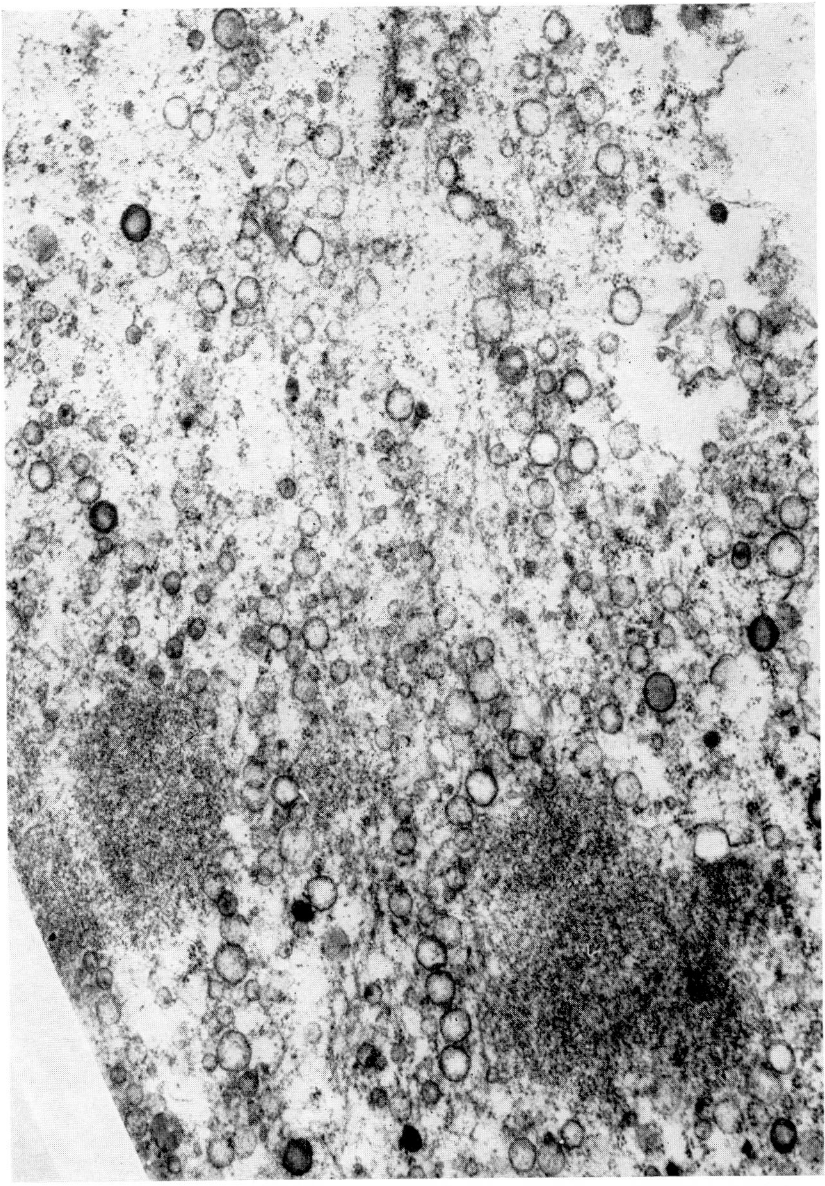

Fig. 1.12 *Closterium ehrenbergii.* E.M. of metaphase chromosomes in mitosis. The chromosomes consist of tangled fibrils. Fine spindle fibres lie singly, not in bundles; they approach the chromosomes and pass between them. There is no centromere structure in the chromosomes. (x 26,000) (E.M. by P. Brandham)

(A)

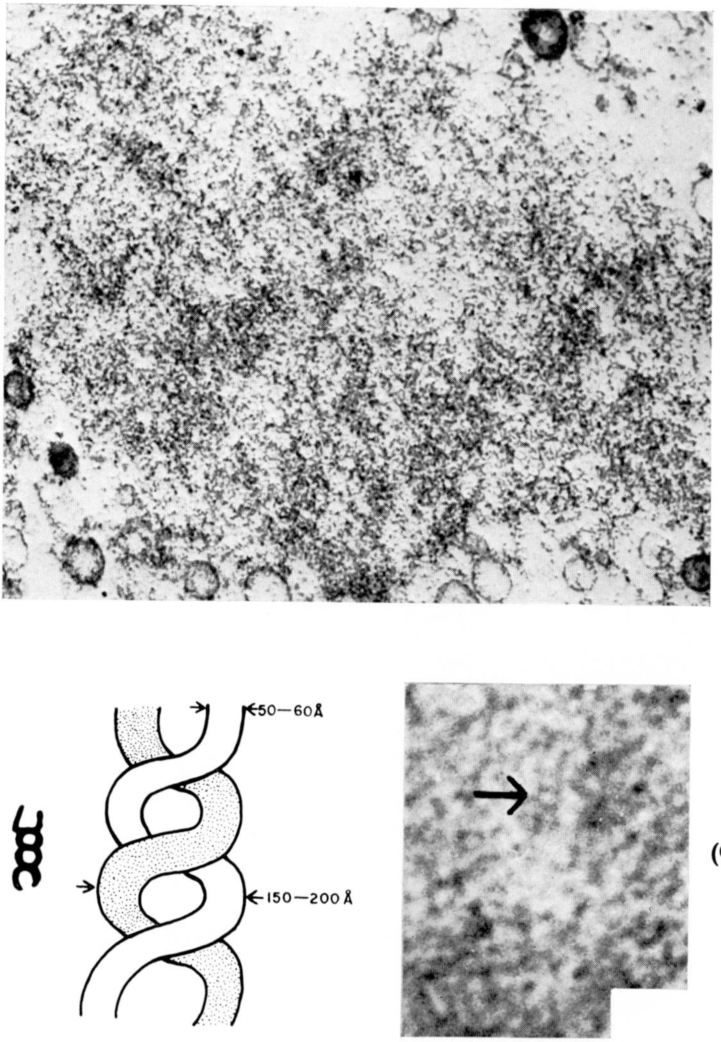

(B) (C)

Fig. 1.13 *Closterium ehrenbergii* mitotic chromosome. **A, B,** and **C.** Detail of the fine structure of the chromosome shows pairs of fine fibrils, in places appearing twisted round each other or spiralled together. The paired fibrils with space between give a compound fibril 150 A in diameter. **A** x 57,500; **C** x 120,000. (E.M. by P. Brandham)

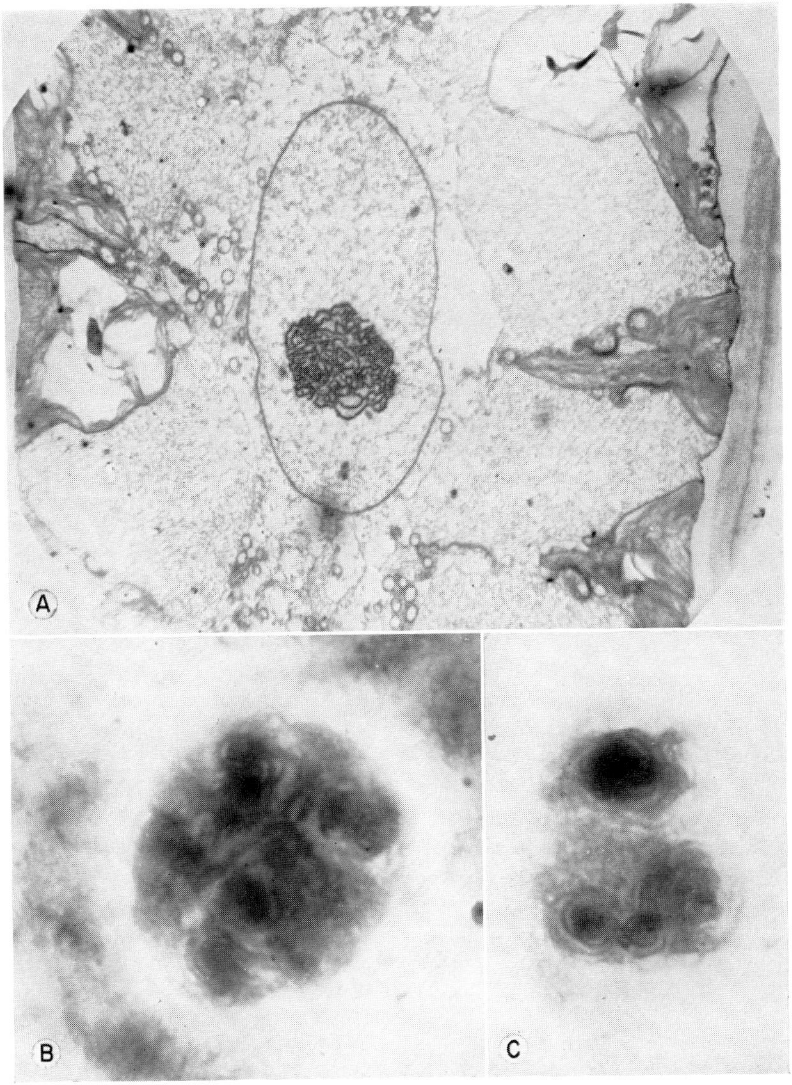

Fig. 1.14 *Spirogyra brittannica* (Godw.). **A** Electronmicrograph (E.M.) showing the nucleus and nucleolus in section. The sponge-like nucleolus shows cavities filled with less dense material, the walls of dense material. **B** and **C** Iron acetocarmine preparations showing the nucleolus by visual light; the 'membranes' are the cavity walls of the E.M. In this squash preparation, the organisation of the membranes round a central axis (the N.O. region of the chromosome, see Fig. 1.7) is clear. (Photographs (x 2,400) and E.M. (x 1,600) by E. G. Jordan)

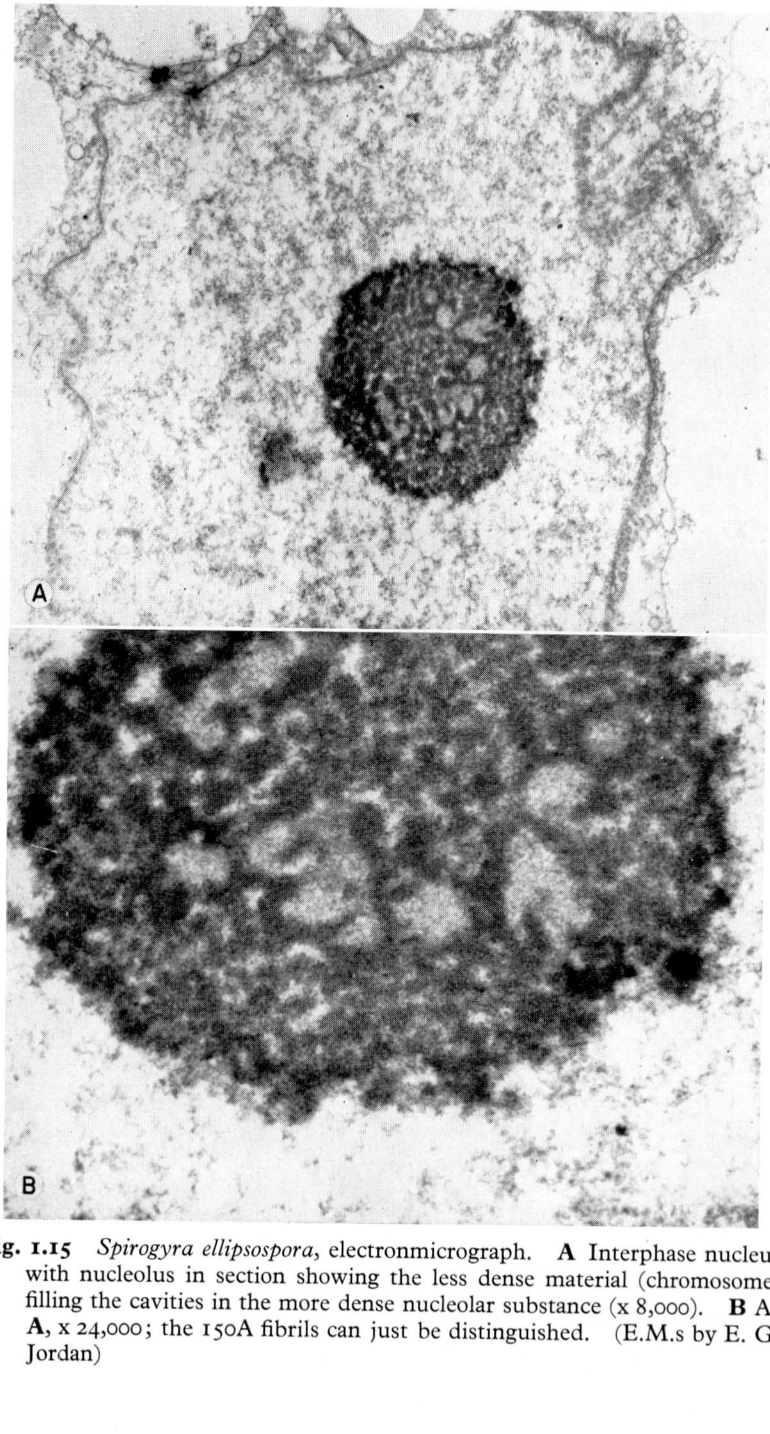

Fig. 1.15 *Spirogyra ellipsospora*, electronmicrograph. **A** Interphase nucleus with nucleolus in section showing the less dense material (chromosome) filling the cavities in the more dense nucleolar substance (x 8,000). **B** As **A**, x 24,000; the 150A fibrils can just be distinguished. (E.M.s by E. G. Jordan)

Recent electron microscopy (Barnicot & Huxley, unpub.; Porter & Ledbetter 1964; Ledbetter 1964) has shown that in chromosomes where there is a localised centromere, a definite dense structure is present in the chromosome at this point, and to it is directed and closely approximated a bundle of spindle

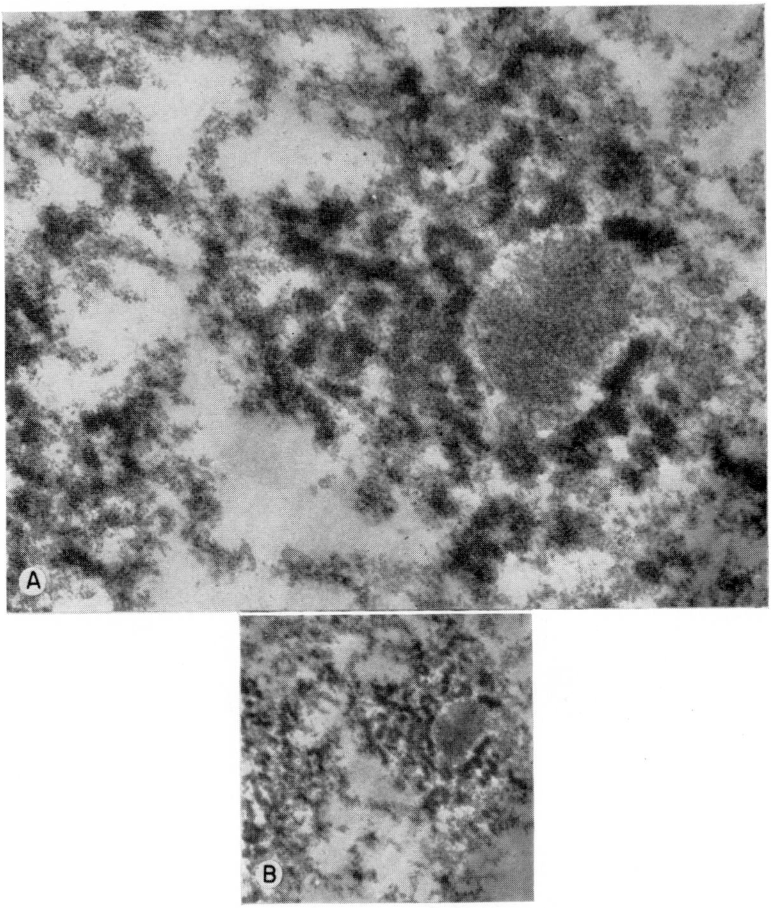

Fig. 1.16 *Spirogyra ellipsospora*, electronmicrograph. Sections of prophase nucleolar material, partly dispersed, showing transverse section of the now contracted chromosome N.O. region. This corresponds to the less dense material in the cavities of the interphase nucleolus. **A** x 24,000; **B** x 8,000. (E.M.s by E. G. Jordan)

fibrils. In the Conjugales, electron microscopy shows that no such structure is found in the chromosome, and the fine spindle fibrils are not in bundles but approach the chromosomes singly (Brandham & Godward in press: Godward & Jordan in press). This is in accord with the hitherto assumed absence of a localised centromere (Godward 1954, 1961) in most Conjugales: and as a result, a parallel separation of the chromatids occurs at mitotic metaphase (Figs. 1.11B and 1.19C). Irradiation fragments the chromosomes but the

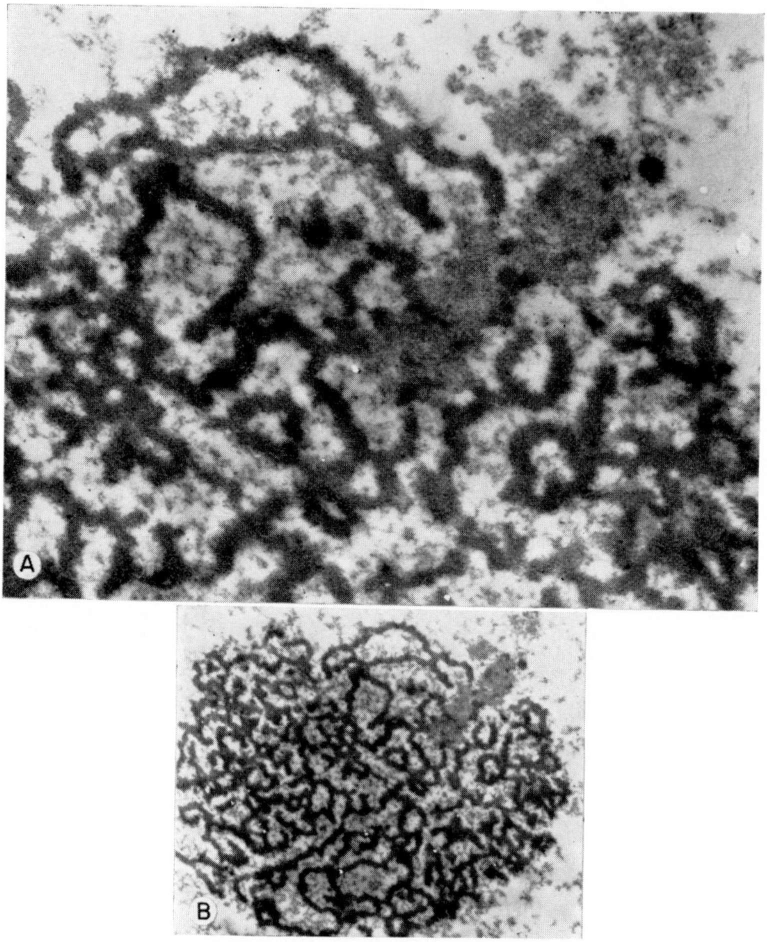

Fig. 1.17 *Spirogyra ellipsospora.* Section of prophase nucleolus passing longitudinally through part of the chromosome. The denser material now forms sheets or strands, the cavities have expanded, the dense material can be seen attached to the chromosome and where sectioned at the attachment, to be embedded in it. The same 150Å fibril can be distinguished in chromosome and dense nucleolar material. **A** x 24,000; **B** x 8,000. (E.M.s by E. G. Jordan)

fragments are not lost where this kind of chromosome is found (Godward 1954; Prasad 1958), new karyotypes continuing in mitosis. The nucleolar substance is partitioned at anaphase and travels to the poles with the chromatids, often obscuring them completely (Fig. 1.15B, C, D and E). In the telophase nuclei, the N.S. appears to become disorganised and dissolved, being reorganised in the N.O. chromosome regions (Godward 1965 in press). Where the chromosomes do appear to have a terminal (Fig. 1.11C)

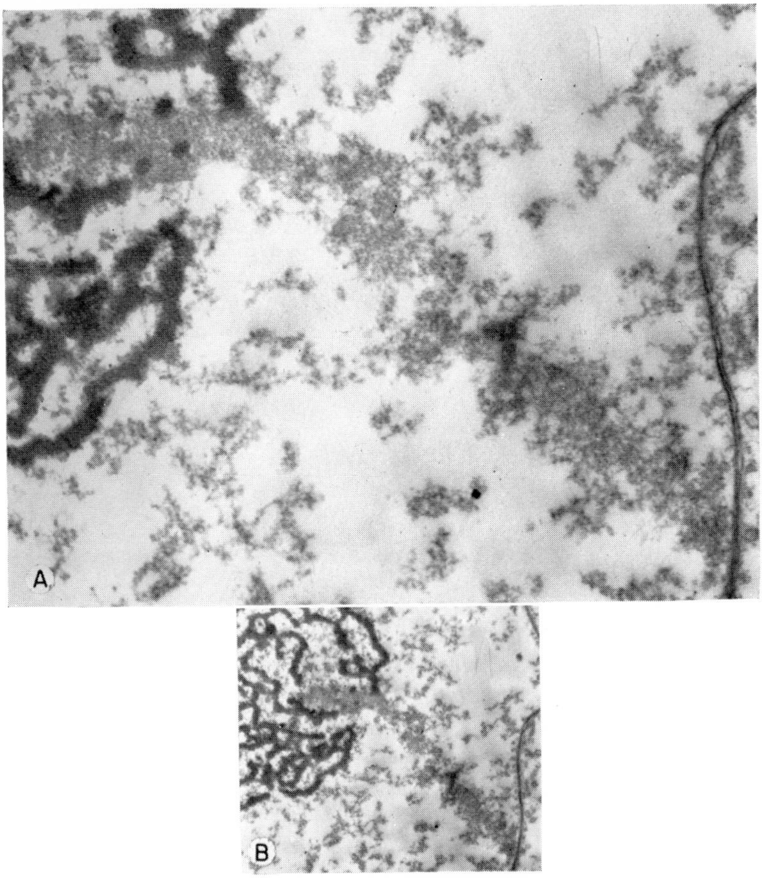

Fig. 1.18 *Spirogyra ellipsospora.* Longitudinal section of the chromosome, showing the N.O. region entering the nucleolus; the long free region abuts on the nuclear membrane. There is a suggestion of helix in the free chromosome. **A** x 24,000; **B** x 8,000. (E.M.s by E. G. Jordan)

or subterminal (Newnham 1962) or indefinite centromere region (Newnham 1962), the behaviour of the nucleolar substance is essentially the same.

Broadly the same features are shown in *Zygnema* and *Mougeotia* (Prasad 1958) and in the Desmids (King 1954; Brandham 1964), although the nucleolus is sometimes compound, i.e. a number of small nucleoli are threaded along the same chromosome (King 1954, 1960; Brandham 1964).

1

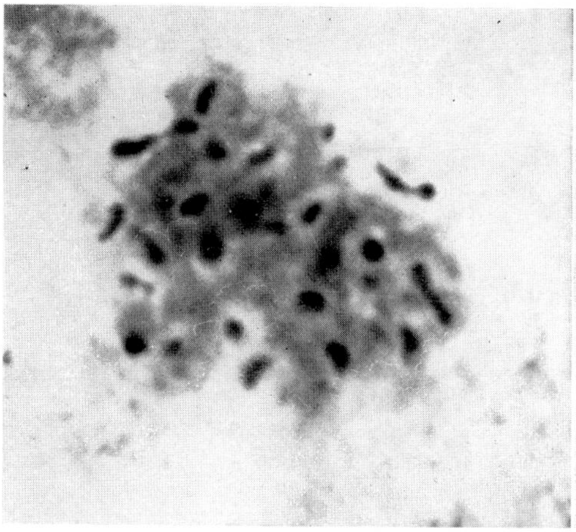

2

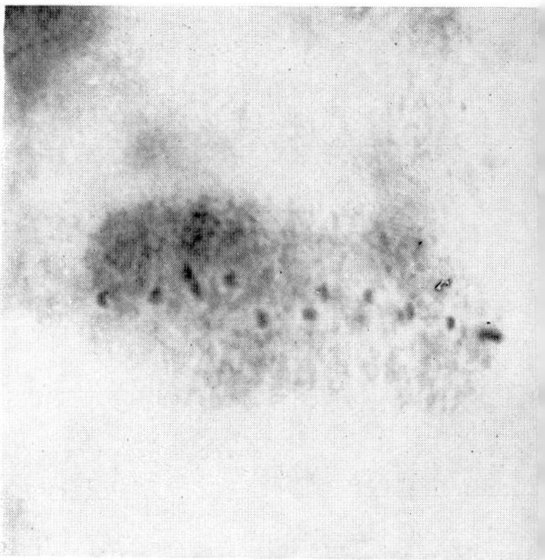

3

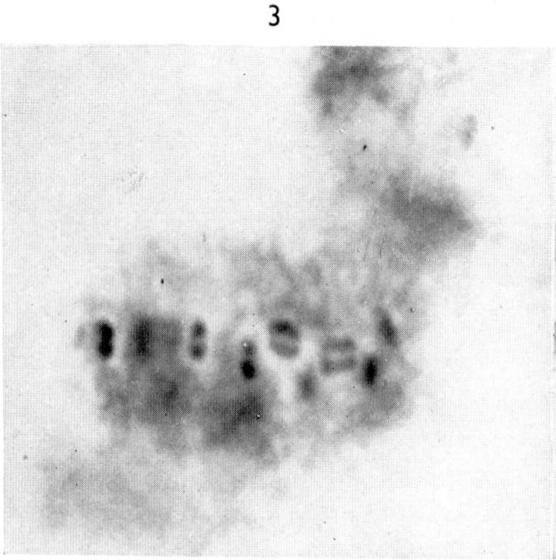

4

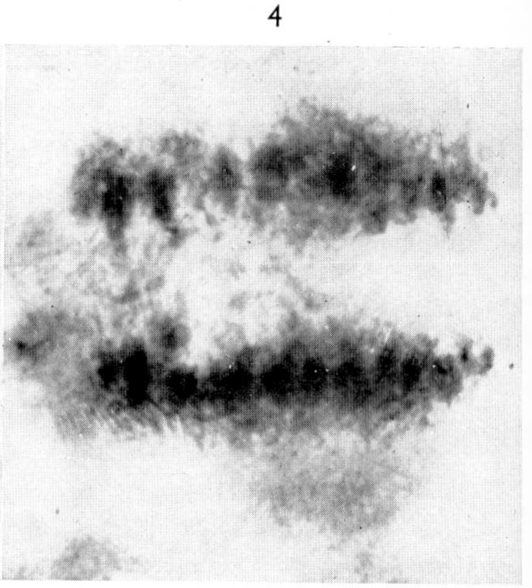

5

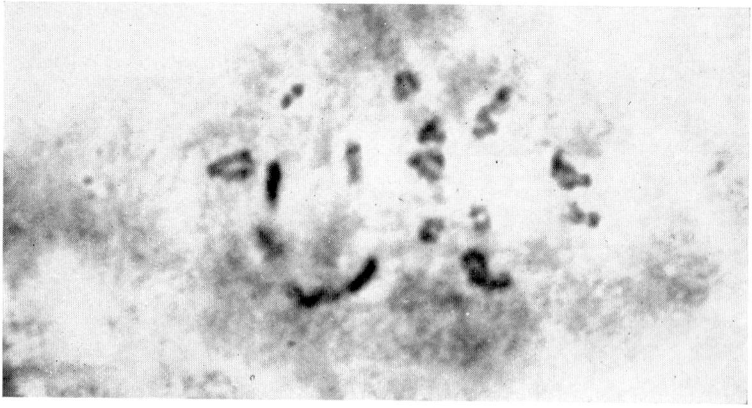

In the filamentous Conjugales, meiosis has been recorded by Tröndle (1911) and Karsten (1908) in *Spirogyra* species, and again by Godward (1961).

In *Spirogyra crassa* (Godward 1961) leptotene, pachytene and diplotene are recognisable but obscure: diakinesis is less so and metaphase and anaphase clear. There is evidence (Godward 1961) that the first meiotic division is equational (Figs. 1.22, 1.24 and 1.25) as in other organisms with similar chromosomes (Malheiros, de Castro & Camara 1947; Hughes-Schrader 1948). Evidence of an equational first meiotic division is also present in the desmid *Cosmarium botrytis* (Brandham & Godward in press; Brandham 1964).

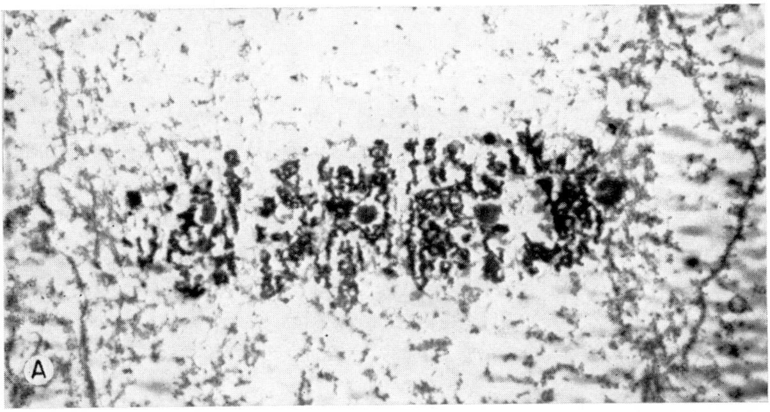

Fig. 1.20 **A** *Spirogyra ellipsospora.* E.M. section through metaphase. The small chromosomes lie on the equator, surrounded by nucleolar substance; this can be seen to resemble the denser material of the prophase nucleolus (x 8,500).

In *S. crassa*, the two to four chiasmata per bivalent observable at diakinesis have all terminalised at metaphase, the bivalents showing all four chromatids. Anaphase I results in separation of 'half-bivalents' (in which the chromatids are entirely separated except at their ends) into two identical-looking anaphase plates, lying parallel to each other (Godward 1961, and Figs. 1.22 and 1.23).

In *C. botrytis*, the bivalents also show two, three or more chiasmata at diakinesis. At metaphase, whether terminalisation is complete or not, some of the chromosomes begin to fall apart while still on the plate. Anaphase separation is not simultaneous for all the chromosomes: some are moving to the poles while others are still associated in bivalents (Brandham 1964; Brandham & Godward in press). The difference in appearance and apparent procedure in the meiotic stages of *S. crassa* and *C. botrytis* is striking,

Fig. 1.19 Metaphases and anaphase showing N.S. accompanying the chromosomes at all stages. (**1**) *Spirogyra majuscula;* (**2** and **4**) *S. ellipsospora;* (**3**) *S. neglecta;* (**5**) *S. punctulata.* (Photos by R. Newnham.) (From Godward and Newnham (1964), *J. Linnean Soc.*)

although neither is of the 'classical' type, neither showing evidence of centromeric action. The homologous chromosomes of Anaphase I of *C. botrytis*

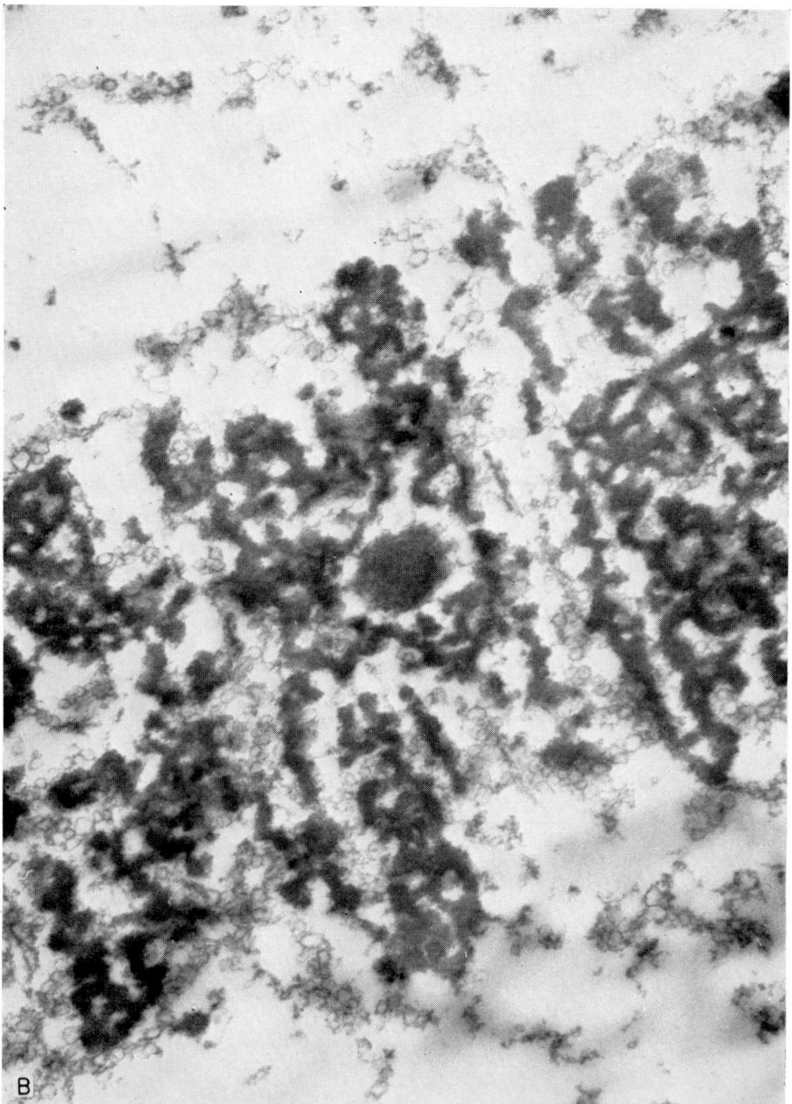

Fig. 1.20 **B** Part of the metaphase of **A**, x 17,000. Fine strands attach the central chromosome to the dense nucleolar substance around it. In detail and in its sponge-like character this substance, now at metaphase, still resembles the N.S. of prophase and interphase. Striations, but scarcely spindle fibres, are seen traversing the metaphase. (E.M.s by E. G. Jordan)

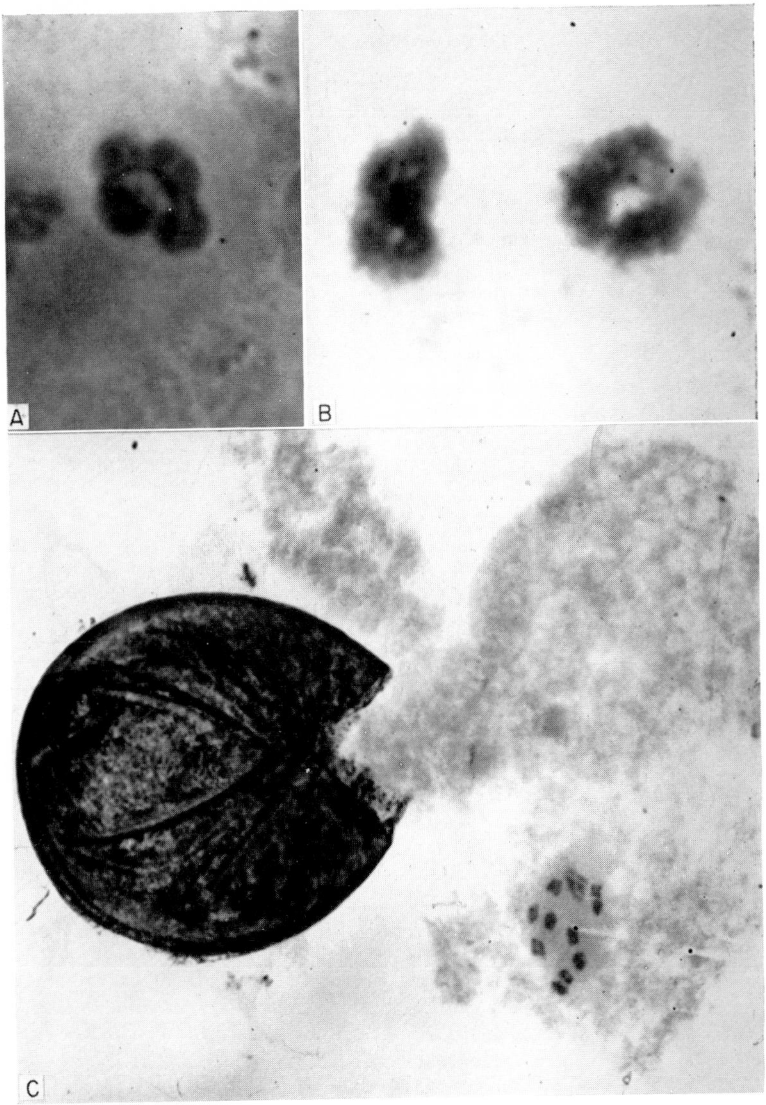

Fig. 1.21 Meiosis in *Spirogyra crassa*. **A** Squashed zygospore with metaphase I, 12 bivalents. **B** Single bivalent with four chromatids. **C** Diakinesis; two bivalents, one with two and one with three chiasmata. (From Godward (1961), *Heredity*)

may in some cases be curved (Brandham 1964; Fig. 1.26A) but since they have already separated before they begin to move there is no pulling apart.

The tables of chromosome numbers in *Spirogyra* also give the numbers of nucleolar-organising chromosomes where this is known. The number can be determined only at mid-prophase or from the maximum number of nucleoli found at interphase or formed at telophase since every N.O. chromosome organises nucleolar material at telophase although fusion of nucleoli usually (in some species) or sometimes (in other species) occurs.

When the chromosome numbers of *Spirogyra*, and also of *Netrium* and *Cosmarium* spp., are surveyed, two trends will be observed: on the one hand towards simple polyploidy: on the other to aneuploidy or something like it.

In *Spirogyra*, we have $n = 6$ in *S. triformis*, *S. jugalis*
$n = 12$ in *S. crassa*, *S.X.*, *S. fuellibornei*
$n = 24$ in *S. columbiana*

These species however have two N.O. chromosomes only, where the number is known: this means that these are not cases of simple polyploidy. Others however could be apparently straightforward polyploid series, e.g.

i { *S. punctulata*, $n = 16$, 2 N.O. chromosomes.
S. majuscula, $2n = 32$, 4 N.O. chromosomes.

ii *S. pratensis* { $n = 11$–15, 1 N.O. chromosome.
$2n = 26$–30, 2 N.O. chromosomes.
$4n = 56$–60, 3 N.O. chromosomes ?+1 (4 would be expected).

Aneuploidy would be suspected in the ten species, all with two N.O. chromosomes, and chromosome numbers ranging from 4 to 70. We have however to bear in mind that these non-centric chromosomes can fragment or fuse and yet survive, so that the peculiar form of polyploidy which has been termed 'agmatoploidy' by Malheiros *et al.* in *Luzula* can exist here. If we look at the chromosome numbers of the clones of desmids the same phenomena appear: the straight polyploidy of *Netrium digitus* is combined with aneuploidy or agmatoploidy: similarly in the clones of *C. botrytis*. A quite remarkable fact nevertheless is that despite the ease with which new karyotypes can arise and persist in culture, there must be a stabilising factor of some force operating in nature, since *S. crassa*, whose chromosomes were first counted by Molle (1870), Strasburger (1898), was at that time and later (Geitler 1930; Godward 1947–58 in four different localities, Newnham 1962) always found to have 12. Similarly, *S. britannica* collected by Godward from several localities, Newnham from more than one, Jordan from more than one (Godward 1956; Newnham 1962; Jordan unpublished) was always found to have 10 of the same numbers of long, medium and short: *S. triformis* collected only by Van Wisselingh (1900) and Godward (1950) was found to have six, of which two were N.O. Geitler's *S.X.*, with 12 chromosomes and highly peculiar mid-prophase features (Geitler 1935) was rediscovered by Newnham (1962) with the same peculiar mid-prophase and somatic characters although in the absence of conjugation, a specific name cannot even yet be given.

These species are identifiable by their chromosomes, apart from other characters.

Another remarkable fact is that in *S. triformis* there are six chromosomes, two N.O. chromosomes, two long, two short; in *S. subechinata* (Godward 1954) four chromosomes, of which two are N.O. each with seven large similarly placed deeply staining bands, and two are short each with five similarly placed deeply staining bands: moreover at mitotic prophase these chromosomes even seem to show some somatic pairing (Godward 1954, and

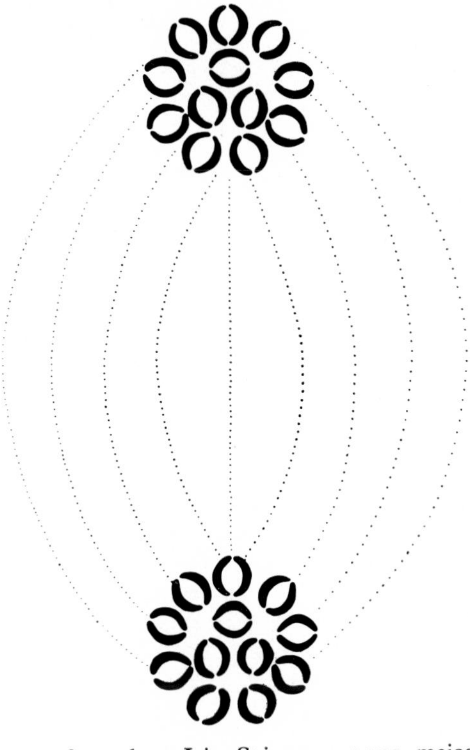

Fig. 1.22 Diagram of anaphase I in *Spirogyra crassa*, meiosis, two identical anaphase plates shown flattened by squashing. (From Godwand (1961), *Heredity*)

Fig. 1.10). Since however there can be no doubt that here as in *S. crassa* which also has two N.O. chromosomes, meiosis occurs in the zygote after fusion of gamete nuclei, the species *S. triformis* and *S. subechinata* are functionally haploid. The evidence in *S. subechinata* that the four chromosomes are in fact two pairs of homologues is overwhelming and it seems likely that the three pairs of *S. triformis* are also homologues. Chromosome duplication in the somatic cells of this group is therefore likely wherever, as usually, there is more than one N.O. chromosome. Similar situations are encountered in the higher plants, where in the amphidiploid, $2n$ is a functional haploid. *S. crassa* also has two N.O. chromosomes in its mitotic complement which might therefore be of the nature of functional haploid of diploid origin: it is the more surprising that meiosis reveals bivalents only: there is no sign of any

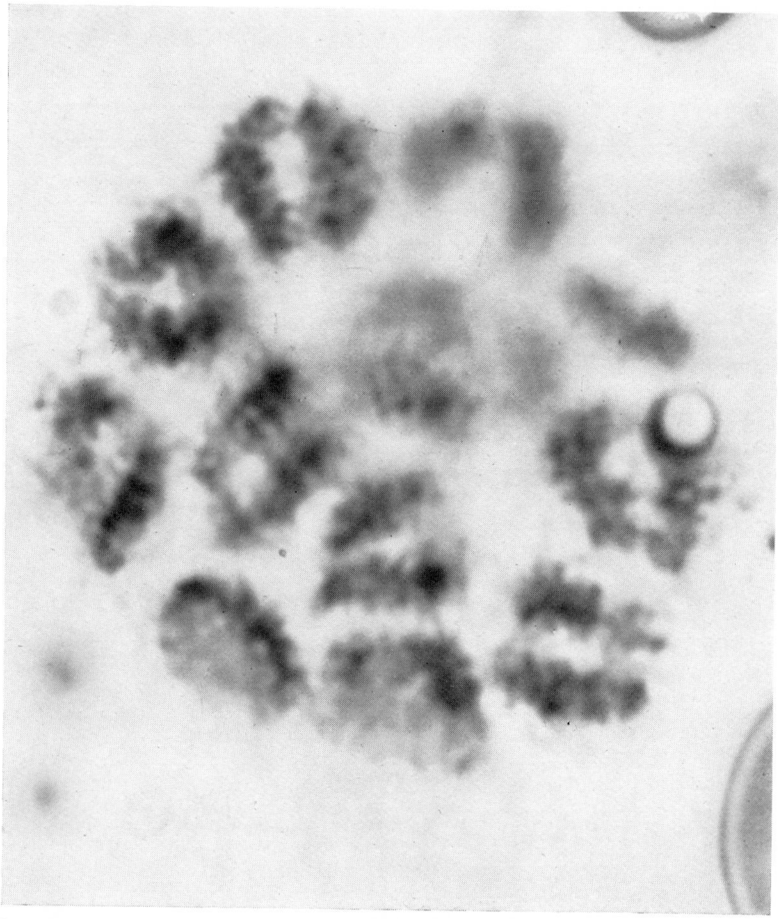

Fig. 1.23 Photograph of one of the anaphase plates (Fig. 1.19); 12 half bivalents are seen, each composed of two chromatids still in most cases terminally associated. (From Godwand (1961), *Heredity*)

tetravalent or even trivalent association. The same is true of *Cosmarium botrytis* (Brandham 1964).

Chromosome numbers in *Spirogyra* and other filamentous forms have usually been obtained after only a few days in culture or in natural water in the laboratory: some were obtained after fixing in the field.

Chromosome numbers in the Desmids have been very largely obtained after some weeks at least in culture, usually in culture media, and not infrequently in clonal cultures. It may fairly be claimed I think that the results observed are at least in part due to this. Examples are the *C. botrytis* series and the *Netrium digitus* series. In the first species (Brandham 1964), five clones have chromosome numbers of 20, 21, 24 and 26, varying in a manner characteristic of aneuploidy. A clear diploid had 42 chromosomes: and another clone had 94, presumably an approximate high polyploid. Similarly in *N. digitus*, recorded chromosome counts are 30, 32 and in separate clonal cultures, 122, 172–82 and 594, the highest chromosome number ever recorded for one nucleus (King 1954). The irregularities of mitosis consequent on

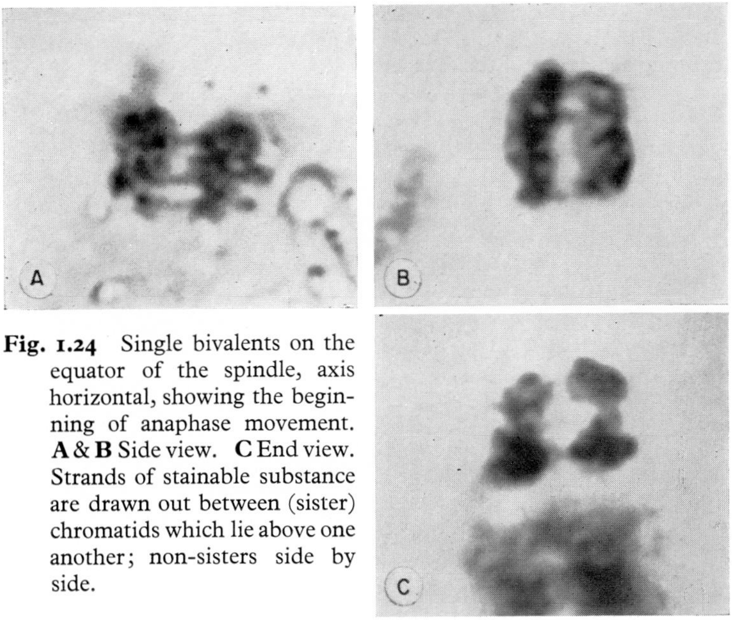

Fig. 1.24 Single bivalents on the equator of the spindle, axis horizontal, showing the beginning of anaphase movement. **A & B** Side view. **C** End view. Strands of stainable substance are drawn out between (sister) chromatids which lie above one another; non-sisters side by side.

culture are, in my opinion, responsible for this development of chromosomal races: one cannot however be in doubt that such races could arise in the field although probably at a much lower rate: and that the rarity or lack of sexuality of many desmids may be due to this (see, however, Brandham & Godward 1965, 'Mating Types in Desmids', *New Phytologist*). It has been shown (Goldstein 1964) that change of chromosome number affects mating type; moreover even if fusion of gametes with different chromosome numbers were possible, the zygote might not be viable. Viable zygotes in *C. botrytis* are from crosses where the chromosome numbers were the same (Brandham 1964).

Disappearance of sex associated with the development of chromosome races has also been postulated in Chaetophorales (Abbas & Godward 1964).

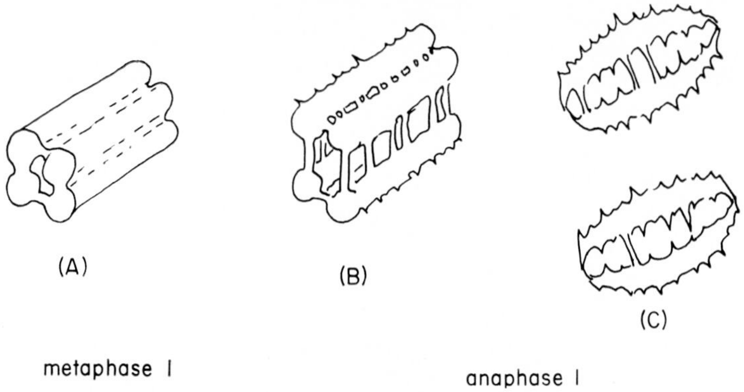

Fig. 1.25 Diagrammatic representation of the bivalent of *Spirogyra crassa*, showing separation of the four chromatids.

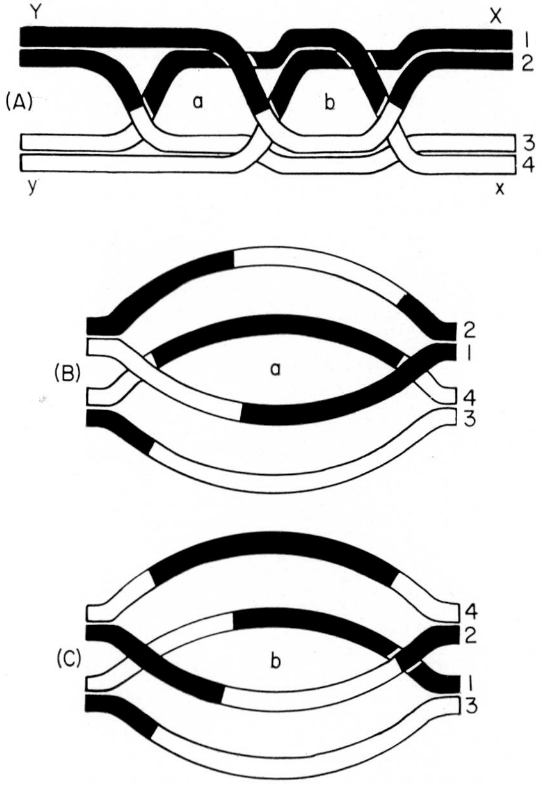

Fig. 1.26 Diagram of bivalent of *Spirogyra* with no localised centromere, showing alternative possibilities of segregation. (From Godward (1961), *Heredity*)

Table 1.8 Chromosome numbers in Spirogyra

Species	Chromosome number	Number of N.O. chromosomes	Author
Spirogyra bellis	14		Merriman 1916
S. britannica Godward	10	2	Godward 1956
S. britannica	10	2	Newnham 1962
S. columbiana Czurda	24		Doraiswami 1946
S. crassa	12		Geitler 1930
S. crassa	12	2	Godward 1961
S. crassa	12	2	Newnham 1962
S. dubia	5		Merriman 1916
S. ellipsospora Transeau	52	2	Newnham 1962
S. fuellibornei Schmidle	12		Doraiswami 1946
S. jugalis	6		Karsten 1908
S. majuscula Kütz. Czurda emend	32	4	Newnham 1962
S. neglecta (Hass.) Kützing	18	2	,, ,,
S. neglecta	12		Trondle 1911
S. oblata	?70	2	Godward 1950
S. paraguayensis Borge	8		Doraiswami 1946
S. porticalis (Muller) Cleve	50	2	Newnham 1962
S. pratensis Transeau	n = 11–15	1	Allen 1958
S. pratensis	$2n$ = 26–30	2	,, ,,
S. pratensis	$4n$ = 56–60	3	,, ,,
S. punctulata Jao	16	2	Newnham 1962
S. setiformis	6		Van Wisselingh,
S. setiformis	less than 12		Geitler 1930
S. subechinata Godward	4	2	Godward 1956
S. submargaritata Godward	38	4	,, ,,
S. submargaritata	38	4	Newnham 1962
S. ternata	4		Merriman 1916
S. triformis Van Wisselingh	6		Van Wisselingh 1900
S. triformis	6	2	Godward 1950
S.X.	12		Geitler 1935
S.X.	12		Newnham 1962
Spirogyra sp.	32		Geitler 1930
Spirogyra sp.	6		Doraiswami 1946
S.D.C.	12	2	Newnham 1962
Spirogyra sp.	84		Godward (unpublished)

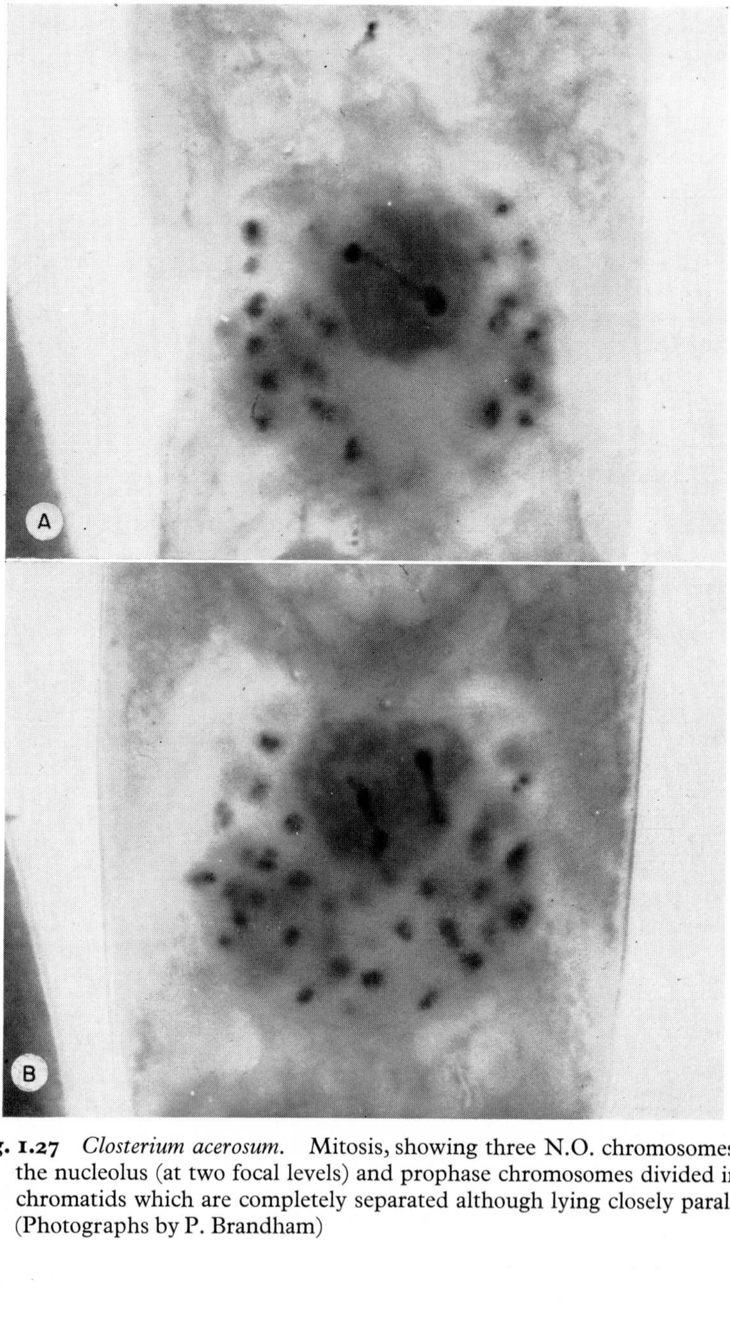

Fig. 1.27 *Closterium acerosum.* Mitosis, showing three N.O. chromosomes in the nucleolus (at two focal levels) and prophase chromosomes divided into chromatids which are completely separated although lying closely parallel. (Photographs by P. Brandham)

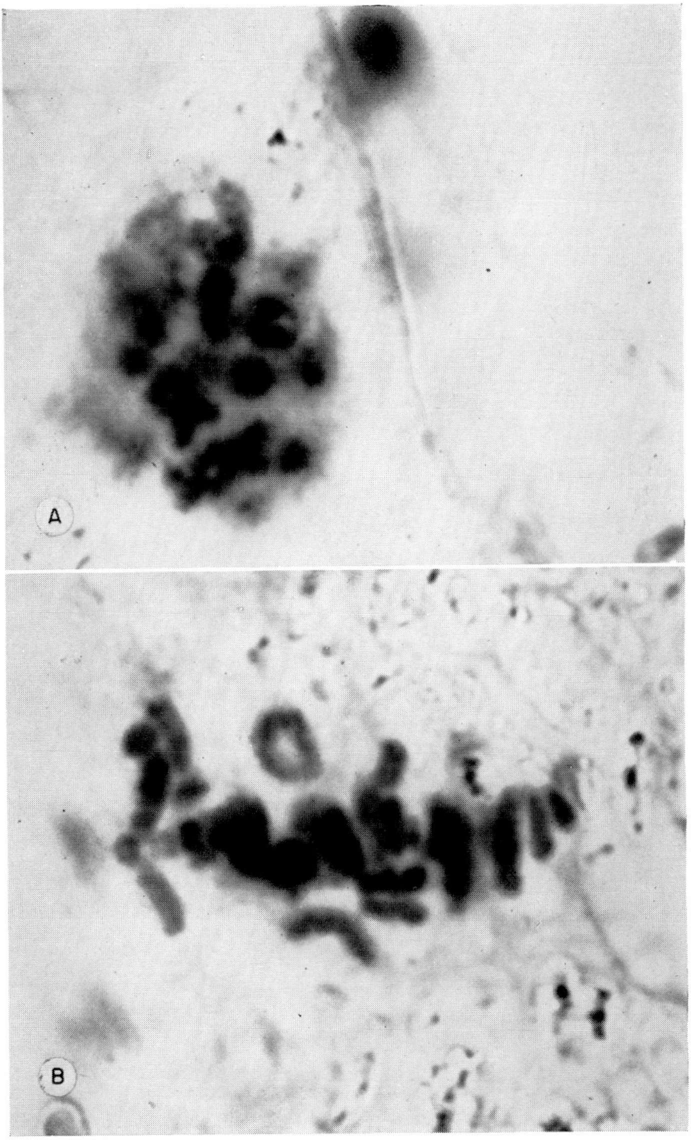

Fig. 1.28 *Cosmarium botrytis* var. *botrytis*. Meiosis. **A** Diakinesis; two bivalents show two chiasmata. **B** Metaphase I, asynchronous separation of homologues; bivalent on the extreme left unseparated; others have fallen apart though still at the equator. (x 3,460) (Photographs by P. Brandham)

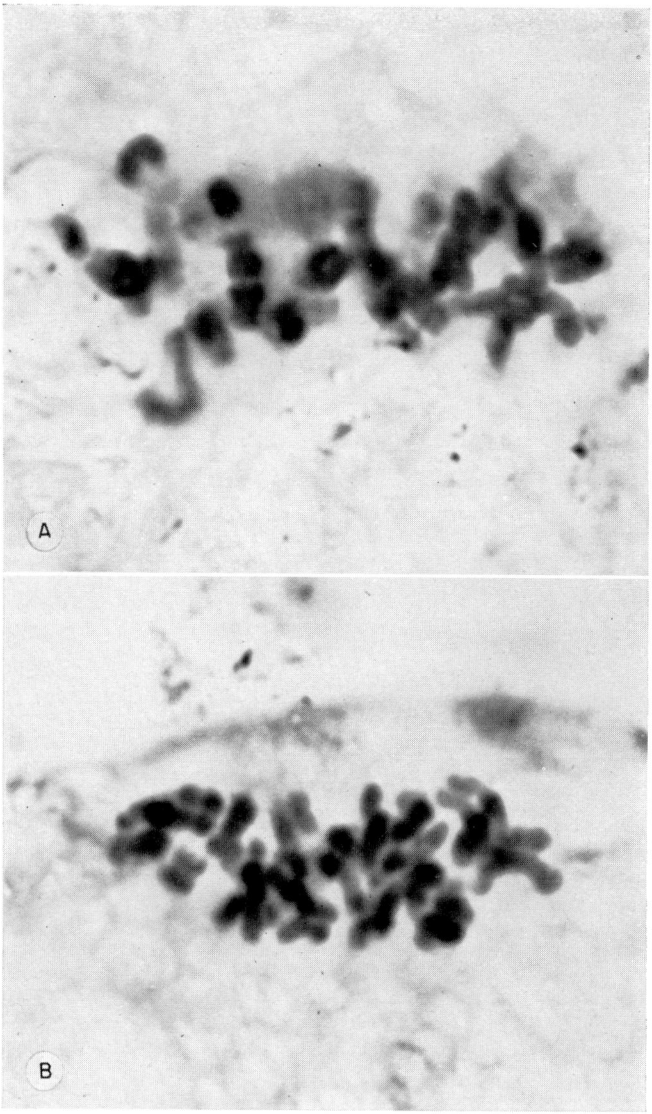

Fig. 1.29 *Cosmarium botrytis* meiosis. **A** Metaphase I, unsynchronous separation; left: two homologues have begun to move to the poles; bottom right: bivalent still unseparated. **B** Metaphase II, separation of chromatids. (x 3,460) (Photographs by P. Brandham)

Table 1.9 Chromosome numbers in the Desmids

Species	Chromosome number	Author
Closterium acerosum	60	Van Wisselingh 1912
Cl. acerosum	c. 60	King 1954, 1960
Cl. acerosum	194	Brandham 1964
Cl. acerosum	220	Fox 1958
Cl. siliqua	86	Brandham 1964
Cl. moniliferum	c. 66	King 1953
Cl. moniliferum Clone O	95	Brandham 1964
Cl. moniliferum Clone D	c. 174	,, ,,
Cl. Ehrenbergii	60	Van Wisselingh 1912 Brandham 1964
Cosmarium botrytis		
Clone A	18	King 1953
Clone R1	20	Brandham 1964
Clone E1	20	,, ,,
Clone D4	21	,, ,,
Clone L3	24	,, ,,
Clone B	26	King 1954
—	30	Karsten 1918
Clone R1 diploid	42	Brandham 1964
Clone C	c. 94	King 1954
Cosmarium cucumis (same clone)	44, 52	,, ,,
C. subtumidum (612/12)	10	Nizam 1960
C. subtumidum (612/11)	12	,, ,,
C. subtumidum (612/8a)	20	,, ,,
C. subtumidum (612/8b)	24	King 1954, 1960
C. impressulum	14	Nizam 1960
C. margaritiferum	18	,, ,,
C. praemorsum	16	,, ,,
C. Turpinii (612/14a)	24	,, ,,
C. Turpinii (612/14b)	12	,, ,,
C. contractum	24	,, ,,
C. tetraophthalum	39	Brandham 1964
C. pseudoconnatum	39	,, ,,
C. difficile	c. 38	,, ,,
Cylindrocystis Brebisonii	c. 20	Kauffman 1941
C. Brebisonii	c. 80	King 1953
Desmidium Swartzii	c. 28	,, ,,
D. cylindricum	33	Brandham 1964
Gonatozygon monotaenium	c. 34	King 1953
G. Kinahini	60	Brandham 1964
Hyalotheca dissiliens f. minor	15	Pothoff 1927
H. dissiliens	c. 12	Acton 1916
H. dissiliens	c. 112	King 1953
Micrasterias Thomasiniana	c. 34–38	Waris 1950
M. angulosa	60–64	,, ,,

Table 1.9 (*continued*)

Species	Chromosome number	Author
M. americana	96 ± 3	Brandham 1964
M. rotata	c. 172	King 1953
M. rotata	c. 200	Waris 1950
Netrium digitus	32	Maguitt 1925
	c. 30	Kopetzky-Rechtperg 1932
Clone C	c. 122	King 1953
Clone M	c. 172–182	" "
Clone W	c. 277	Brandham 1964
Clone M	592	King 1953
Pleurotaenium minutum	24	Nizam 1960
P. trabecula	104	King 1953
Spondylosium pulchellum	c. 18	King 1953
Sp. papillosum	9	Brandham 1964
Sphaerozoma vertebratum	c. 20	King 1953
Staurastrum gracile	c. 14	" "
S. tohopekaligense	103 ± 5	Brandham 1964
S. orbiculare	42	Nizam 1960

ZYGNEMA AND MOUGEOTIA

The list of chromosome numbers and other data for *Mougeotia* (Table 1.11) and *Zygnema* (Table 1.10) is entirely due to B. N. Prasad (1958). Zygotes were observed only in the species asterisked: these therefore are the only ones named with certainty. Other names are those given in the Cambridge Type Culture Collection: code numbers and localities are given for others. It is possible that *Mougeotia* species M VI, M XII and M I are one: *Zygnema* species 'Malham' and '*cylindricum*' are one, WA-4B and *peliosporum* also. There is a general trend for increase in cell diameter to be accompanied by increase in chromosome number and increase in chromosome size, in both genera. The first feature would indicate approximate polyploidy: the latter is rather puzzling, especially since the reverse is true in *Spirogyra*. All the chromosomes are, however, very small. Most *Zygnemas* seem to have one nucleolus: most *Mougeotias* can have more than one, up to eight: this indicates the presence of more than one N.O. chromosome and therefore possible polyploidy. Most counts are approximate but within one or two of the probable number unless otherwise stated. Although this first list contains no really low numbers, it is but a small sample from the two genera.

Table 1.10 Chromosome numbers in the Zygnema

Species	Width of cell	Chromosome number	Size	Number of nucleoli
Zygnema WA-4N (Grasmere)	12–16μ	25	0·17–1·5 μ	1
*Z. cylindrospermum**	15–18	42	0·25–0·7	1
Z. sub-clyindrospermum * Prasad	15–20	37	0·3–1·0	1
Z. W.7 (Wray)	17–19	43	0·25–1·0	1
Z. W.11 (Coniston)	18–22	16–20	0·25–1·0	1–2
Z. circumcarinatum	20–22	19	0·17–0·35	1
Z. verrucopunctatum * Prasad	20–23	39	0·3–1·3	1
*Z. sub-tenue** Prasad	20–24	40	0·4–1·0	1
Z. WA-4B (Grasmere)	20–28	28	0·5–1·5	1
Z. peliosporum	23–30	28	0·5–1·0	1
Z. W.6–A	24–30	29–34	— —	1
Z. sp. 'Malham'	28–32	72	0·3–1·5	1
Z. B.10 (Ogwen)	28–32	44	0·6–1·6	1
Z. cylindricum	28–33	70	0·5–1·8	1
Z. Z.6 (Golding's Hill)	28–34	46	0·5–1·2	1
*Z. cruciatum**	30–36	43	0·5–1·2	1–2
Z. Z.5 (Millport)	34–46	82	0·5–1·5	1

Table 1.11 Chromosome numbers in Mougeotia

Species	Width of cell cell	Chromosome number	Size	Number of nucleoli
*Mougeotia viridis**	6–9μ	51	0·2–1·0μ	
*M. nummuloides**	8–16	32	0·3–1·2	1–2
M. W.5 B (Wray)	13–15	46	0·3–1·0	1
M. WX-Z (Wray)	20–22	40 app.	0·5–2·0	1–2
M. W.10 (Wray)	20–25	35–45	— —	1–4
M. M VI (Dytchleys)	23–25	94 app.	0·5–2·0	1–3
M. M XII (Flatford Mill)	24–30	82	0·5–2·0	1–8
M. M I (Cambridge Culture Coll.)	30–37	92	0·5–2·0	1–4

SIPHONALES AND SIPHONOCLADALES

by SIMONE PUISEUX-DAO

Laboratoire de Biologie Cellulaire Végétale, Paris

Chlorophyceae with a siphoneous thallus are usually marine, living in a warm or temperate climate. The diversity of their life-cycles which are gradually becoming known, although as yet this knowledge is incomplete, has led to recasting of the classification of the long-established groups, Siphonocladales and Siphonales (Chadefaud 1960; Feldmann 1963) which will not be discussed here. The maintenance of cultures of these algae in the laboratory has proved to be difficult since their growth is slow and their nutritive requirements little known. This difficulty still limits their biological and cytological study but should progressively diminish.

Their cellular structure appears simple and constant at first glance. A voluminous central vacuole is surrounded by the very thin cytoplasm which it is itself constituted by more or less fine trabeculae containing nuclei, plastids, mitochondria, dictyosomes and diverse inclusions. Numerous small vacuoles separate the cytoplasmic filaments: they are practically in contact with the surrounding medium and indicate an intense activity of pinocytosis: a paraplasmic membrane, partitioned or not, supports the whole.

Study of nuclear behaviour appears impossible without dividing the siphoneous algae into two groups: the first includes the multinucleate forms such as *Siphonocladus*, *Bryopsis*, *Caulerpa*; the second group comprises the Dasycladaceae which are uninucleate for a longer or shorter part of their life.

I MULTINUCLEATE FORMS

(*a*) *Nuclear stages and life-cycles*

The very small size of the nuclei (2–6 μ usually) does not facilitate observation: nevertheless the appearances of the resting nuclei are known: by contrast nuclear division is seldom observed, whether because the material was not collected at a period of mitotic or meiotic activity or because the culture conditions were not favourable.

Life-cycles are of two kinds (Fritsch 1948; Chadefaud 1960; Feldmann 1963).

A alternation of generations with two types of thallus, diploid and producing zoospores (*Derbesia*), haploid and producing gametes (*Halicystis*) [digenetic cycle].

B one type of thallus, diploid, producing gametes following meiosis; the zygote develops into the diploid alga again (*Valonia*) [monogenetic cycle].

Protosiphon botryoides constitutes an exception, the thallus being haploid and meiosis probably occurring on germination of the zygote (Bold 1933).

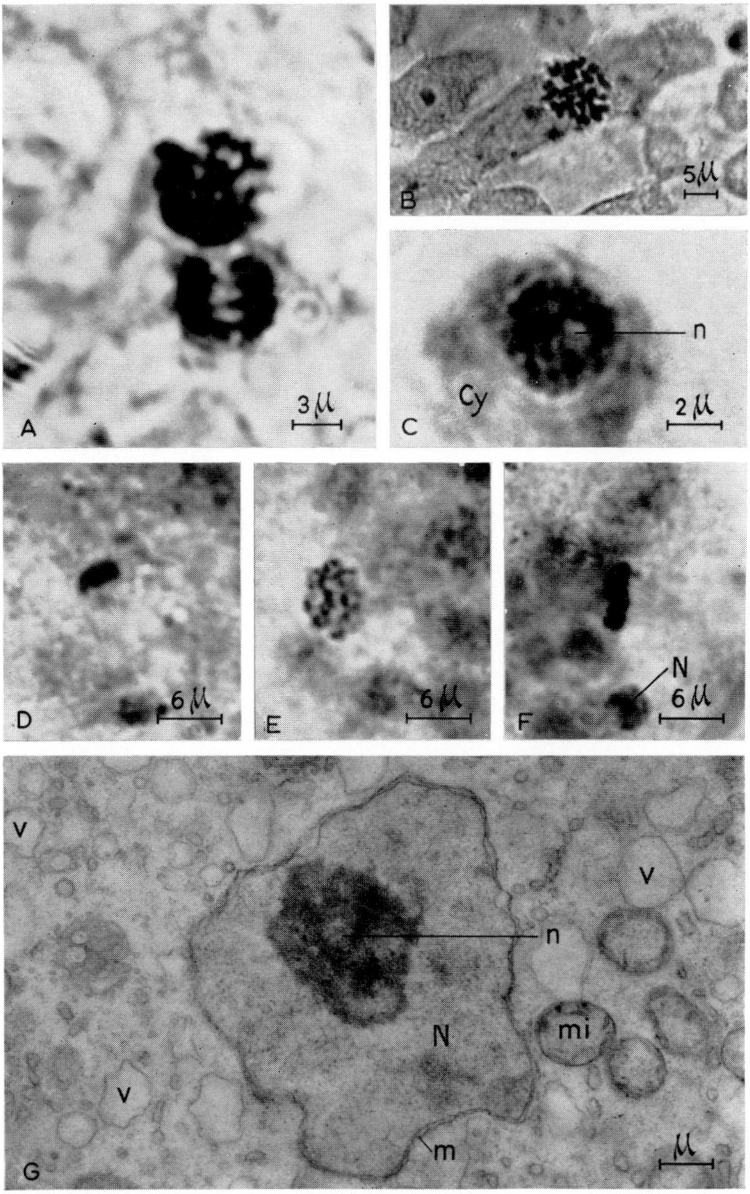

Fig. 1.30 **A** Mitoses in *Boergensenia forbesii*. Metaphase plate and anaphase (Feulgen, after Valet). **B** Metaphase plate in *Siphonocladus pusillus* (Feulgen). **C** Nucleus of germinating zoospore in *Batophora oerstedii* (Feulgen). The 'chromatin' is still visible at this stage. **D** Anaphase observed in the reproductive organs before the formation of cysts in *B. oerstedii* (Feulgen). **E** and **F** Mitoses in the cysts of *B. oerstedii*; on the left, end of prophase; on the right metaphase (Feulgen). **G** Resting nucleus in *Bryopsis plumosa*. *N*, nucleoplasm; *n*, nucleolus; *m*, nuclear membrane; *mi*, mitochondrion; *v*, vacuole in the parietal cytoplasm (glutaraldehyde postosmified; Giraud).

Most species can also reproduce by accidental or regular fragmentation, the latter associated with the phenomenon of segregative division described in the Siphonocladaceae and Valoniaceae, or with the formation of propagules as in *Codium*. Thus the biological observations indicate the nuclear divisions which are available for study.

There are mitoses in growing thalli, more or less numerous according to the rate of growth; multiplication by fragmentation is accompanied by nuclear

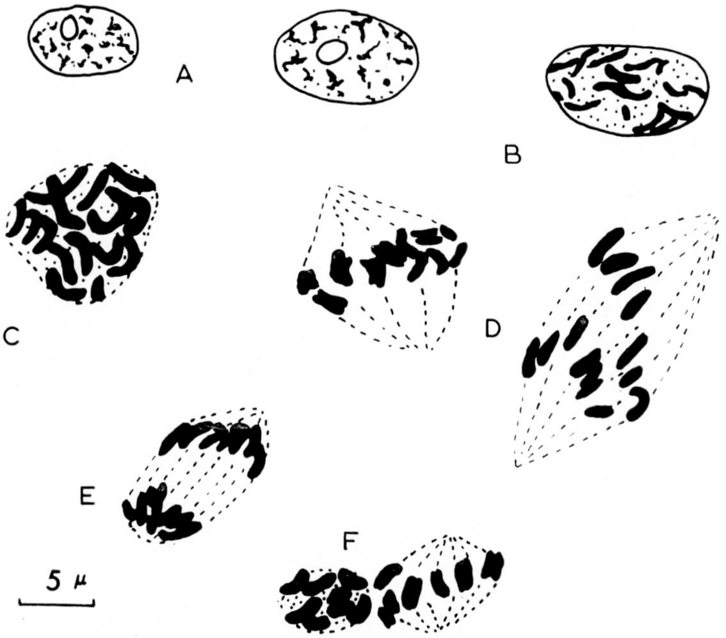

Fig. 1.31 *Siphonocladus pusillus.* Mitotic figures observed in a coenocytic filament during the course of sporogenesis (original). 1, resting nuclei; 2, prophase; 3, metaphase plate; 4, metaphase and beginning of anaphase at the start of sporogenesis; 5, anaphase at the end of sporogenesis; 6, metaphases in the material whose chromosomic stock has been reduced by half (Feulgen).

divisions; finally, formation of zoospores is preceded by intense mitotic activity. These mitoses concern diploid or haploid nuclei.

Meioses occur with the formation of zoospores in diploid thalli of digenetic species, with the formation of gametes in monogenetic species.

(*b*) *The resting nucleus*

The nucleus, usually containing a nucleolus, shows almost without exception a chromatic structure in the form of an (apparent) network with numer-

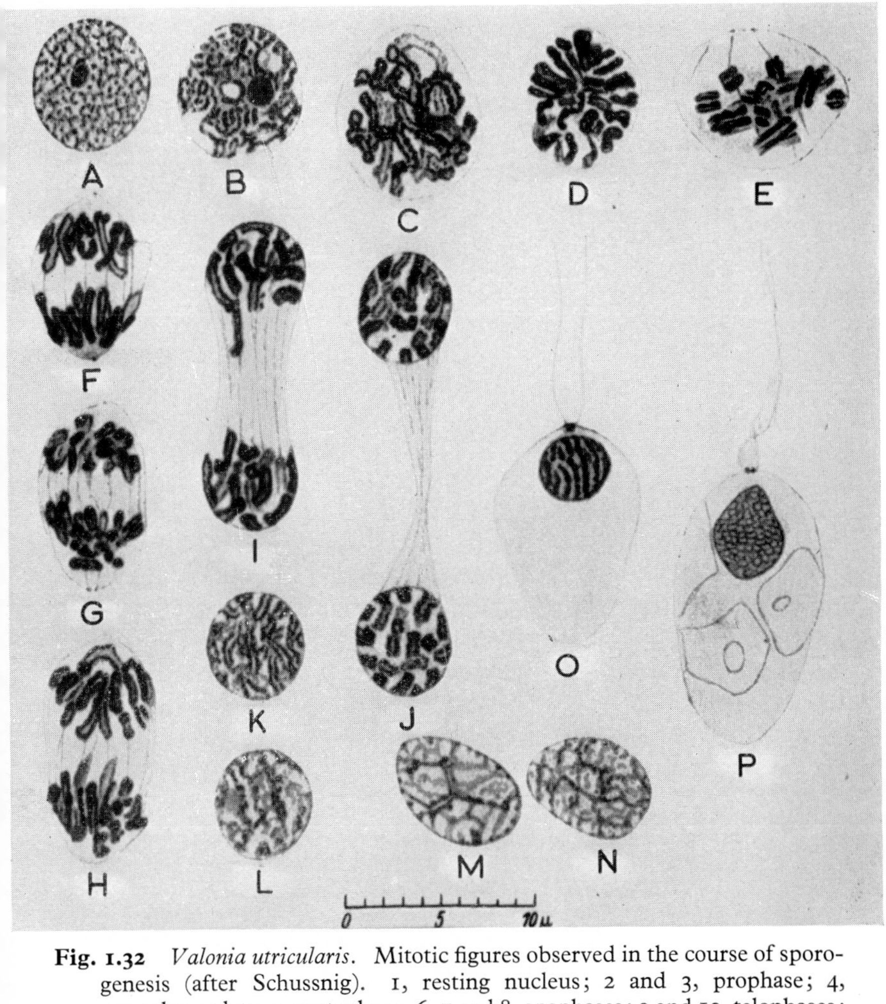

Fig. 1.32 *Valonia utricularis*. Mitotic figures observed in the course of sporogenesis (after Schussnig). 1, resting nucleus; 2 and 3, prophase; 4, metaphase plate; 5, metaphase; 6, 7 and 8, anaphases; 9 and 10, telophases; 11–14, telophase nuclei approaching interphase; 15 and 16, zoospores (haematoxylin).

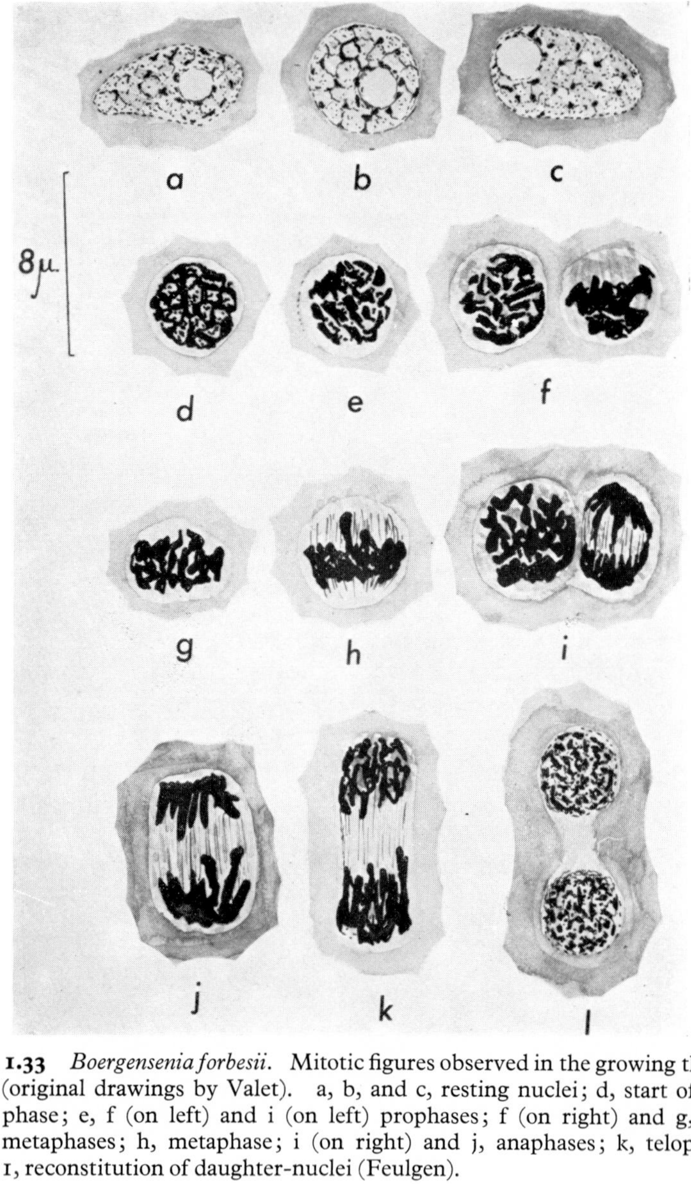

Fig. 1.33 *Boergensenia forbesii*. Mitotic figures observed in the growing thallus (original drawings by Valet). a, b, and c, resting nuclei; d, start of prophase; e, f (on left) and i (on left) prophases; f (on right) and g, prometaphases; h, metaphase; i (on right) and j, anaphases; k, telophase; l, reconstitution of daughter-nuclei (Feulgen).

ous chromocentres. This structure, shown by various nuclear stains, is known for the following species:

Protosiphon botryoides (Bold 1933)
Siphonocladus pusillus (Jonsson, Puiseux-Dao 1959)
S. rigidus (unpublished)
Anadyomene stellata (Jonsson unpublished)
Microdictyon tenuis
Valonia utricularis (Schussnig 1938)
Boergensenia forbesii (Valet unpublished)
Codium tomentosum (Williams 1925)
C. elongatum (Schussnig 1932)

Magne (1964) has shown that *Derbesia Lamourouxii* possesses a nucleus without reticulum but with small (eu) chromocentres.

Unpublished observations (Giraud, Descomps) indicate that the network structure is visible under the electron microscope (Fig. 1.30, 1.37, and 1.38E). The 'chromatin' appears after fixation with glutaraldehyde, postosmified, as a more or less lax trellis of fibrils and granules (*Bryopsis*, *Codium*, *Halimeda*). The density of the network is increased at the approach of mitosis.

(c) *Mitosis*

The mitoses associated with vegetative growth are identical with those leading to the formation of zoospores, but while in the first case the nuclei maintain normal dimensions, in the second, the rapid succession of nuclear divisions is accompanied by a reduction in size, the nuclear diameter falling from 4–6 μ to 0·5–2 μ.

The different phases of mitosis proceed on the classic plan, the spindle being squat, the chromosomes contracting considerably during prophase, and at metaphase they appear as short rods, more or less incurved: V shapes are also seen. The haploid chromosome number varies from 8 to 20; numbers are given in the following table according to the authors already cited.

Siphonocladus pusillus	$2n$ = 16 (Figs. 1.30, 1.31 and 1.32)
Microdyction tenuis	$2n$ = 32–36
Valonia utricularis	$2n$ = 32 (Schechner-Fries)
	$2n$ = 28 (Fig. 1.32, Schussnig)
Boergensenia forbesii	$2n$ or n = 15–18 (Figs. 1.30, 1.31A)
Codium tomentosum	$2n$ = 20
C. elongatum	$2n$ = 40

Asynchronous mitoses have been observed in *Boergensenia forbesii* (Valet unpublished) in those parts of a vegetatively growing culture which are fragmenting actively by segregative division. In other species, the descriptions

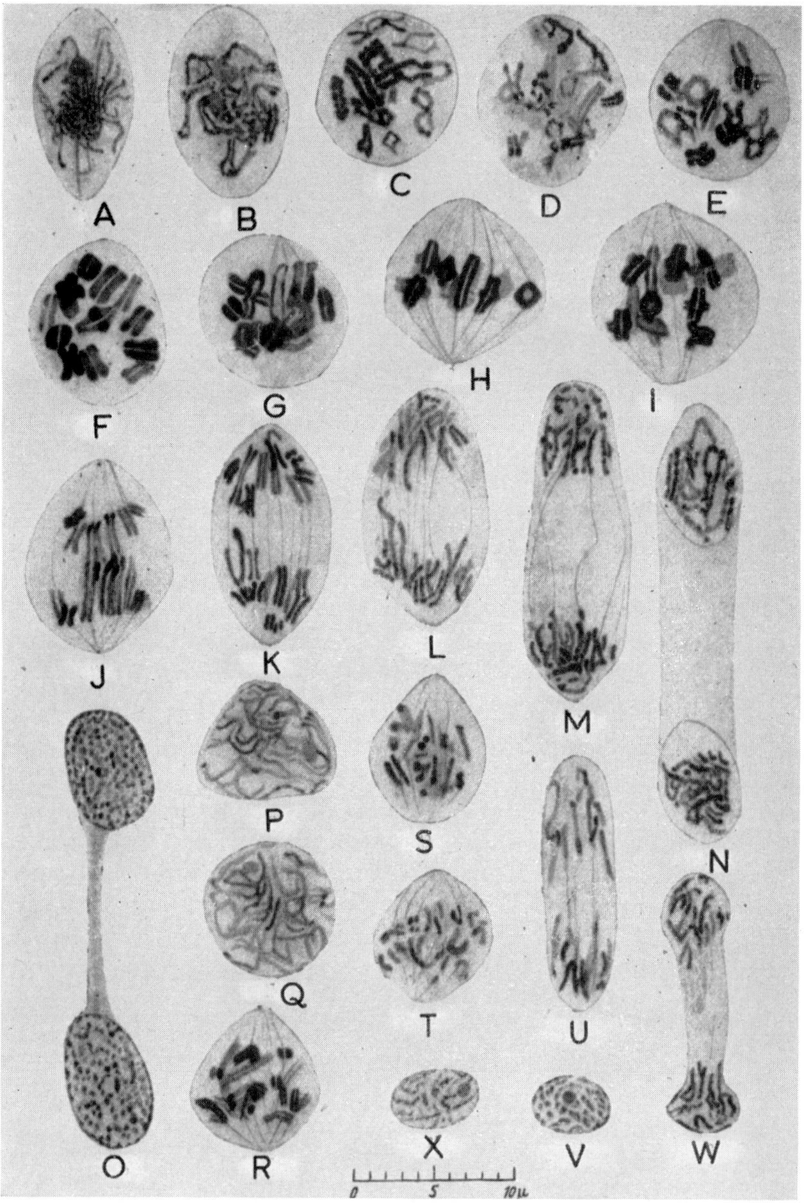

Fig. 1.34 *Valonia utricularis.* Meiotic figures observed during gametogenesis (after Schussnig). 1 and 2, prophases; 3–5; diakinesis; 6–9, metaphase I; 10–12, anaphase I; 13–15, telophase; 16–17, prophase of the homoeotypic mitosis; 18 and 19, metaphase II; 20 and 21, anaphase II; 22, telophase; 23 and 24, tetrad nuclei (haematoxylin).

of mitosis usually are of those leading to zoospore formation. In *Siphonocladus pusillus*, for example, in the coenocytes derived from segregative division, whose contents have become reticulate, numerous asynchronous nuclear divisions are also produced: the cytoplasm is cleaved around the nuclei and biflagellate swarmers are thus formed which develop directly, via a germination like that of the parent alga—a reproduction by means of zoospores. It is possible that in this case, meiosis might have occurred obscurely, as one is led to think by the presence among other nuclei, of a few nuclei with half the number of chromosomes. Because of this, one cannot decide whether *Siphonocladus* belongs to group A or B.

Valonia macrophysa also seems to reproduce itself indefinitely by asexual zoospores, although these are quadriflagellate: it is not possible here to say if meiosis takes place or not.

By contrast, in *V. utricularis*, the mitotic figures which have been recorded (Schussnig 1938) lead to the formation of biflagellate swarmers like those of *Siphonocladus*. These zoospores germinate to give an alga identical with that from which they originated. Nevertheless it is certain that *Valonia* is monogenetic diploid since the same thalli can produce gametes after a meiosis. These gametes are elaborated in vesicles of the segregative type in *Valonia*: in *Codium*, they are formed in gametangia, which are lateral dilatations of the thallus in which meiosis has been observed and described.

(d) *Meiosis*

Reduction division is known only for the two last species. It follows the classic form as Fig. 1.34 shows. At diakinesis the bivalents are much contracted and look like curved rods. They are well separated and the chromosome count should be reliable. Meiosis precedes the appearance of tetrads of haploid nuclei which undergo a variable number of mitoses before gamete-formation.

The assembled observations on the multinucleate siphoneous algae indicate that, most of the time, the thalli observed in nature are diploid. The absence of the haploid generation seems to be a frequent character of this group of algae: this is true also of the Dasycladaceae. The general tendency to vegetative reproduction by fragmentation or asexual diploid zoospores is also common to this group and the Dasycladaceae.

II THE DASYCLADACEAE

(a) *Nuclear stages and the life-cycle*

The very peculiar Dasycladaceae (except for *Cymopolia*) remain uninucleate throughout their vegetative life. The 'primary' nucleus becomes greatly enlarged, then divides in an aberrant manner at the time of reproduction which usually occurs in two stages. First resting cysts are formed in specialised organs (reproductive spheres of *Batophora* and *Bornetella*, heads or 'umbrellas' of various *Acetabularias*). In these cysts, after resting periods of varying length, zoospores are formed, which germinate to form an alga like the parent, or gametes of two kinds which fuse, the resulting zygotes producing, like the zoospores, algae resembling the parent.

The different stages of development are marked by well-defined nuclear states. During germination, the primary nucleus undergoes a number of endomitoses, then enters a long period of rest. After formation of the reproductive organs, the primary nucleus disintegrates into very numerous daughter-nuclei which undergo a large number of mitoses of the ordinary type. This results a cloud of small nuclei which are carried into the reproductive organs by ascending cytoplasmic currents. Mitoses continue for a time, then come to an end: around each nucleus a cyst becomes organised. This consists of cytoplasm containing a portion of the central vacuole; and becomes surrounded by a thick membrane. The cyst-nucleus thus formed usually divides to 20 or 30 nuclei which remain dormant in the cyst.

At maturity, these enter on intense asynchronous mitotic activity, and the numerous small nuclei thus formed acquire cytoplasm and constitute zoospores. Certain chromosome configurations which have been seen have given support to the possibility that, when gametes are formed in the cysts, the last mitoses are followed by a meiosis giving haploid nuclei, which perhaps divide yet again before the gametes are constituted. Nuclear fusion in the zygotes leads to the production of a diploid chromosome complement. The life-cycle of Dasycladaceae is therefore monogenetic; it can be short-circuited by the formation of asexual zoospores in the cysts, meiosis being eliminated: also by fragmentation, due to the direct germination of cysts to give normal plants.

(b) *The primary nucleus*

Extensive observations of this have been made in *Acetabularia mediterannea*, *A. Wettsteinii*, and in *Batophora oerstedii* (Schulze 1939; Vanderhaeghe thesis; Puiseux-Dao 1962–63). The single nucleus, 2–5 μ in diameter, seen on germination, has the classic 'network' with numerous chromocentres. This nucleus enlarges to a diameter of 100 μ or more, while the nucleolus increases in volume (Fig. 1.35, 1.38A and 1.38B). At the same time, the deep staining of the 'chromatin' by the Feulgen technique in young germlings becomes diluted and it is impossible to detect it in 100 μ nuclei. This disappearance has led certain authors to think that the primary nucleus remains diploid (Schulze 1939). Nevertheless, in plants produced by direct germination of cysts in *Batophora*, endomitosis has been detected (Puiseux-Dao 1962) which suggest that the primary nucleus is about $32n$, $2n$ being approximately 16. It is possible that the polyploidy may be of the same order as in the

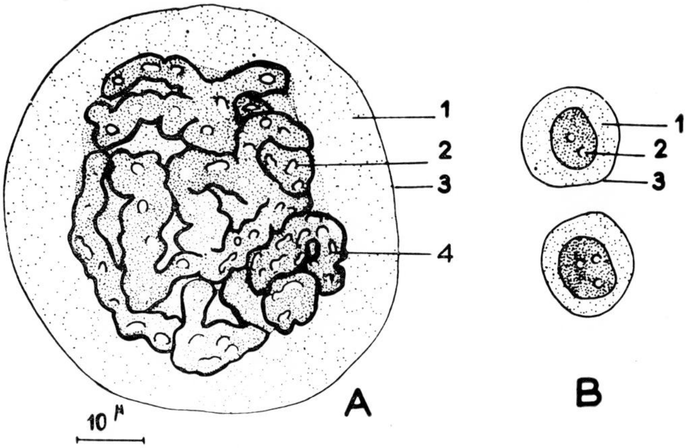

Fig. 1.35 *Acetabularia mediterranea.* Primary nuclei (after Puiseux-Dao). **A** Primary nucleus of the mature alga: 1, nucleoplasm; 2, nucleolus; 3, nuclear membrane; 4, 'nucleolar vacuole'. **B** Primary nucleus of a very young germling (100 µ) (anthracene blue)

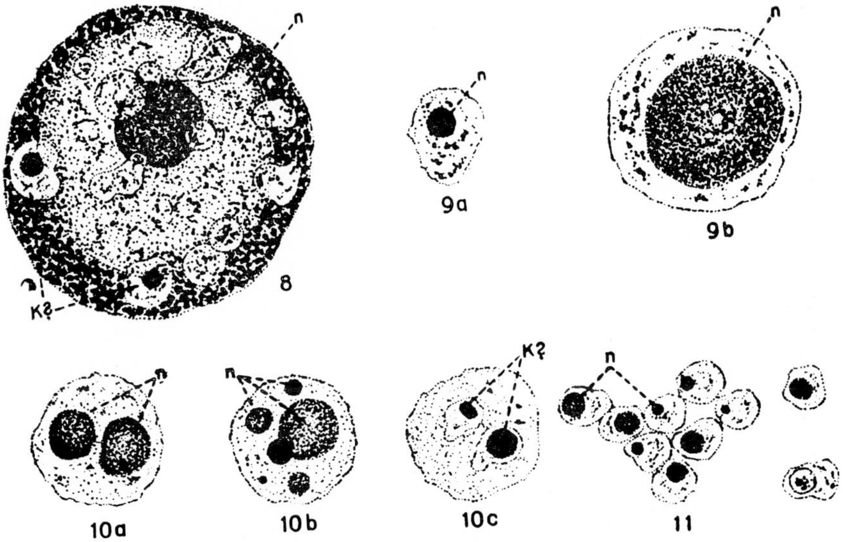

Fig. 1.36 *Cymopolia barbata.* Division of the primary nucleus and production of the daughter nuclei in the rhizoids (after Werz). 8, primary nucleus in which small nuclei are being produced (K); 9a, small secondary nucleus which has emerged from the primary nucleus; 9b, secondary nucleus whose volume has increased; 10a and 10b, partition of the nucleolus in a secondary nucleus; 10c, appearance of small daughter-nuclei (K) in a secondary nucleus; 11, small nuclei apparently formed in a secondary nucleus and liberated following breakdown of the nuclear membrane (8, 9 and 11, anthracene blue; 10, acetic azocarmine).

Acetabularias: in fact if the chromatic volume were multiplied by 16, in a nucleus where the nuclear volume is multiplied by 1,000, it is readily conceivable that the chromosome material would no longer be detectable in the large primary nuclei.

In *Cymopolia barbata* plants of one to several millimetres in length, the nucleus, after enlarging, becomes dissociated into small daughter-nuclei. These nuclei, identical with those found in germlings arising from zygotes, distribute themselves little by little throughout the alga, and increasing in volume in their turn, acquire an appearance much like that of the primary nucleus, without becoming quite so large ($2R = 30$–$50\ \mu$). Then they also become disintegrated into daughter-nuclei similar to those of germinating zygotes (Fig. 1.36). Very probably these processes of growth and multiplication with mitosis continue as long as the thallus survives (Werz 1953).

In *Neomeris annulata*, the voluminous primary nucleus usually persists for a very long time, but in some cases during germination it becomes broken up without apparent mitosis into daughter-nuclei, as in *Cymopolia*. In this case however the number of nuclei formed is very restricted (Dao 1958).

ENDOMITOSES

While studying the nuclei of the cysts which germinate directly into young plants instead of entering on a dormant period, it has been possible to reveal several successive stages of endomitosis; the cysts then contain a single nucleus like that of an ordinary germination although larger ($2R = 10\ \mu$). Endomitotic prophase is characterised by the appearance of about 16 long, fine chromosomes. A 'pseudometaphase' follows during which the chromosomes contract and appear to become double, the nucleolus meantime emits evaginated material. In the next stage, endomitotic anaphase, the nuclear volume is increased, the chromosomes are thinner once again and some are more or less parallel. Their number has apparently doubled and the evaginated nuclear material becomes drawn out as if for detachment. Most of the bigger nuclei which contain 2 nucleoli and 32 chromosomes have apparently thus originated. Following stages are difficult to interpret on account of the increase in chromosome number. Study of the nucleolus leads to the conclusion that the nucleus undergoes 16 endomitoses before becoming stabilised as a primary nucleus of considerable volume (Puiseux-Dao 1962; Fig. 1.37, 1.38C).

When observing the nuclear stages of *Cymopolia*, Werz thought that the nuclei when enlarging underwent a certain number of endomitoses. The nuclear mass thus produced divided to score a dozen or more diploid daughter-nuclei which in their turn were the seat of endomitosis. The absence of stages in which these chromosomes could be recognised did not allow him to be more precise (Fig. 1.36). Personal observations tend to confirm his statements. In the branchings of the whorls of *Cymopolia*, nuclear figures are met with which we have interpreted as follows. The secondary nuclei, derived from the primary nucleus by a process already described, enlarge while 'chromatin' threads appear in their nucleoplasm—a stage identical with the 'pseudoprophase' observed in *Batophora*.

The 'pseudometaphase' is characterised by contraction of the chromosomes, their duplication and the budding of a daughter-nucleolus from the pre-existing nucleolus—here also the course of events is as in *Batophora*.

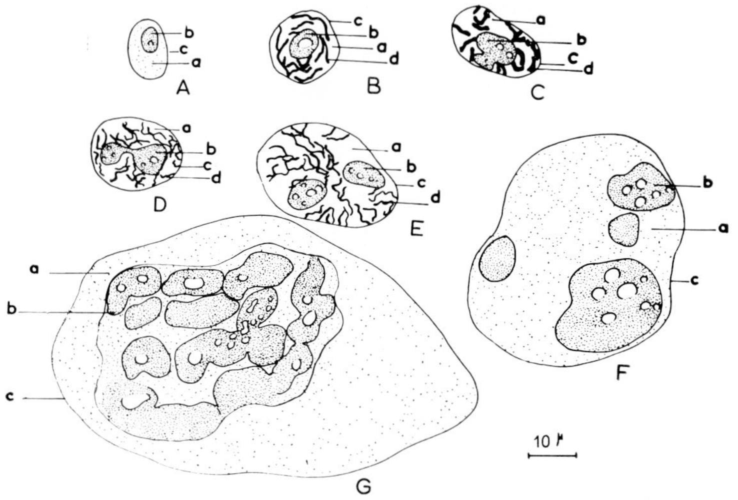

Fig. 1.37 *Batophora oerstedii.* Succession of nuclear stages during the course of polyploidisation of the primary nucleus (after Puiseux-Dao). 1–6, primary nucleus of the young germlings of *B. oerstedii*; 1, resting stage; 2, endomitotic stage equivalent to a prophase (pseudo-prophase); 3, 'pseudo-metaphase' during which the short chromosomes become longitudinally divided and the nucleolus emits a satellite nucleolus; 4, 'pseudo-anaphase' showing numerous thread-like chromosomes and two nucleoli still joined by a filament of nucleolar material; 5, 'pseudotelophase' with 'chromatic filaments' twice as numerous as in nuclei 2 and 3, two nucleoli; 6, stage undoubtedly corresponding to a nucleus with eight nucleoli; 7, primary nucleus of adult *Batophora*—a, nucleoplasm; b, nucleolus; c, nuclear membrane; d, 'chromatic filament' (acetic azocarmine).

During 'pseudoanaphase' the chromosomes separate from their replicates as do the two nucleoli: the 'pseudo-telophase' which follows leads to the simple pulling apart of the original nucleus into two daughter-nuclei (Figs. 1.30B, C and G and 1.39).

However, most commonly, after the first endomitosis, the same nucleus undergoes others, recognisable from the appearance of the nucleoli; but in *Cympolia*, while further endomitosis is proceeding, small nuclei resulting from

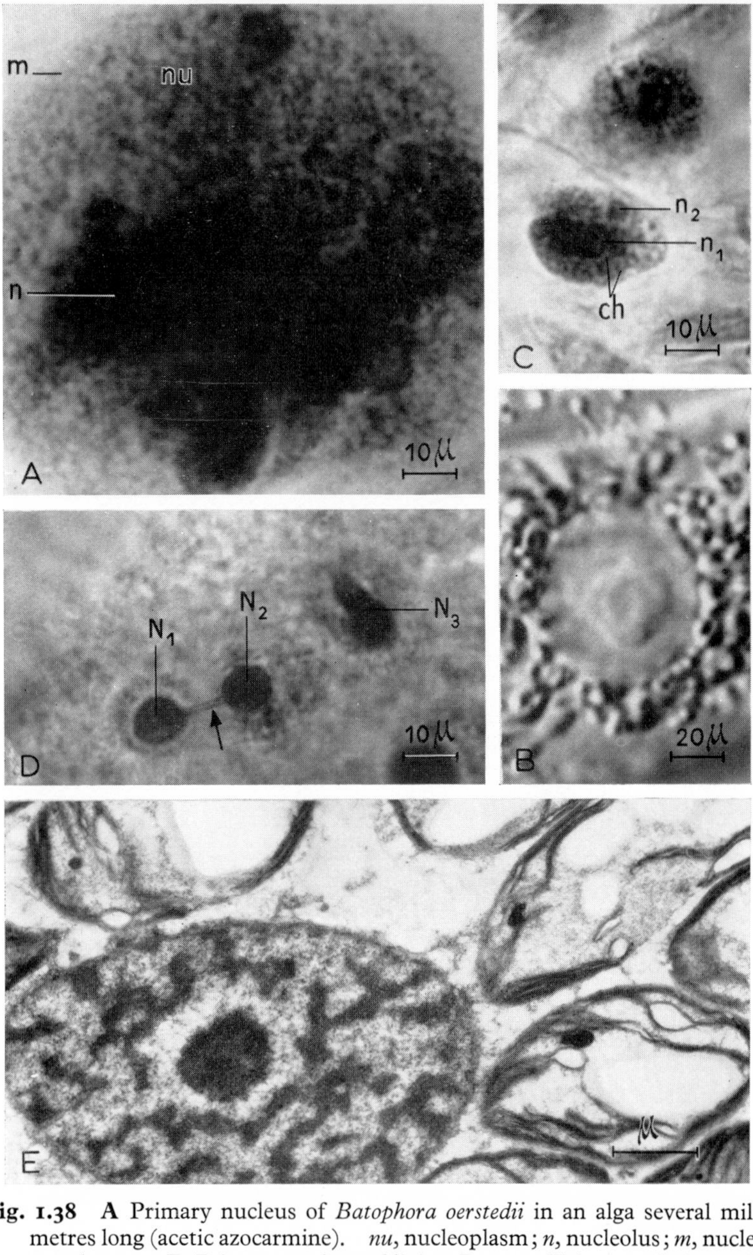

Fig. 1.38 **A** Primary nucleus of *Batophora oerstedii* in an alga several millimetres long (acetic azocarmine). *nu*, nucleoplasm; *n*, nucleolus; *m*, nuclear membrane. **B** Primary nucleus of living *B. oerstedii* (stage a little earlier than that of Fig. 1.37). **C** Endomitoses in the germination of *B. oerstedii* occurring in the direct development of cysts. A large irregular nucleolar mass can be seen (N_1) as well as a smaller rounded nucleolus (N_2) which has probably been detached from the main mass. 'Chromatic' filaments can also be seen (*ch*) (acetic azocarmine). **D** Endomitoses in the whorls of *Cymopolia barbata*. In the nucleus on the upper right, an irregular nucleolar mass (N_3). The two other nuclei are separating by a process apparently like amitosis; the nucleoli are still attached by a thin strand (acetic azocarmine). **E** Resting nucleus of *Codium tomentosum* surround by plastids. The 'chromatin' is denser than in *Bryopsis* (glutaraldehyde postosmified; Giraud).

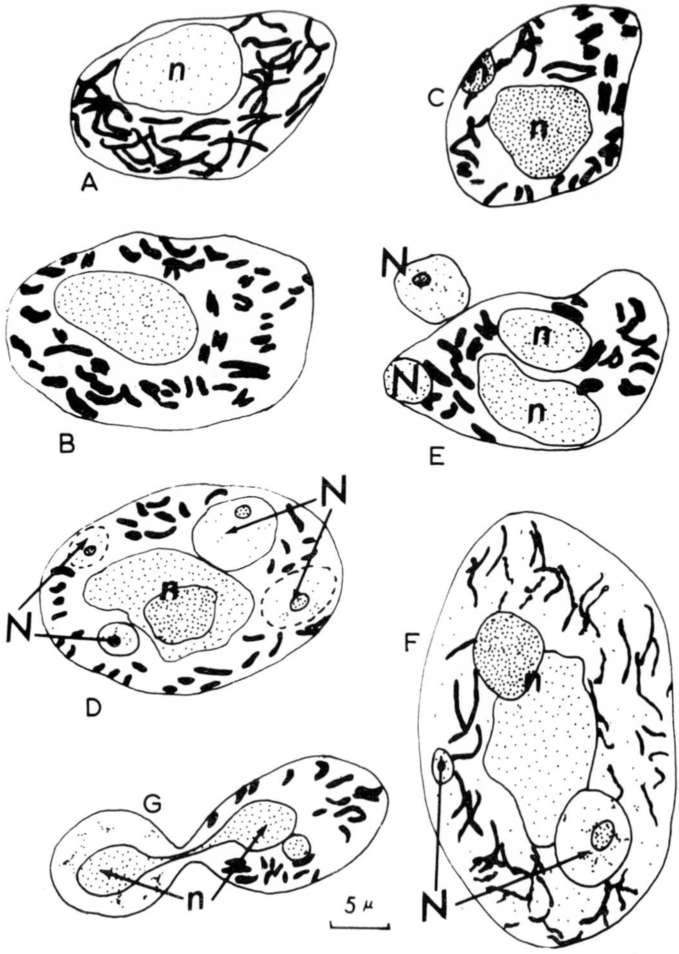

Fig. 1.39 *Cymopolia barbata*. Endomitosis in the whorled hairs (original). 1, secondary nucleus of large volume in which the chromosomes have become visible—'pseudoprophase'; 2, pseudometaphase; the short chromosomes become doubled, the nucleolus is still solitary; 3, 'pseudoanaphase', the duplication of chromosomes, often still associated in pairs, is complete, a small nucleolus has formed beside the first which is still larger; 4, 'pseudometaphase', accompanied by the elaboration of small daughter-nuclei ready to be emitted into the cytoplasm; the contracted chromosomes have not yet separated into chromatids but the daughter-nucleolus is already enlarging; 5, end of the preceding stage; the chromosomes and their replicates are separating, the nucleoli are already separated, two daughter-nuclei (N) constituted by the preceding endomitosis are in one case already expelled outside the nucleus, in the other in course of expulsion; 6, 'pseudotelophase'; the thin chromosomes become indistinct, the daughter-nucleolus is thus clearly visible as well as the two nuclei ready to be ejected into the cytoplasm; 7, two nuclei are separating from each other by a process resembling amitosis; the attached nuclei are not in the same state; on the right, there is a pseudometaphase with formation of pairs of chromosomes and daughter-nucleoli, on the left a resting stage (azoacetocarmine).

earlier endomitotic cycles are expelled into the cytoplasm, usually in pairs and at different times (Fig. 1.39D, E and F).

It is thus possible to regard the primary nucleus of Dasycladaceae as polyploid. Polyploidy is brought about by intranuclear replication of the chromosomes accompanied by the elaboration of new nucleoli. These nucleoli often fuse together to form an irregular globular or serpentine nucleolar mass. This nucleolus is metabolically active: the different nucleoli separate once again from one another when their size is reduced by a diminution of the metabolic activity.

There is certainly a state of equilibrium in the course of which the polyploid nuclei persist, till little-known physiological factors provoke the eruption of nuclear enlargement and numerous daughter-nuclei. This eruption occurs generally only once in the Acetabularias and in *Batophora*; but in the *Cymopolias* it is credible that several successive cycles of endomitosis, life in the polyploid state and abnormal divisions, occur.

The case of *Neomeris* is probably intermediate, the dividing-up of the primary nucleus before reproduction seeming to be accidental.

THE DIVISION OF THE PRIMARY NUCLEI

This division without a sign of mitosis is totally aberrant as in all the polyploid nuclei.

The simplest case is found in *Cymopolia*, where the nucleus becomes pulled out and separates into two masses, apparently following a process similar to amitosis, the daughter-nucleoli separating in the same way (Figs. 1.38D and 1.39G). In *Neomeris*, the mode of division seems identical.

Most frequently, in *Cymopolia*, rounded masses, surrounded by a membrane and including a more or less important piece of nucleolar material, become cut off inside the large nuclei. These rounded portions are emitted at the outside of the large nucleus or quite often this nucleus breaks down with their liberation (Fig. 1.30G).

In the Acetabularias and *Batophora*, the breakdown of the enormous primary nucleus occurs in this latter manner; however the delimitation of the daughter-nuclei, called secondary nuclei and extremely numerous (several thousand) is far from being as complete at the start of the breakdown. Basophilic lobules detach themselves from the primary nucleus which then has the appearance of a homogeneous mass. In these lobules appear little by little small resting nuclei or mitoses. A great part of the nuclear substance is abandoned without being used up (Fig. 1.40).

MITOSES OF THE SECONDARY NUCLEI

In the *Cymopolias*, the secondary nuclei undergo endomitoses and return to the polyploid state until the period of reproduction. At this moment, by contrast, they divide mitotically and the daughter-nuclei are enclosed in the developing cysts. In the other genera, *Acetabularia* and *Batophora*, as soon as they have appeared, the secondary nuclei enter asynchronously on to

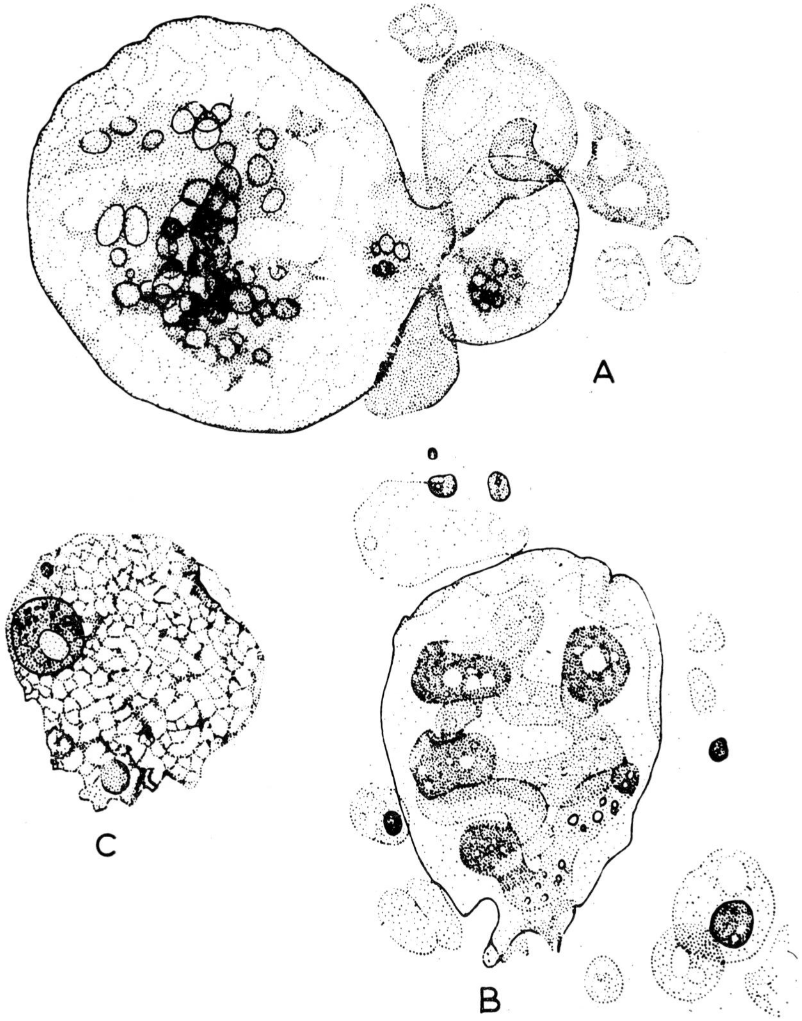

Fig. 1.40 Division of the primary nucleus in *Acetabularia wettsteinii* (1 and 3) and *A. mediterranea* (2) (after Schulze). 1 and 2, start of division, the nucleus becomes dis-aggregated into lobules of varying size; 3, the remains of the nucleus not used up in the formation of secondary nuclei. (1 and 2, anthracene blue; 3, carmine and chrome alum).

mitosis. Their diameter is then about 3–5 μ in *Acetabularia*, 7–10 μ in *Batophora*. The start of prophase is easily recognised by the presence of one or two very densely staining granules: then the 'chromatin' threads become visible at the same time that the nuclear volume diminishes, especially in *Batophora* where the diameter of the nucleus is sometimes reduced by one-quarter.

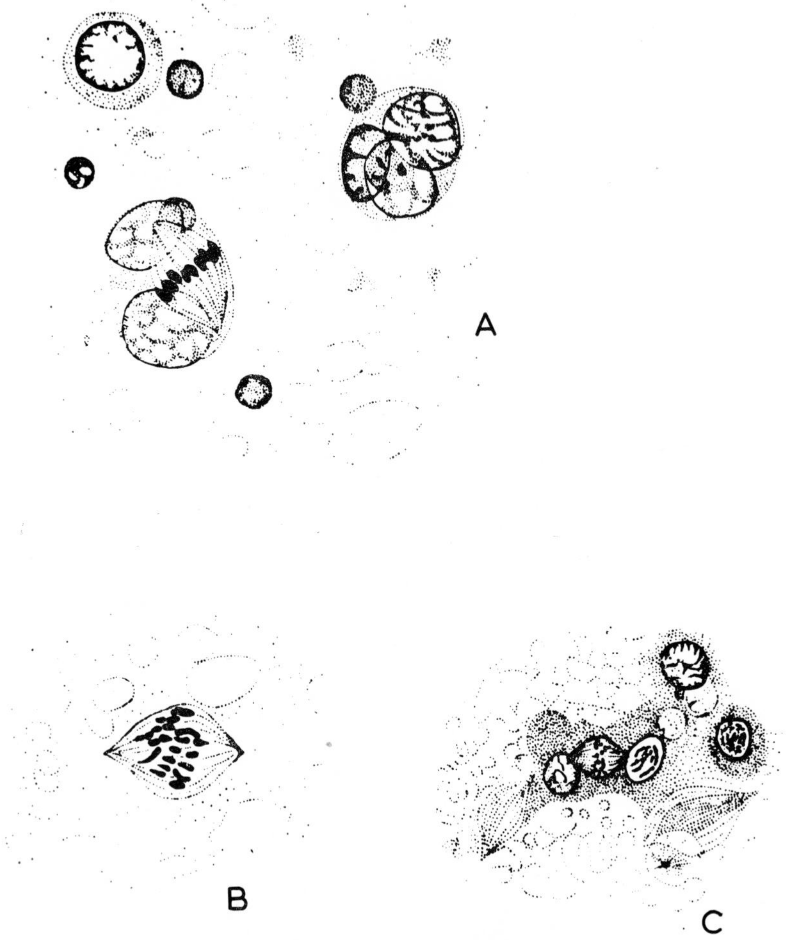

Fig. 1.41 Appearance of secondary nuclei in *Acetabularia mediterranea* (1 and 2) and *A. wettsteinii* (3) (after Schulze). 1 and 3, resting nuclei and mitosis in the lobules originating in division of the primary nucleus and situated in the rhizoids where this is situated; 2, secondary nucleus in mitosis (carmine after chrome alum).

When the metaphase plate is organised, there is again a general expansion of the nucleus and the membrane disappears: nevertheless Schulze indicates that in *Acetabularia* this membrane can persist for a longer time (Fig. 1.41). The chromosomes are short and slightly incurved in *Batophora*; thinner and

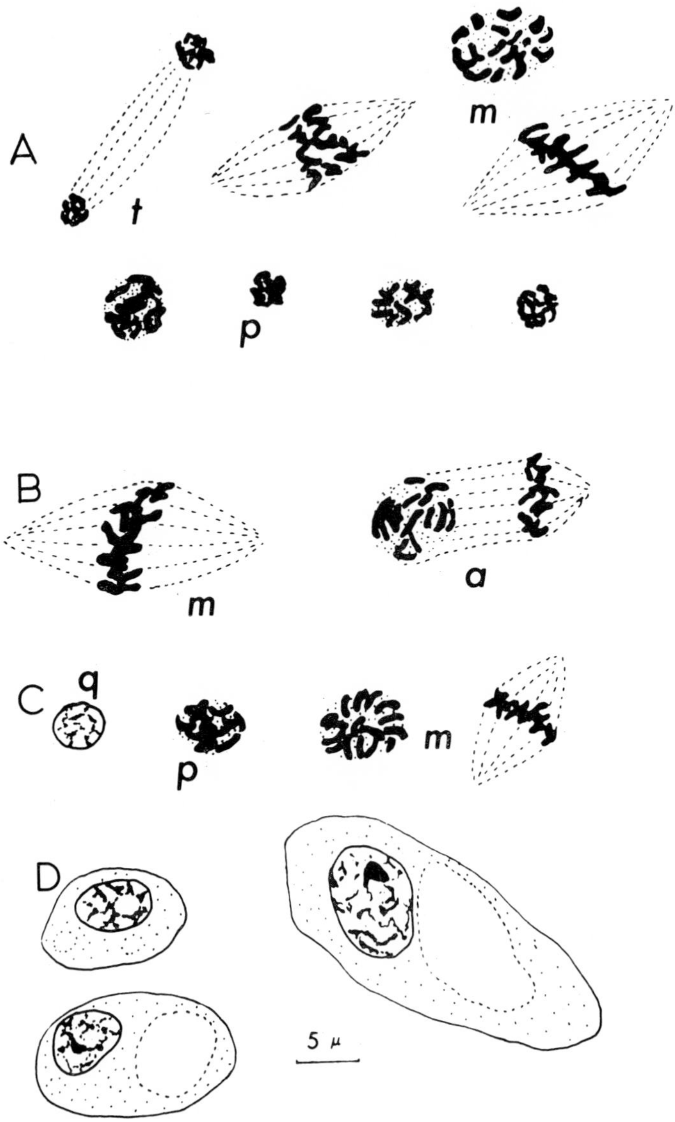

Fig. 1.42 *Batophora oerstedii*. Secondary nuclei in mitosis observed in different situations (original). 1, mitoses localised in the reproductive organs before cyst-formation; 2, mitosis in cysts fixed before their entry into the dormant state; 3, mitoses produced at the end of sporogenesis; 4, three stages of development of zoospores—t, telophase; m, metaphase; p, prophase; a, anaphase; q, resting nucleus (Feulgen).

longer in *Acetabularia*. The spindle, large and squat at the beginning of metaphase, becomes longer in anaphase and telophase (Fig. 1.42). Telophase nuclei look like the prophase ones—as resting stage is reached they enlarge slightly. Chromosome numbers are as follows:

Acetabularia mediterranea	2*n* = 20 (Schulze)
	2*n* = 8–10 (Puiseux-Dao)
Batophora oerstedii	2*n* = 16 (Puiseux-Dao)
Cymopolia barbata	2*n* = 14 (Werz)

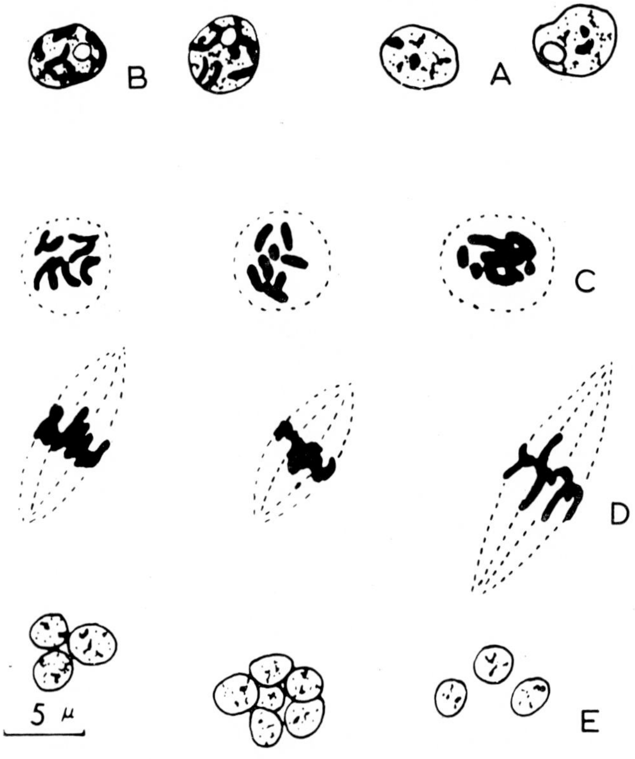

Fig. 1.43 *Acetabularia mediterranea*. Nuclei in mitosis observed in the cysts during the course of sporogenesis (original). 1, resting nuclei in which lie two granules deeply stained by the Feulgen technique—2, prophase; 3, metaphase plates; 4, metaphase; 5, future zoospore nuclei still grouped together (Feulgen).

Ascending cytoplasmic currents carry the mitotic nuclei up to the reproductive organs of these algae. As a general rule, when the daughter-nuclei have entered on a period of rest, cysts are delimited around each one of them, although such delimitation is not always regular and certain large cysts contain several nuclei from the start. Nuclear division begins again in the cysts

(Fig. 1.42), producing 20–30 nuclei which distribute themselves regularly before entering on a resting period.

Sporogenesis is preceded by considerable mitotic activity: the mitoses always show the same characters but the size of nuclei becomes progressively less (Figs. 1.42 and 1.43). The cytoplasm breaks up into swarmers, each containing a single nucleus: cytoplasmic cleavage often starts before the nuclei have finished dividing. After liberation, these swarmers germinate to give a plant like the parent which had produced the cysts.

MEIOSIS AND GAMETOGENESIS

In certain cysts, the swarmers are gametes which fuse among themselves: the zygotes develop to give rise again to a plant like that which had produced the cysts, therefore uninucleate for a longer or shorter period of its existence: the gametes usually contain a miniature nucleus (1–2 μ across), study of which is difficult. Nuclear fusion within the egg has been revealed for *Acetabularia mediterranea* (Puiseux-Dao 1962) and *Cymopolia barbata* (Werz 1953). On the other hand, the meiosis which all authors regard as occurring during the last division in the gametogenic cysts, has never been described. Certain nuclear configurations have been observed by Schussnig, Schulze and Puiseux-Dao, but all stages of meiosis could not be followed, the nuclei being extremely small and some hardly distinguishable from pycnotic nuclei on the way to degeneration.

Just as in the Valoniaceae, Codiaceae and Caulerpaceae, in the Dasycladaceae there is only one kind of thallus and the mode of development of the zygotes supports the view that this thallus is diploid in origin. Nevertheless the fusion nucleus becomes polyploid in the course of the growth of the alga; the polyploid nucleus remains stable and therefore unique in all species except in *Cymopolia* where nuclei at different stages of polyploidisation are observed. Reproduction induces nuclear division in nuclei of raised chromosomic stock and at this stage classic nuclear figures occur. But sometimes it happens that some of these normal nuclei become polyploid again under the influence of unknown factors; then plants of normal type for example from cytoplasm not used up in cystformation or even from the cysts themselves. Further, the failure of reduction division to take place, suggested for *Siphonocladus*, occurs very often in Dasycladaceae at least in culture, since frequently the cysts produce zoospores which germinate directly. In spite of the absence of precise observations concerning meiosis, this interpretation of the life-cycle of Dasycladaceae is probably correct. In fact the only other possible place for meiosis would be the moment of initiation of division in the primary nucleus; but two arguments are against this, namely, the comparability of the nuclear stages in zoospores and zygotes, and the behaviour of the nuclei in *Cymopolia*.

It may be noted in passing, that all authors agree in regard to gametogenesis in Dasycladaceae: the gametes are usually isogamous or slightly anisogamous.

Exceptionally, in *Acetabularia mediterranea* a markedly anisogamous state has described. When one considers the chromosome number given for this species, it is obvious that there are at least two different races.

CONCLUSION

In the siphoneous Chlorophyceae, the facts which have been uncovered regarding the nuclei, nuclear division, and life-cycles, are still fragmentary. Nevertheless such nuclear figures as have been obtained are typically classic except in Dasycladaceae where the polyploidisation complicates matters. One character appears quite constant in all these algae: the nuclei behave independently of each other and nuclear divisions are always asynchronous. To sum up, the absence of the haploid thallus is evident in many species and even sexual reproduction is often suppressed, the diploid thalli multiplying very easily by fragmentation or by diploid zoospores when the conditions are favourable for growth.

REFERENCES

ABBAS, A. (1963). Ph.D. thesis, London University.

ABBAS, A. and GODWARD, M. B. E. (1963). Cytology in relation to taxonomy in *Chaetophorales*. *J. Linn. Soc.* (*Bot.*), **58**, 499–506.

ADAMS, K. J. and GODWARD, M. B. E. (1965) (in press).

ALLEN, M. A. (1958). Ph.D. thesis, Indiana University.

BARNICOT, N. A. and HUXLEY, H. E. (University College, London) unpublished.

BĚLAŘ, KARL (1926). 'Der Formwechsel der Protistenkeine.' Gustav Fischer, Jena.

BENDIX, S. (1964). Phenotypic variability in certain *Chlorella pyrenoidosa* strains. *Phycologia*, **4**, 84–91.

BOLD, H. C. (1933). The life history and cytology of *Protosiphon botryoides*. *Bull. Torrey Bot. Club*, **60**, 241–299.

BRANDHAM, P. E. (1964). Ph.D. thesis, London University.

BRANDHAM, P. E. and GODWARD, M. B. E. (1965). *Meiosis in Cosmarium botrytis* (in press).

— — (1965). *Electron microscopy of a desmid nucleus* (in press).

BUFFALOE, N. P. (1958). A comparative cytological study of four species of *Chlamydomonas*. *Bull. Torrey Bot. Club*, **85**, 157–178.

BURDETT, R. M. and TURNBULL, L. P. (1960). The effect of gibberellic acid on the growth of *Chlamydomonas moewusii*. *Brit. Phycol. Bull.*, **2** (No. 1), 13.

BURLEW, J. S. (1953). *Algal Culture from Laboratory to Pilot Plant*. Carnegie Institution, Washington D.C.

CAVE, M. S. and POCOCK, M. A. (1951). Karyological studies in the *Volvocaceae*. *Amer. J. Bot.*, **38**, 10, 800–811.

— — (1956). Variable chromosome number in *Astrephomene gubernaculifera*. *Amer. J. Bot.*, **43**, 2.

CHADEFAUD, M. (1960). *Traité de Botanique systématique*, Vol. I. Masson.

CHAPMAN, V. J. (1956). The marine algae of New Zealand. *J. Linn. Soc.* (*Bot.*), **55**, (360), 333–501.

CHRISTENSEN, T. (1962). *Systematisk Botanik, II Alger.* Copenhagen.

— (1964). General consideration of algal phylogeny. *Xth Int. Bot. Cong. Edinburgh*, 107–108 (Abstract).

CONARD, H. *et al.* (1959). Effects of auxin and gibberellic acid on growth of *Ulothrix. Nature*, **184**, 556–557.

DAO, S. (1958). Recherches caryologiques chez le *Neomeris annulata* Dickie. *Rev. Algol. Nlle. série*, **3**, 192–201.

DODGE, J. D. (1960). Ph.D. thesis, London University.

DROOP, M. R. (1957). Auxotrophy and organic compounds in the nutrition of marine phytoplankton. *J. gen. Microbiol.*, **16**, 286.

— (1958). Optimum relative and actual ionic concentrations for growth of some Euryhaline algae. *Proc. Int. Assoc. Limnol.*, **13**, 722–730.

— (1958). Requirement for thiamine among some marine and supralittoral protista. *J. biol. Ass., U.K.*, **37**, 323–329.

— (1959). Chemical and ecological considerations in the design of synthetic culture media for marine algae. *Proc. IX Inter. Bot. Congress*, 96–97.

FELDMAN, J. (1963). *Précis de botanique.* Masson.

FOTT, B. (1959). *Algenkunde.* Veb Gustav Fischer, Jena.

— (1964). Evolutionary tendencies among algae and their position in the plant kingdom. *Xth Int. Bot. Cong., Edinburgh*, 140 (Abstract).

FRIEDMANN, I. (1959). Structure, life-history, and sex determination of *Prasiola stipitata suhr. Ann. Bot., Lond.*, N.S., **23**, No. 92.

FRITSCH, F. E. (1948). *The Structure and Reproduction of the Algae*, Vol. I. Cambridge.

GEITLER, L. (1930). Uber die kernteilung von *Spirogyra. Arch. f. Protist.*, **71**, 10–18.

— (1935). Neue untersuchungen uber die mitose von *Spirogyra. Arch. f. Protist.*, **85**, 10–19.

— (1936). Vergleichende untersuchungen uber den feineren kern und chromosomen bau der *Cladophoraceen. Planta*, **35**, 530–578.

GODWARD, M. B. E. (1948). Iron alum acetocarmine method for algae. *Nature Lond.*, **161**, 203.

— (1950). On the nucleolus and nucleolar-organising chromosomes of *Spirogyra. Ann. Bot., Lond*, N.S., **14**, 39–53.

— (1953). Geitler's nucleolar substance in *Spirogyra. Ann. Bot., Lond.*, N.S., **17**, 403–416.

— (1954a). The diffuse centromere or polycentric chromosomes in *Spirogyra. Ann. Bot., Lond.*, N.S., **18**, 143–156.

— (1954b) Irradiation of *Spirogyra* chromosomes. *Heredity*, **8**, 293.

— (1956). Cytotaxonomy of *Spirogyra* I: *S. submargaritata, S. subechinata* and *S. britannica*, spp. Novae. *J. Linn. Soc. (Bot.)*, **55**, 532–546.

— (1961). Meiosis in *Spirogyra crassa. Heredity*, **16**, 53–62.

— (1962). Invisible radiations. In *Physiology and Biochemistry of Algae*, LEWIN, R. A., Ed. Academic Press, New York and London.

— (1965). Problems of mitosis in the Algae. In *Viewpoints in Biology*, Butterworth, London.

GODWARD, M. B. E. and NEWNHAM, R. E. (1965). Cytotaxonomy of *Spirogyra II. S. neglecta* (Hass.) Kütz., *S. punctulata* Jao, *S. majuscula* (Kütz.) Czurda emend., *S. ellipsospora* Transeau, *S. porticalis* (Müller) Cleve. *J. Linn. Soc. (Bot.)*, **59**, 99–110.

GODWARD, M. B. E. and JORDAN, E. G. (1965). Electron microsopy of the nucleolus of *Spirogyra. Jl. Roy. microse. Soc.* **84**, 347–60.

GOLDSTEIN, M. (1964). Speciation and mating behaviour in *Eudorina*. *J. Protozool.*, **11** (3), 317–344.
GOLTERMAN, H. L. (1960). Studies on the cycle of elements in freshwater. *Acta Bot. Neerl.*, **9**, 1–58.
GRIFFIN, D. N. (1958). The effect of GA upon *Euglena*. *Proc. Oklahoma Acad. Science*, **38**, 14–15.
HENNINGSEN, H. (1965). Chromosome numbers in five species of *Oedogonium*. *Phycologia*, **3**, 29–36.
HOFFMAN, L. (1965). Cytological studies of *Oedogonium I*. Oospore germination in *O. foveolatum*. *Amer. J. Bot.*, **52**, 2.
HOLLANDE, A. (1942). Etude cytologique et biologique de quelques flagellees libres. *Arch. Zool. Exp. Gen.*, **83**, 1–268.
— (1954). Classe des *Cryptomonadineae*. *Traite de Zoologie*, I, GRASSE, P., Ed. 285–308.
HOWARD, A. and HORSLEY, R. J. (1960). Filamentous green algae for radiobiological study. *Int. J. Rad. Biol.*, **2**, 319–330.
HUTNER, S. H. and PROVASOLI, L. (1951). The phytoflagellates. In *Biochemistry and Physiology of Protozoa*. **1**, 27–128. Academic Press, New York and London.
HUTNER, S. H., PROVASOLI, L., SCHATZ, A. and HASKINS, C. P. (1950). Some approaches to the study of the role of metals in the metabolism of microorganisms. *Proc. Amer. Phil. Soc.*, **94**, 152–170.
JAMES, T. W. (1961). Continuous culture of micro-organisms. *Ann. Rev. Microbiol.*, **15**, 27–46.
JAMES, T. W. and COOK, R. (1960). *Exp. Cell Res.*, **21**, 585.
JONSSON, S. and PUISEUX-DAO, S. (1959). Observations morphologiques et caryologiques relatives à la reproduction chez le *Siphonoclacdus pusillus* (Kütz.) Hauck, Siphonocladacées, en culture. *C.R. Acad. Sci.*, **249**, 1383–1385.
KALLIO, P. (1951). The significance of the nuclear quantity in the genus *Micrasterias*. *Ann. Bot. Soc. Zool. Bot. Fenn*, **24**, 1–122.
KARSTEN, G. (1908). Die entwicklung der zygoten von *Spirogyra jugalis* Kütz. *Flora*, **99**, 1–11.
KIM, W. K. and GREULACH, V. A. (1961). Promotion of algal growth by IAA, GA and Kinetin. *Plant Physiol.*, **36** (Suppl.), 14.
KING, G. C. (1954). Ph.D. thesis, London University.
— (1959). The nucleoli and related structures in the desmids. *New Phytol.*, **58**, 20–28.
— (1960). The cytology of desmids: the chromosomes. *New Phytol.*, **59**, 65–72.
KING, R. and BEAMS, H. (1940). Comparison of the effects of colchicine on division in protozoa and other cells. *J. Cell, Comp. Physiol.*, **15**, 252–254.
KINOSHITA, S. and TERMOTO, K. (1958). On the efficiency of gibberellin on the growth of *Porphyra* frond. *Bull. Jap. Phycol. Soc.*, **6**, 85–88.
LEDBETTER, M. C. (1964). The form and distribution of cytotubules in plant cells. *Abstr. Int. Bot. Congress*, 1964.
LEEDALE, G. F. (1957). Ph.D. thesis, London University.
LEVAN, A. (1938). The effect of colchicine on root mitosis in *Allium*. *Hereditas*, **24**, 471–485.
— (1940). The effect of acenaphthene and colchicine on mitosis of *Allium* and *Colchicum*. *Hereditas*, **26**, 262–276.

LEVAN, A. and SANDWALL, C. (1943). Quantitative investigations on the reactions of yeast to certain biologically active substances. *Hereditas*, **29**, 164–178.

LEVINE, R. P. and EBERSOLD, W. T. (1960). The genetics and cytology of *Chlamydomonas*. *Ann. Rev. Microbiol.*, **14**, 187–215.

MAGNE, F. (1964). Recherches caryologiques chez les Floridées (Rhodophycées). *Cahiers de Biologie marine*, V, 467–663.

MAINX, F. (1931). Physiologische und genetische untersuchungen an *Oedogonium I*. *Zeitschr. Bot.*, **24**, 481–527.

MOEWUS, F. (1939). Untersuchungen uber die sexualitat von algen. *Biol. Zbl.*, **59**, 40–58.

— (1950). Sexualitat und sexualstoffe bei einem einzelliger organismus. *Zeit. f. Sexualforsch.*, pp. 1–26.

MOLLE (1870). See Van Wisselingh, 1900.

MYERS, J. (1946). Culture conditions and the development of the photosynthetic mechanism. IV. Influence of Light Intensity on Photosynthetic Characteristics of *Chlorella*.

— (1953). Growth characteristics of Algae in relation to the problem of mass culture. In *Algal Culture from Laboratory to Pilot Plant*. BURLEW, J. S., Ed. Carnegie Institution, Washington D.C.

— (1962). Laboratory cultures. In *Physiology and Biochemistry of Algae*. LEWIN, R. A., Ed. Academic Press, New York and London.

NEWNHAM, R. A. (1962). M.Sc. thesis, London University.

NIZAM, J. (1960). Ph.D. thesis, London University.

PATEL, R. J. (1961). Ph.D. thesis, London University.

PORTER, K. R. and LEDBETTER, M. C. (1964). The fine structure of dividing cells. *Abstr., Int. Bot. Congress*, 1964.

PRASAD, B. N. (1958). Ph.D. thesis, London University.

PRINGSHEIM, E. G. (1946a). *Pure Cultures of Algae*. University Press, Cambridge.

— (1946b). The biphasic or soil water culture method for growing algae and flagellates. *J. Ecol.*, **33**, 193–204.

— (1951). Methods for cultivation of algae. In *Manual of Phycology Chronica Bot. Wiltham, Mass.*, 347–357.

PROVASOLI, L. (1958a). Effect of plant hormones on *Ulva*. *Biol. Bull.*, **144**, 375–384.

— (1958b). Nutrition and ecology of Protozoa and Algae. *Ann. Rev. Microbiol.*, **12**, 279–308.

PROVASOLI, L. and HUTNER, S. H. (1964). Nutrition of Algae. *Ann. Rev. Plant Physiol.*, **15**, 37–56.

PROVASOLI, L., MCLAUGHLIN, J. J. A. and DROOP, M. R. (1957). The development of artificial media for marine algae. *Arch. Mikrobiol.*, **25**, 392–428.

PROVASOLI, L., MCLAUGHLIN, J. J. A. and PITNER, I. J. (1954). Relative and limiting concentrations of major mineral constituents for the growth of algal flagellates. *Trans. N.Y. Acad. Sci.*, **16**, 412.

PUISEUX-DAL, S. (1962). Recherches biologiques et physiologiques sur quelques Dasycladacées. *Rev. Gén. Bot.*, **819**, 409–503.

— (1963). Les Acétabulaires, matériel de laboratoire. Les résultats obtenus avec ces Chlorophycées. *L' Année Biologique, II*, **3–4**, 100–154.

RAYNS, D. G. (1961). Ph.D. thesis, London University.

— (1962). Alternation of Generations in A *Coccolithophorid*, *Cricosphaera*

Carterae (*Braarud & Fagerl.*) *Braarud*. *J. mar. biol. Ass., U.K.*, **42**, 481–484.

RODHE, W. (1948). Environmental requirements of fresh water plankton algae; Experimental studies in the ecology of phytoplankton. *Symb. Bot. Upsaliensis*, **10** (1), 1–149.

SAGER, R. (1962). Streptomycin as a mutagen for non-chromosomal genes. *Proc. Nat. Acad. Sci.*, **48**, 2018–2026.

SAGER, R. and ROMINIS, Z. (1963). The particulate nature of non-chromosomal genes. *Proc. Nat. Acad. Sci.*, **49**.

SARMA, Y. S. R. K. (1958). Ph.D. thesis, London University.

SCHECHNER-FRIES, M. (1934). Der Phasenwechsel von *Valonia utricularis* (Roth) *Ag. Osterr. Botan. Zeitschrift*, **83**, 241–254.

SCHULZE, K. L. (1939). Cytologische Untersuchungen am *Acetabularia mediterranea* und *Acetabularia wettsteinii*. *Arch. Protistenkde*, **92**, 179–225.

SCHUSSNIG, B. (1928). Die reduction teilung bei *Cladophora glomerata*. *Osterr. Botan. Zeitschrift*, **57**, 1, 62–67.

— (1930). Der chromosomencyclus von *Cladophora Suhriana*. *Osterr. Botan. Zeitschrift*, **79**, 3, 273–277.

— (1938). Der kernphasenwechsel von *Cladophora gracilis*. *Biol. Generatis*, **59**, 129–144.

— (1951). Der kernphasenwechsel von *Cladophora glomerata*. *Svensk Botan. Tidskrift*, **45**, 597–602.

— 1953. Handbuch der Protoyhytenkunde, Bd. I. Gustav Fischer, Jena.

— (1954). Gonidiogenese, gametogenese und meiose bei *Cladophora glomerata* (L.) Kütz. *Arch. Protistenk.*, **100**, 287–322.

— B. (1932). Der Generations- und Phasenwechsel bei den Chlorophyceen. III. *Osterr. Botan. Zeitschrift*, **18**, 296–298.

— (1938). Der Kernphasenwechsel von *Valonia utricularis* (Roth) *Ag. Planta*, **28**, 43–59.

SELBY, C. H. (1956). Ph.D. thesis, London University.

SINHA, J. P. (1958). Ph.D. thesis, London University.

— (1963). Cytological studies on *Oedogonium cardiacum* Wittrock and one another *Oedogonium*. *Cytologia*, **28**, No. 2, 194–200.

SMITH, G. M. (1946). The nature of sexuality in *Chlamydomonas*. *Amer. J. Bot.*, **33**, 625–630.

STARR, R. C. (1954a). Heterothallism in *Cosmarium botrytis var. subtumidum*. *Amer. J. Bot.*, **41**, 8, 601–607.

— (1954b). Inheritance of mating type and a lethal factor in *Cosmarium botrytis var. subtumidum* Wittr. *Proc. Nat. Acad. Sci.*, **40**, 11, 1060–1063.

— (1955b). Zygospore germination in *Cosmarium botrytis var. subtumidum*. *Amer. J. Bot.*, **42**, 577–581.

— (1959). Sexual reproduction in certain species of *Cosmarium*. *Arch. Protistenk.*, **104** (1), 155–164.

STEIN, J. R. (1958). A morphological study of *Astrephomene gubernaculifera* and *Volvulina steini*. *Amer. J. Bot.*, **45**, 388–397.

STRASBURGER, E. (1898). *See* Van Wisselingh, 1900.

TAMIYA, H. (1957). Mass cultures of algae. *Ann. Rev. Plant Physiol.*, **8**, 309–334.

— (1963). Control of cell division in micro-algae. *J. Cell Comp. Physiol.*, **62**, 157–174.

THAKUR, M. (1964). Ph.D. thesis, London University.

THOMAS, P. T. (1940). The aceto-carmine method for fruit material. *S.T.*, **15**, 167–172.

TRÖNDLE, A. (1911). Uber die reduktionsteilung in den zygoten von *Spirogyra. Zeitschr. Bot.*, **3**, 593–619.

TSCHERMAK, E. (1943). Vergleichende und experimentelle cytologische untersuchungen an der Gattung *Oedogonium. Chromosoma*, **2**, 493–518.

VAN WISSELINGH, C. (1900). Uber kernteilung bei *Spirogyra. Flora*, **87**, 355–377.

WERZ, G. (1953). Uber die Kernverhältnisse der Dasycladaceen, besonders von *Cymopolia barbata* (L.) *Harv. Arch. Protistenkde*, **99**, 198–155.

WETHERELL, D. F. and KRAUSS, D. W. (1956). Colchicine induced polyploidy in *Clamydomonas. Science*, **124**, 25.

WILLIAMS, M. M. (1925). Cytology of the gametangia of *Codium tomentosum. Proc. Linn. Soc.*, **50**, 91--111.

2 The Euglenophyceae

GORDON F. LEEDALE
B.Sc., Ph.D.
Reader, Department of Botany,
University of Leeds

The peculiarities of nuclear structure and division in the euglenoid flagellates were first reported upon by Blochmann in 1894 and Keuten in 1895. In the three-quarters of a century since then, investigations of the euglenoid nucleus have been the source of much speculation and controversy. Results and theories produced by the many workers in this field have been summarised and evaluated in a series of papers (Leedale 1958a, 1958b, 1959a, 1959b, 1959c, 1961, 1962) and reference should be made to these for an historical review and exhaustive bibliographies.

The present summary is based upon light microscopical studies of living and fixed nuclei of 25 euglenoid species, drawn from a dozen genera (see Leedale 1958b for a list of species studied and for details of cultivation, cytological and experimental techniques). Nuclear structure and mitosis are described for *Euglena gracilis* Klebs, a research organism of major importance, and the details compared with idiosyncrasies of structure and behaviour exhibited by other species. Despite these specific variations, there emerges a basic pattern of euglenoid mitosis which is common to, and typical of, all euglenoid flagellates. This process is discussed in general terms with regard to its nature, mechanism and significance. In addition, other patterns of nuclear behaviour in the Euglenophyceae ('amitosis', meiosis) have also been studied and these are briefly considered at the end of this survey.

NUCLEAR STRUCTURE AND MITOSIS IN *EUGLENA GRACILIS*

Interphase The interphase nucleus of *E. gracilis* lies in the centre or posterior half of the cell (Fig. 2.1A).* It is an approximately spherical body, averaging 10 μ in diameter. The chromosomes remain condensed and stainable throughout the nuclear cycle, appearing as granular threads in interphase. The nucleus also contains a single, large, spherical endosome ('nucleolus', see p. 83) and is limited by a nuclear envelope. Modern methods

* Figs. 2.1–2.7. All cells prepared by methanol fixation and aceto-carmine staining, with ferric acetate mordant (see p. 3).

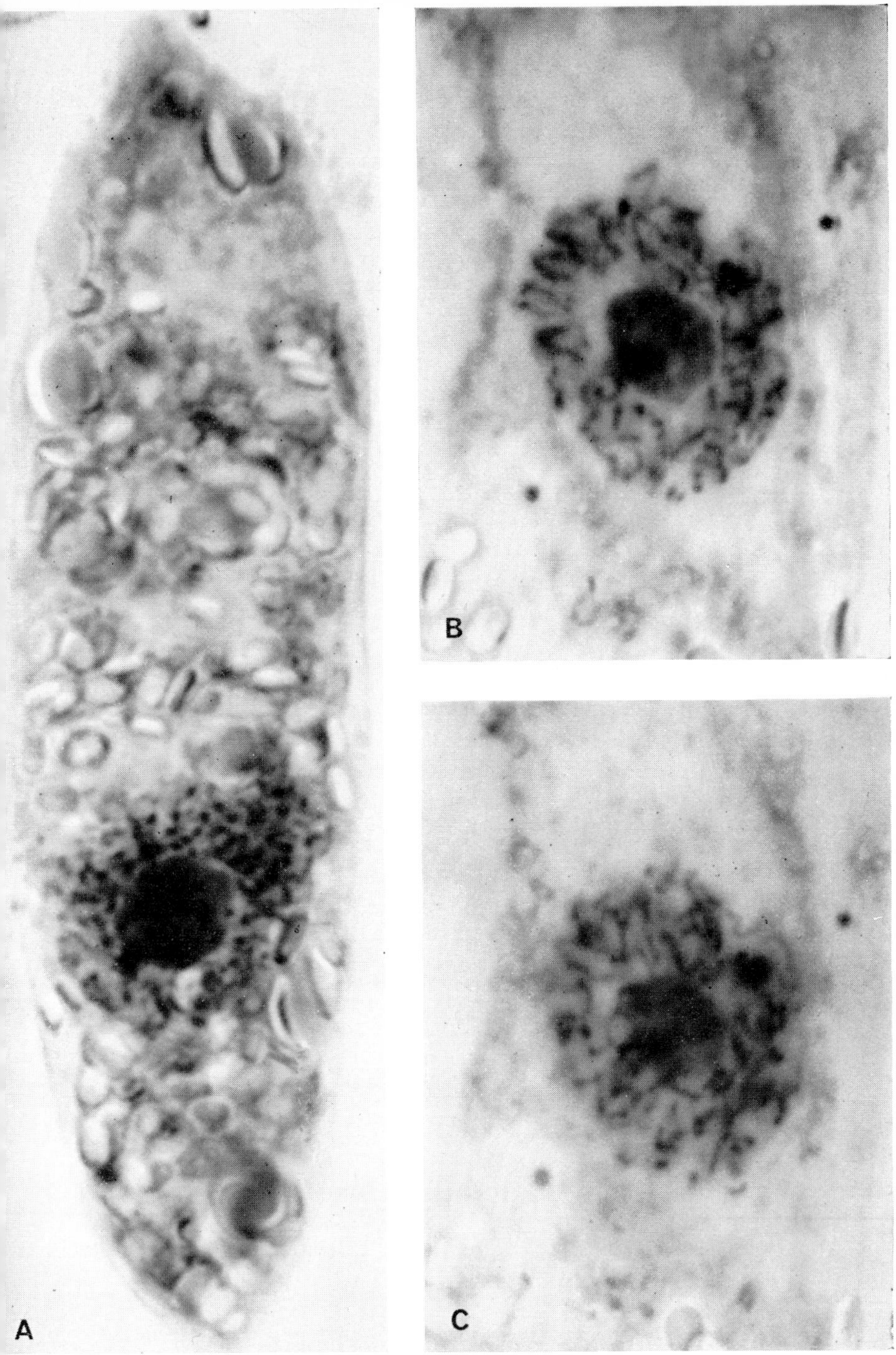

Fig. 2.1 *Euglena gracilis.* Mitosis. **A** Cell showing position and structure of the interphase nucleus. **B** and **C** Two focal levels of a nucleus in prophase. (x 3,000)

of microscopy fail to reveal structures which can be interpreted as 'rhizoplasts', though these connections from nucleus to flagellar bases were recorded by a few earlier workers (see Leedale 1958b for a discussion of this point).

Prophase Mitosis begins with movement of the nucleus from its interphase position towards the anterior end of the cell, prophase* being initiated as the nuclear migration proceeds. During prophase the chromosomes become more obviously filamentous, finally appearing as a sphere of tangled threads around the still spherical endosome (Fig. 2.1B and C).

Early Metaphase The endosome starts to elongate along the division axis (Fig. 2.2A), perpendicular to the long axis of the cell, whilst the chromosomes orientate into the metaphase position. The prophase chromosomes showed no signs of double structure (Fig. 2.1B and C) but during late prophase and early metaphase the chromosomes replicate longitudinally and can be seen to consist of paired chromatids, relationally coiled.† As the chromatid pairs orientate to the metaphase position, separation and segregation of most of the chromatids occurs so that the final metaphase circlet (Fig. 2.2B) is of *single* chromatids.

Metaphase The metaphase figure consists of chromatids lying along the division axis, parallel to one another and to the now dumbbell-shaped endosome (Fig. 2.2B). If such a figure is squashed out, the endosome is clearly displayed and most of the chromatids are seen to be separate with only a few still associated in pairs (Fig. 2.2C).

Anaphase Anaphase begins with the movement of individual chromatids to the poles (Fig. 2.2D). Chromatid migration is staggered, so that some chromatids reach the poles whilst others are still at the equator. Endosomal material flows to the poles and the elongated endosome becomes more markedly dumbbell-shaped (Fig. 2.3A). As anaphase continues, a central gap appears in the belt of chromatids (Fig. 2.3A). Further movement to the poles produces two distinct groups of chromatids arranged at opposite ends of the endosome (Fig. 2.3B), often with one or two lagging chromatids still at

* The terms 'prophase', 'metaphase', 'anaphase' and 'telophase' have been retained for the stages of euglenoid mitosis as a matter of convenience, but they must not be taken to imply the chromosome structure and arrangement typical of 'classical' mitosis.

† In *E. gracilis* the paired condition shows clearly in living nuclei under Anoptral contrast microscopy but is masked by fixation and staining. It can, however, be clearly seen in fixed cells of other species as, for example, in Fig. 2.5C and D.

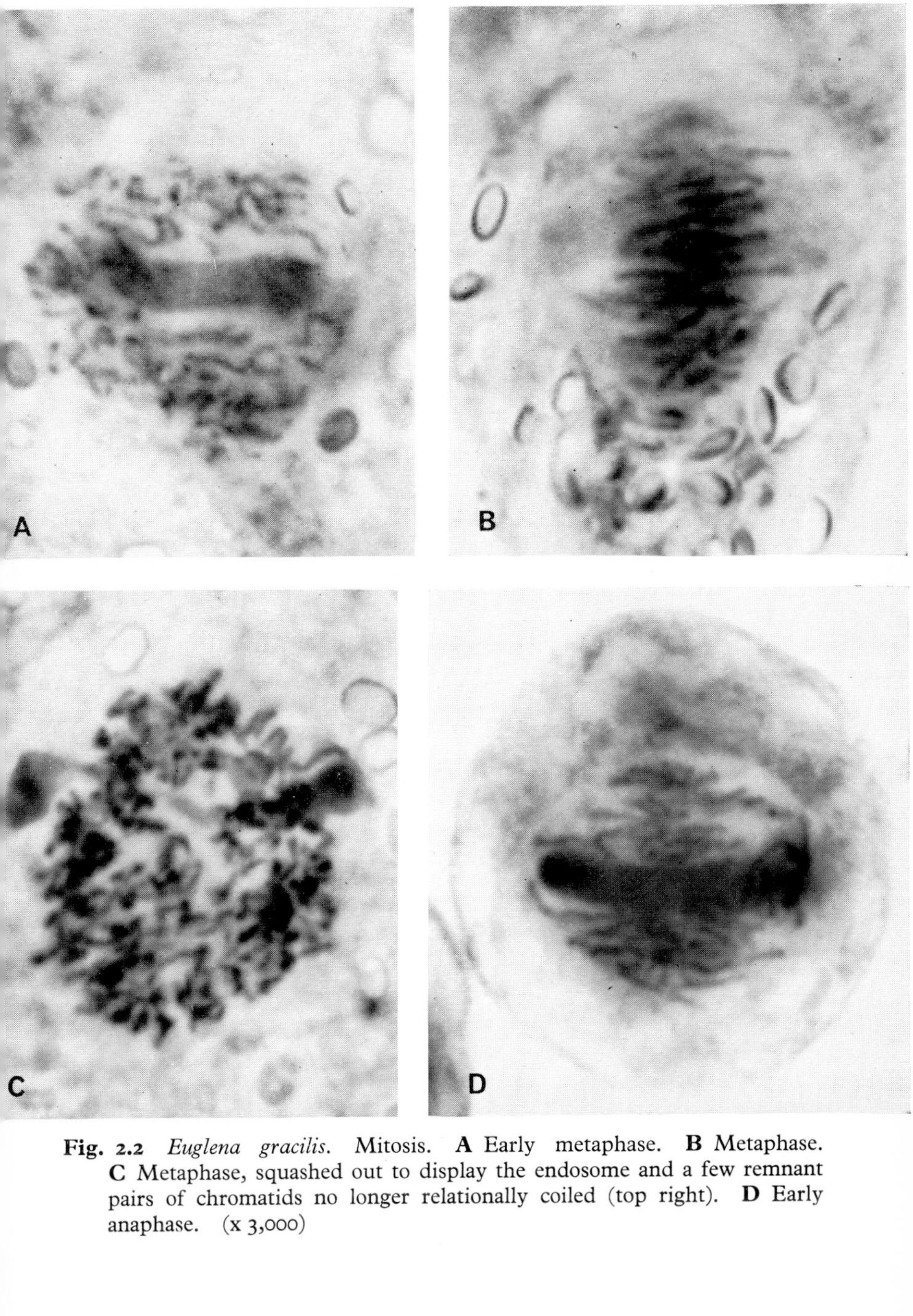

Fig. 2.2 *Euglena gracilis.* Mitosis. **A** Early metaphase. **B** Metaphase. **C** Metaphase, squashed out to display the endosome and a few remnant pairs of chromatids no longer relationally coiled (top right). **D** Early anaphase. (x 3,000)

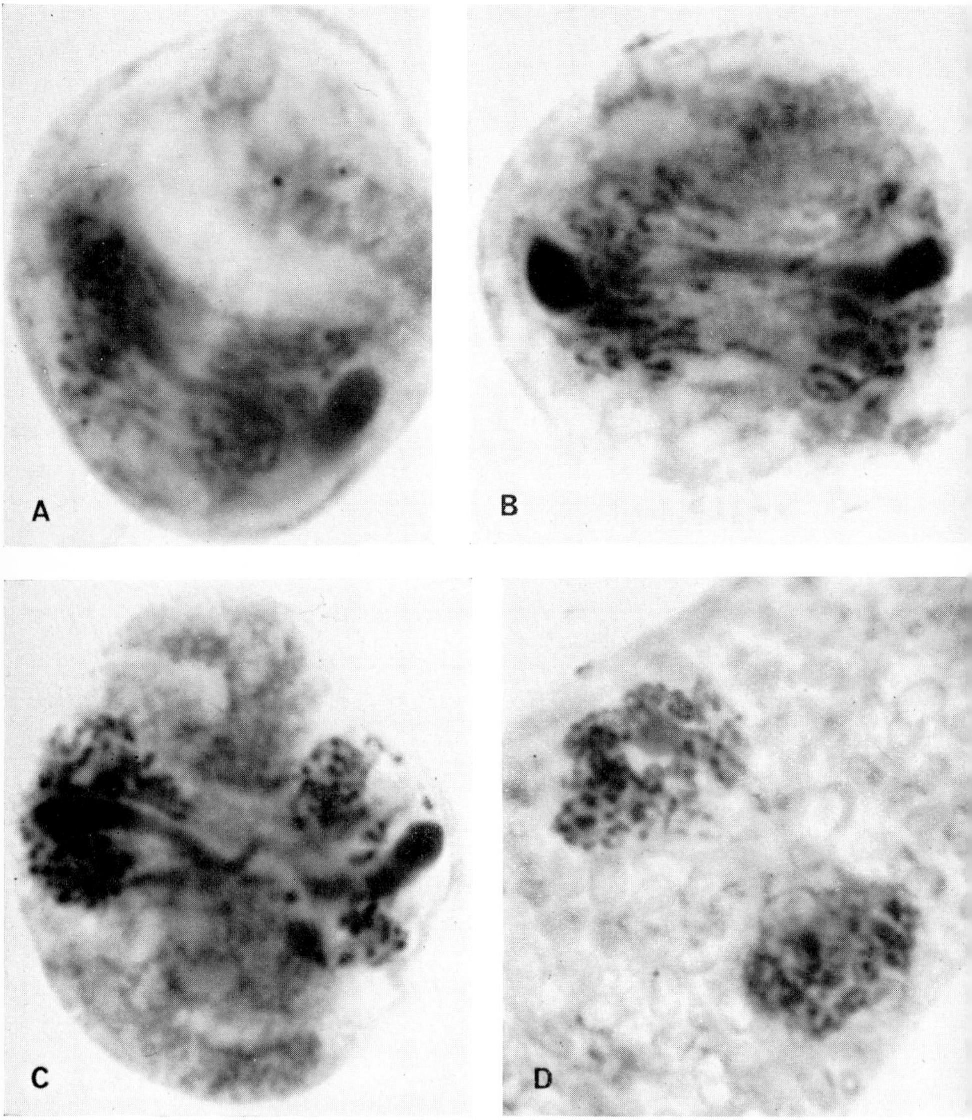

Fig. 2.3 *Euglena gracilis*. Mitosis. **A** Mid-anaphase. **B** Late anaphase. **C** Late anaphase/early telophase. **D** Telophase. (x 3,000)

the equator. The chromatids are now becoming less uniform in thickness and when anaphase is completed (Fig. 2.3C) the chromatids have reassumed the granular appearance of interphase chromosomes. Elongation of the endosome continues and it often buckles in the mid-region (Fig. 2.3C).

Telophase The end of anaphase is marked by a sudden flowing of the central region of the endosome to the poles, and the two portions of endosome round off to become daughter-endosomes in the telophase nuclei (Fig. 2.3D). The nuclear envelope apparently persists throughout the mitosis (see especially Figs. 2.2B and D and 2.3C) and presumably seals around the daughter nuclei to separate them as the nuclei of telophase.

Observationally, at no stage of this division process is there any evidence that the chromosomes have centromeres or that a spindle is present. Experimentally, absence of spindle is suggested by the total lack of effect of colchicine and other spindle inhibitors on mitosis in *E. gracilis* (and other species, see Leedale 1958b, 1961) and by the time-scale of the mitosis (Leedale 1959a). The average duration of mitotic stages in *E. gracilis* is: prophase, 17 min.; metaphase, 12 min.; anaphase, 86 min.; telophase, 4 min.; cell cleavage, 133 min. The maximum velocity of chromatids separating in anaphase is 0·1 μ per min. As in other euglenoid flagellates (see p. 87), the anaphase duration is longer and chromatid velocity is slower than in all other organisms and tissues for which records exist (see Leedale 1959a). The significance of all these findings is discussed below (pp. 91–92).

Finally, it should be mentioned that *E. gracilis* in biphasic culture (Pringsheim 1946) under a natural day/night cycle has a regular periodicity of cell division, with mitosis strictly confined to the dark period (Leedale 1959b). The rhythm is exogenous since it can be immediately removed by growth in artificial light or continuous darkness (resulting in no mitosis) or in a rich organic medium (resulting in rapid mitosis at a constant rate).

SELECTED FEATURES OF NUCLEAR STRUCTURE AND MITOSIS IN OTHER EUGLENOID SPECIES

Interphase Interphase nuclei of euglenoid flagellates (Fig. 2.4) show a range of sizes, shapes, positions and structure but all have chromosomes which remain condensed and stainable. The chromosomes are more obviously threadlike in some species (Fig. 2.4A and B) than others (Fig. 2.4D), but even nuclei with a granular appearance reveal the individualised chromosomes on squashing (Fig. 2.4C). Many species have only one endosome (Fig. 2.4C), others have several (Fig. 2.4B and D). Endosomes are similar to nucleoli in

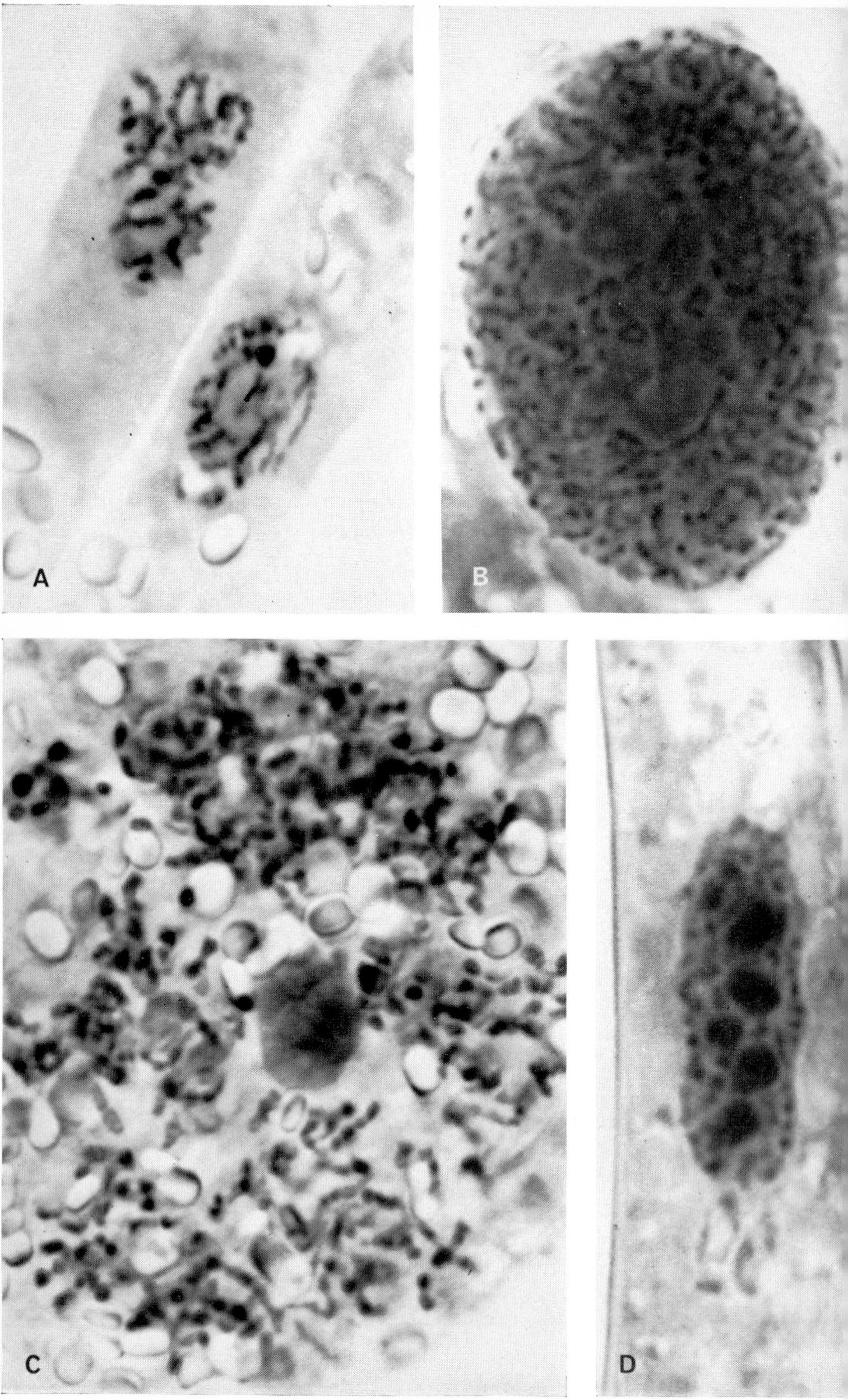
A
B
C
D

their shape and position in the interphase nucleus (Figs. 2.1A and 2.4B, C and D), in their ability to fuse and fragment (see below), in their staining affinities and in containing RNA but no DNA (see Leedale 1958b for techniques used). However, endosomes differ from nucleoli in their persistence and division during mitosis, in their retention of RNA during mitosis and in apparently not being associated with special nucleolar-organising chromosomes.

Prophase All euglenoid species have an anterior migration of the nucleus as a prelude to mitosis, with fusion of endosomes occurring in most polyendosomal nuclei. Some speces of *Euglena*, *Peranema* and *Phacus* regularly have several endosomes dividing separately in each nucleus.

Metaphase Metaphase begins with elongation of the endosome (or endosomes) and the chromosomes orientate to form a metaphase 'plate' of a shape and extent typical for each species. This orientation occurs in one of three ways. *Lepocinclis ovum* var. *buetschlii* Conrad (Huber-Pestalozzi) and *Peranema trichophorum* (Ehrenberg) Stein have orientation of the *Euglena gracilis* type, with pairs of chromatids from late prophase forming a metaphase circlet of *single* chromatids (Fig. 2.5A), separation and segregation of the daughter-chromosomes having occurred during orientation. In *Astasia klebsii* Lemmermann, *Colacium mucronatum* Bourrelly & Chadefaud, *Distigma proteus* Ehrenberg, *Euglena acus* Ehrenberg, *Euglena deses* Ehrenberg, *Euglena spirogyra** Ehrenberg and *Phacus pyrum* (Ehrenberg) Stein, orientation is of single chromosomes from prophase into a metaphase circlet, in which position they then duplicate into chromatids (Fig. 2.5D). In the third group of species, orientation is of *pairs* of chromatids (duplication having occurred in the previous telophase or interphase) into a metaphase circlet of such pairs. This sequence takes place in *Euglena viridis* Ehrenberg, *Eutreptia pertyi* Pringsheim, *Eutreptia viridis* Ehrenberg, *Lepocinclis steinii* Lemmermann (Conrad) and *Trachelomonas grandis* Singh (Fig. 2.5B and C). The metaphase figure

* The mitotic cycle in this species has been summarised in a recent paper (Leedale, Meeuse & Pringsheim 1965).

Fig. 2.4 **A** *Astasia klebsii.* Interphase nuclei of two cells, showing the relatively few, thick, granular chromosomes. **B** *Euglena ehrenbergii klebs.* Interphase nucleus (unsquashed), showing the many chromosomes, numerous central endosomes of different shapes and sizes, and the nuclear envelope. **C** *Trachelomonos grandis.* Squashed interphase nucleus, showing the single spherical endosome and the granular chromosomes. **D** *Euglena acus.* Elongated interphase nucleus, showing the granular chromosomes and the central row of endosomes. (x 3,000)

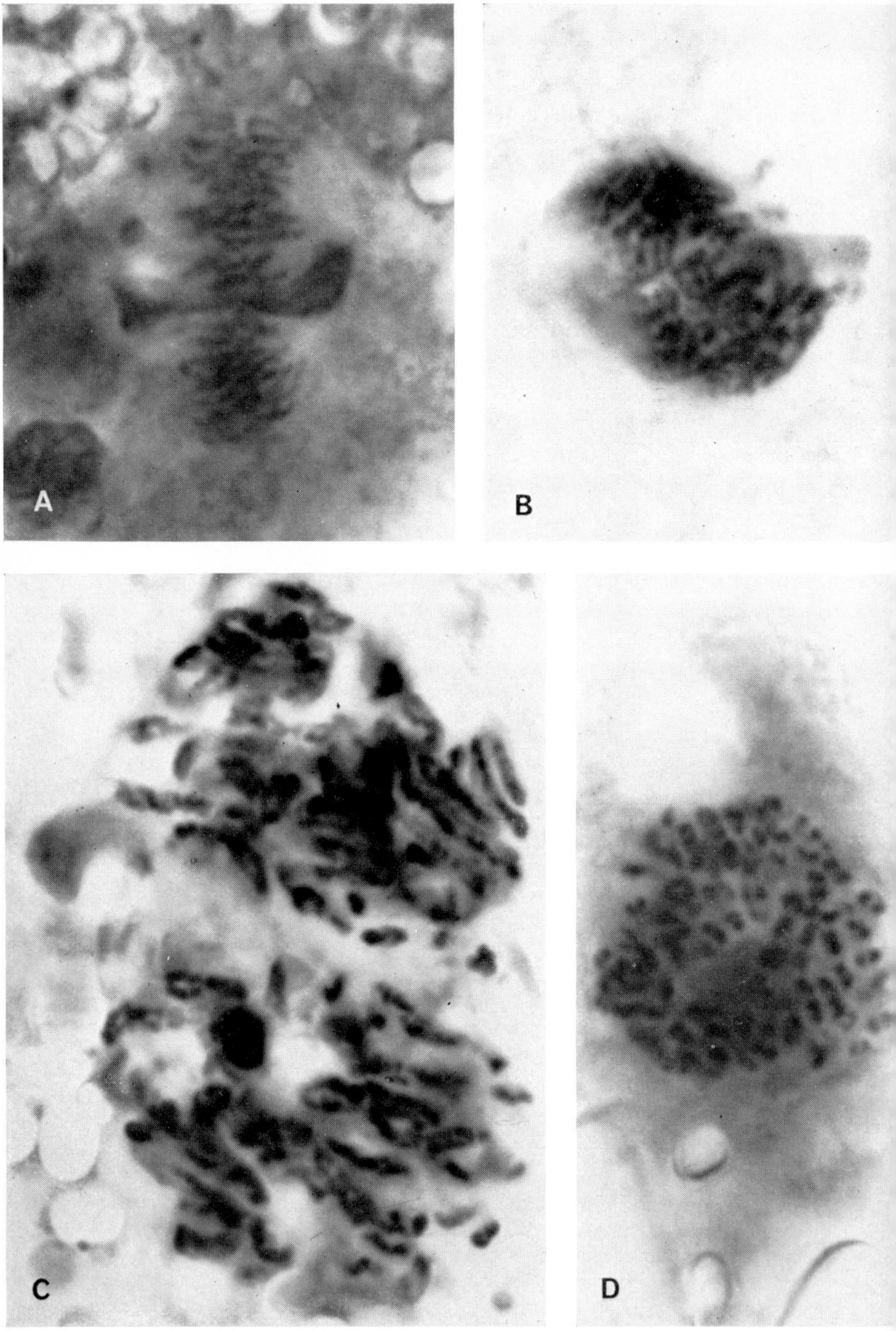
A
B
C
D

produced in *Eutreptia viridis* bears no resemblance to an equatorial plate, consisting of pairs of parallel chromatids arranged at all angles in a dense matrix of nucleoplasm (Fig. 2.5B), whilst the elongated endosome is a thin rod of uniform thickness. Similarly, in *Lepocinclis steinii* the pairs of relationally coiled chromatids are spread from pole to pole of the division figure though most lie more or less parallel to the endosome (Fig. 2.5C).

Anaphase With orientation of the *Euglena gracilis* type, chromatid separation and segregation takes place during orientation (Fig. 2.5A). In species of the latter two groups described above, chromatids separate and segregate into the two daughter-nuclei during anaphase from the metaphase position. Staggering of chromatid separation, segregation and anaphase migration is found in all euglenoid flagellates and a typical mid-anaphase picture of euglenoid mitosis is a spread of chromatids surrounding a dumbbell-shaped endosome from equator to poles (Fig. 2.6). During anaphase movement (Figs. 2.6, 2.7 and 2.8), chromatids appear as straight rods, curving threads or U-shapes, with no constrictions which could be interpreted as centromeres. Anaphase movement in *Eutreptia viridis* is of blocks of chromatids still embedded in dense nucleoplasm (Fig. 2.7B). The chromatids have separated and segregated in early anaphase and now show duplication into the daughter chromosomes of the *next* mitosis. In species with obviously non-homologous chromosomes, sister chromatids can be seen segregating to opposite poles and into different daughter-nuclei (Fig. 2.7C).

Anaphase of euglenoid mitosis occupies from 47 to 86 min. in different species, compared with 1 to 26 min. in all other cells for which records exist (Leedale 1959a), whilst the absolute velocity of chromatids in anaphase varies between 0·06 and 0·15 μ per min. in different euglenoid species, as compared with 0·3 to 6·0 μ per min. in all other cells.

Fig. 2.5 Euglenoid mitosis. **A** *Peranema trichophorum.* Metaphase/early anaphase; separation of daughter chromosomes during orientation produces a narrow belt of straight, curved and U-shaped chromatids, seen here in optical section at the level of the endosome; 10 focal levels are necessary to include all the chromatids and the total number countable is c. 350, giving a chromosome count for this species of c. 175. **B** *Eutreptia viridis.* Metaphase, showing a 'muff' of paired chromatids spread around the rod-shaped endosome. **C** *Lepocinclis steinii.* Metaphase, showing relationally coiled pairs of chromatids lying more or less parallel to the elongated endosome. **D** *Euglena spirogyra.* Metaphase, figure recognised in side view and then rotated in the preparation to give a polar view; this focal level shows the chromosomes in optical transverse section, with most of them arranged parallel to the slightly off-centre endosome and showing the longitudinal 'split' into two chromatids. This figure gives a chromosome count of 86 for *Euglena spirogyra.* (x 3,000)

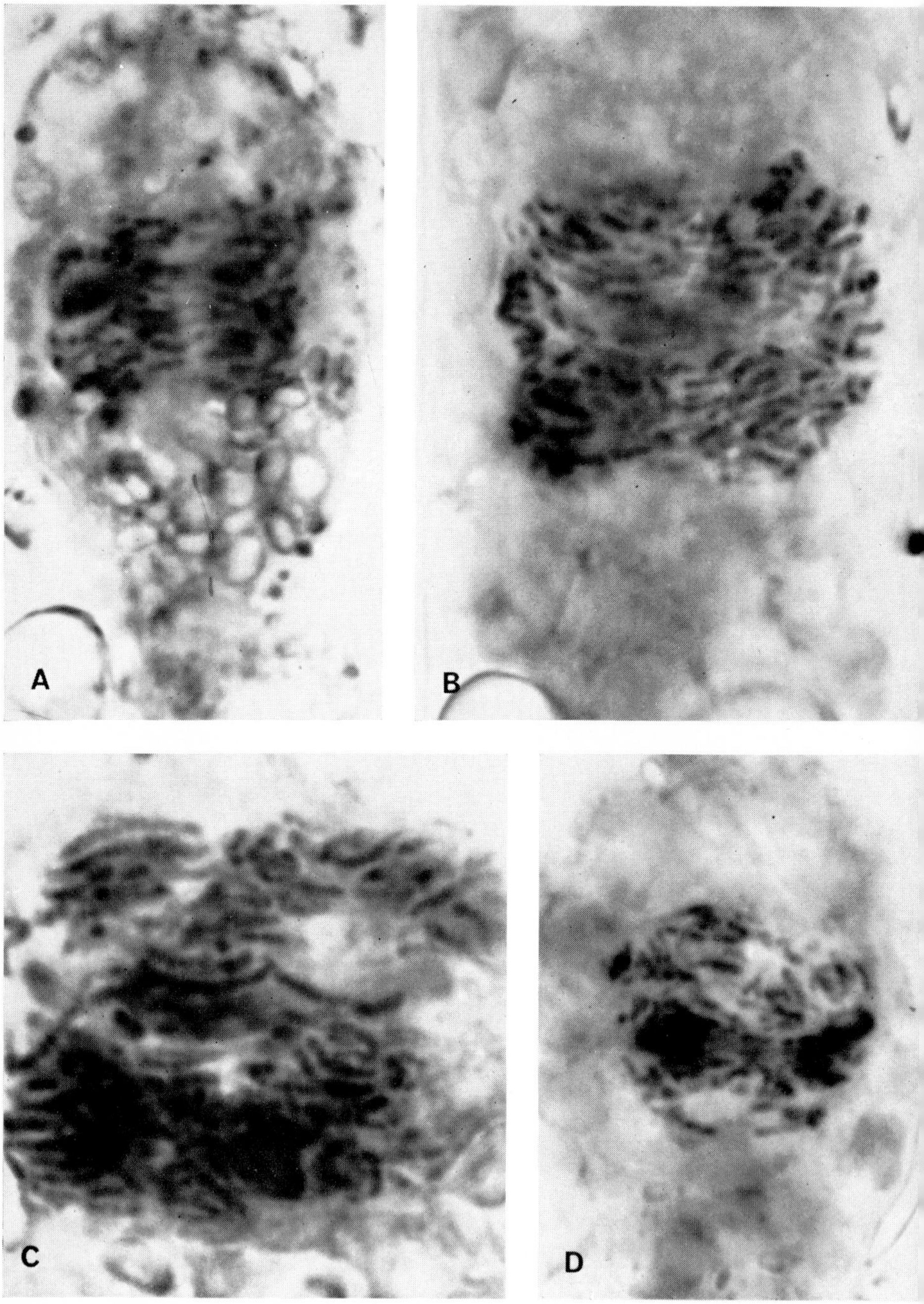
A
B
C
D

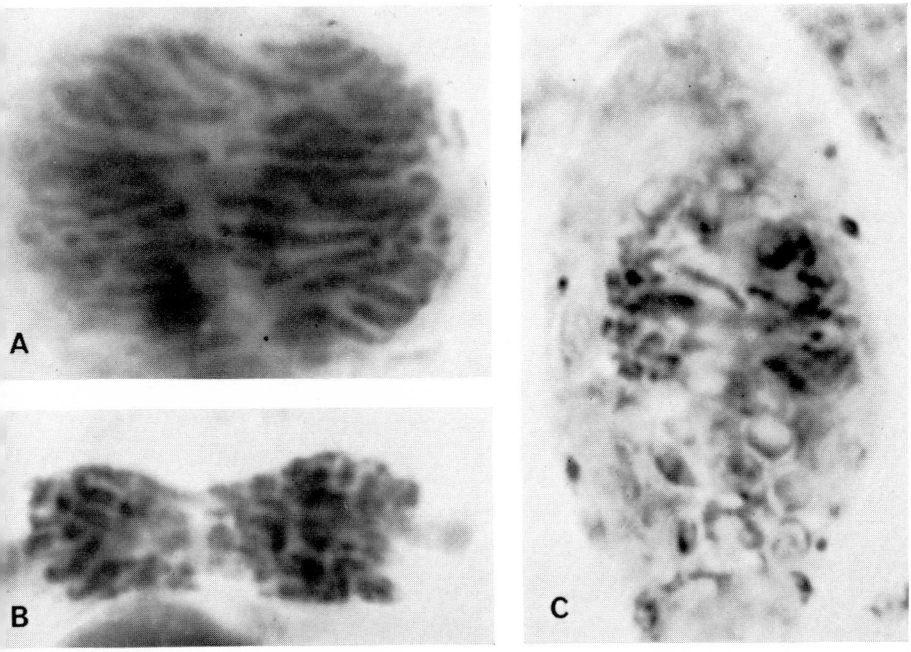

Fig. 2.7 Euglenoid mitosis. **A** *Eutreptia pertyi*. Late anaphase, showing a well-marked equatorial gap and rod-shaped, curved and U-shaped chromatids passing to the poles, mostly parallel to the endosome. **B** *Eutreptia viridis*. Late anaphase, showing migrating blocks of chromatids around the rod-shaped endosome, with a central gap appearing (see p. 87). **C** *Colacium mucronatum*. Late anaphase, showing sister chromatids of the one long chromosome, one projecting from one daughter group of chromatids, the other from the other (see p. 87). (x 3,000)

Fig. 2.6 Euglenoid mitosis **A** *Colacium mucronatum*. Mid-anaphase, showing the spread of chromatids from equator to poles, with an equatorial gap just appearing. **B** *Euglena spirogyra*. Mid-anaphase, showing a complete spread of chromatids from equator to poles; compare the thickness of the migrating chromatids with the chromatin elements in Fig. 2.5D. **C** *Eutreptia pertyi*. Mid-anaphase, showing various shapes of migrating chromatids. **D** *Phacus pyrum*. Mid-anaphase spread of chromatids. (x 3,000)

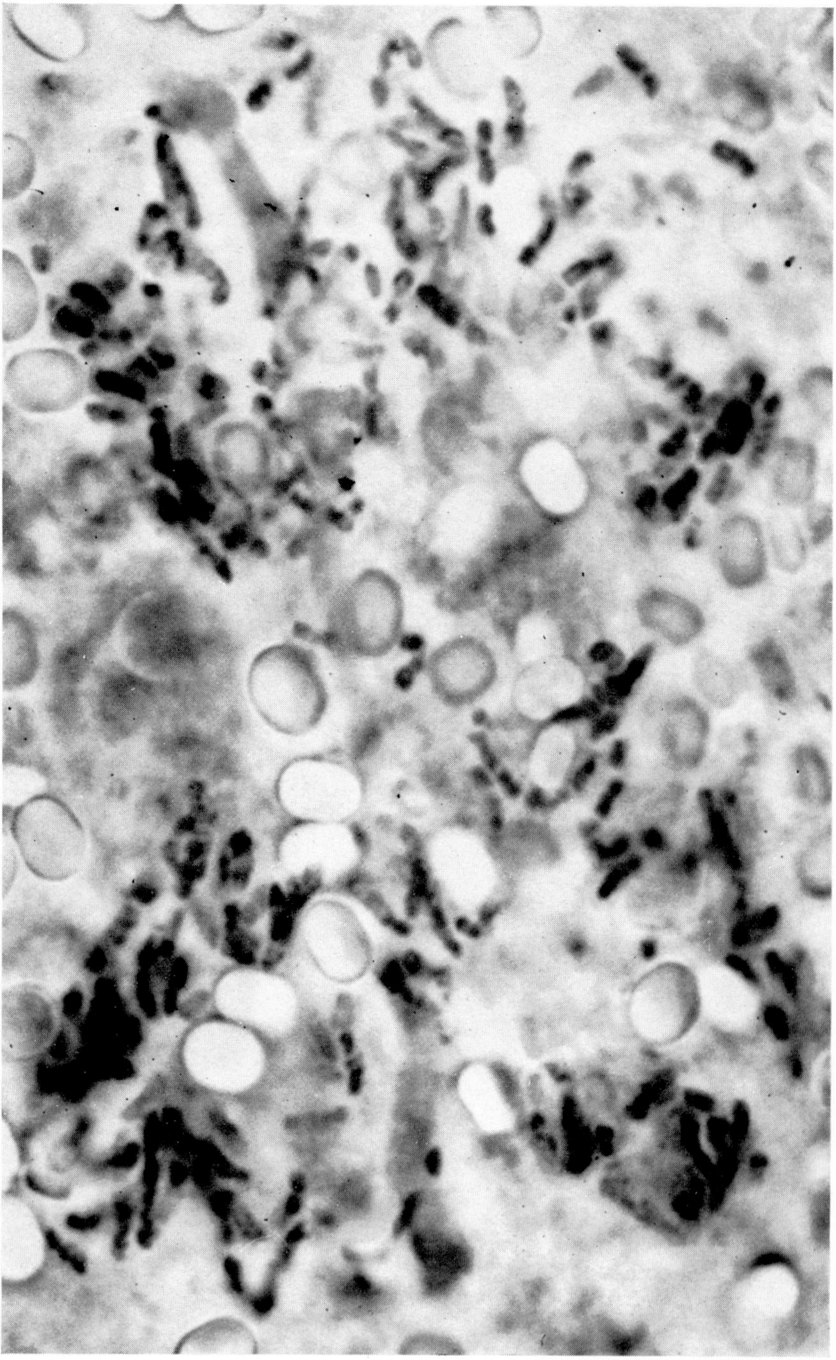

Telophase Anaphase proceeds into telophase and the daughter nuclei are formed in the way already described for *Euglena gracilis.* Adjustment of nuclear material, in some species involving fragmentation of the endosome and/or chromosome duplication ready for the next mitosis, restores the interphase structure typical for the species.

Further cytological features of the species chosen for illustration are commented on in the legends to the figures, but special attention might be paid to Figs. 2.5C and D which clearly show chromosomes with longitudinal 'cleavage', the occurrence of which was denied by some authors until quite recently (see Leedale 1958b for details).

The mitotic periodicity in biphasic culture described above for *Euglena gracilis* is found in all green euglenoid species, with mitosis beginning one to two hours after the onset of darkness and up to 7% of the cells in a culture dividing in one night. Colourless euglenoid flagellates in biphasic culture show no rhythmic response to any light regime, but have bursts of up to 10% mitosis followed by periods of low mitotic activity. These phenomena (see Leedale 1959b) are presumably a simple reflection of energy relationships in cells with different modes and rates of nutrition.

DISCUSSION ON EUGLENOID MITOSIS

Euglenoid nuclear division fulfils the essential criteria of mitosis in that individualised chromosomes duplicate themselves longitudinally and the sister chromatids thus formed segregate into different daughter-nuclei. Accounts of transverse cleavage of a continuous chromatin strand or of individual chromosomes have finally been disproved by contrast microscopy of living cells and by photographs showing longitudinal duplication of chromosomes at some stage of the mitotic cycle.

It can now be categorically stated that euglenoid nuclear division is a mitotic process, albeit a peculiar one. Euglenoid mitosis differs from 'classical' mitosis in the persistence and division in the nucleus of an achromatic body (the endosome); the retention of RNA by this body during mitosis; the apparent absence of spindle and centromeres; the arrangement of chromosomes parallel to the division axis at metaphase and the absence of a true equatorial plate; the staggering of chromatid separation, segregation and

Fig. 2.8 *Trachelomonas grandis.* Squashed out late mitotic anaphase, showing the elongated endosome of uniform thickness and the daughter chromosomes returning to a granular condition. (x 3,000)

anaphase migration; the long duration of anaphase; the slow chromatid velocity at anaphase; and the apparent retention of the nuclear envelope.

Evidence for the absence of the spindle typical of mitosis in most other organisms is provided by the lack of any inhibition of euglenoid mitosis by colchicine and the irregularity and slowness of anaphase movement of chromatids (see Leedale 1959a). So far there is little supporting or conflicting evidence from electron microscopy. Investigations at present in progress (see Leedale, Meeuse and Pringsheim 1965) will be reported elsewhere when completed.*

In the apparent absence of centromeres and spindle, I originally suggested (Leedale 1958a, 1958b) that endosome division and chromatid movement are autonomous in the Euglenophyceae, mutual repulsion by sister chromatids leading to anaphase. If such repulsion starts at different stages of the division process in different species, the several forms of chromosome orientation and segregation are explained. Continuous repulsion between sister chromatids should ensure their incorporation into different daughter-nuclei and retention of the nuclear envelope result in the repelling chromatids becoming marshalled into two groups. As these move apart and the endosomal material flows to the poles, the stretched nuclear envelope will meet between the two groups to separate two daughter-nuclei which are cytologically and genetically equivalent.

This theory does not explain the autonomous anterior migration of the nucleus or the constant orientation of the division axis. It is tempting to cite the nuclear movement as evidence that the flagellar bases on the wall of the reservoir act as division centres and determine the division axis. However, mitosis is structurally in progress as the nucleus is moving towards the anterior end of the cell. Evidence on these points should be provided by current electron microscopical investigations of dividing cells (see footnote below).

Studies of euglenoid nuclear cytology published too recently for inclusion in my review (1958b) each deal with only a single species, and the authors seem not to have appreciated the peculiar nature of the chromosomal behaviour in these organisms. Singh (1958) failed to see the details of the chromosome cycle in *Trachelomonas grandis*, whilst Ueda (1958) presupposes the nuclear division of *Euglena gracilis* to be similar to mitosis in higher plants and interprets it as such. Saito (1961) is an author who produces elegant photographs, clearly showing relational coiling of chromatids in *Euglena viridis*. However, he claims to see localised centromeres and decides that nuclear division in *Euglena viridis* is essentially similar to that

* Note added in proof: Preliminary results from electron microscopy of dividing cells (as yet unpublished) indicate that 'spindle elements' (i.e. microtubules) of some sort *are* present in the mitotic nucleus. There is evidence of structural connection between the microtubules and the flagellar basal bodies, but no indication that the microtubules are organised into a 'conventional' spindle.

in somatic cells of higher plants and animals. None of these authors undertook any experimental investigation.

That euglenoid mitosis has many peculiar cytological features cannot now be doubted. Other departures from the cytology of 'classical' mitosis are found in various protista (Grell 1964), though many of these have a spindle-organised mitosis. The peculiarities of euglenoid mitosis are most closely reflected in the mitosis recorded for some dinoflagellates (see pp. 101–110) and for the somatic nuclei of many fungi (Robinow 1962). Excursions into the cytology of less common organisms are showing more and more that 'classical' mitosis is not necessarily 'normal' mitosis, and the undoubted differences of euglenoid mitosis are taking their place as fringe variations of a basic pattern of nuclear division in eucaryotic cells.

Perhaps the real comparative significance of euglenoid mitosis is as a demonstration of the high degree of autonomous activity that can be possessed by chromosomes. This may be a more important phenomenon in the mechanism of 'classical' mitosis than has hitherto been supposed.

OTHER PATTERNS OF EUGLENOID NUCLEAR BEHAVIOUR

Several species of *Euglena* exhibit a process of nuclear fragmentation ('amitosis') in biphasic culture, resulting in occasional binucleate cells (Leedale 1959c). At subsequent mitoses in *E. acus* and *E. spirogyra* the half-nuclei divide simultaneously. Cell cleavage produces two binucleate cells, though occasional miscleavage results in cells with either one half-nucleus or three half-nuclei. These cells are viable and their asexual progeny retain the characteristics of the species. This suggests that these species of *Euglena* are highly polyploid, cells being fully viable with much less than the normal chromosome complement. Normal cells of *E. spirogyra* have 86 chromosomes (Fig. 2.5D); the 'half-nuclei' in a binucleate cell contain 40 to 45 chromosomes.

Grell's difficulty in reconciling these observations of amitosis and mitosis in the same species (Grell 1964) is apparently due to his misinterpretation of the significance of the amitotic process. It should be emphasised that amitosis in *Euglena* is merely a nuclear fragmentation, occurring as a rare phenomenon in response to unfavourable conditions of growth. The process is not connected with reproduction.

The evidence for a meiotic process in euglenoid flagellates has been recently reviewed (Leedale 1962). In that account, cells of *Hyalophacus ocellatus* Pringsheim are described which contain either a nuclear figure consisting of a double complement of highly condensed chromosomes arranged in pairs in the anterior half of the cell, or a huge posteriorly placed nucleus consisting of long, granular chromosomes which also show signs of pairing. These nuclear figures are quite unlike interphase nuclei or stages in mitosis and are interpreted as stages in euglenoid meiosis. The validity of this interpretation is strengthened by the fact that the figures in *Hyalophacus* are very similar to those described as stages of meiosis in *Phacus pyrum* by Krichenbauer (1937). He produces evidence that this meiosis follows an autogamy (the fusion of two nuclei which are the mitotic products of one cell).

Chromosome counts of the *Hyalophacus* nuclei suggest that if this is a meiotic process, then it is following autogamy or sexual fusion of gamete nuclei rather than preceding the formation of gametes. In fact, no evidence has been obtained for a sexual fusion of gametes or cells and all previous accounts of sexuality in the Euglenophyceae are suspect. It seems probable that sexuality is lacking from the group as a whole and, if meiosis does occur, it does so as a rare phenomenon following autogamy.

Table 2.1 Chromosome numbers in the Euglenophyceae (Leedale 1957)

COUNTS	
Euglena spirogyra Ehrenberg	86
Euglena viridis Ehrenberg	42
Eutreptia pertyi Pringsheim	90
Eutreptia viridis Ehrenberg	44
Hyalophacus ocellatus Pringsheim	92
Phacus pusillus Lemmermann	42
ESTIMATES	
Astasia klebsii Lemmermann	18
Colacium mucronatum Bourrelly & Chadefaud	35
Euglena gracilis Klebs	45
Lepocinclis ovum var. *buetschlii* Conrad (Huber-Pestalozzi)	34
Menoidium cultellus Pringsheim	15
Peranema trichophorum (Ehrenberg) Stein	177
Trachelomonas bulla Stein (Deflandre)	25
Trachelomonas grandis Singh	40–60

Counts by previous authors published between 1902 and 1930 are listed in Leedale (1957).

REFERENCES

BLOCHMANN, F. (1894). Über die Kernteilung bei *Euglena viridis*. *Biol. Zbl.*, **14**, 194–197.

GRELL, K. G. (1964). The protozoan nucleus. In *The Cell*, Vol. VI (Ed. J. BRACHET and A. E. MIRSKY). Academic Press, New York and London.

KEUTEN, J. (1895). Die Kernteilung von *Euglena viridis*. *Z. wiss. Zool.*, **60**, 215–235.

KRICHENBAUER, H. (1937). Beitrag zur Kenntnis der Morphologie und Entwicklungsgeschichte der Gattungen *Euglena* und *Phacus*. *Arch. Protistenk.*, **90**, 88–123.

LEEDALE, G. F. (1957). Thesis, Division Cytology in the Euglenineae, Ph.D., University of London.

— (1958a). Mitosis and chromosome numbers in the Euglenineae (Flagellata). *Nature, Lond.*, **181**, 502–503.

— (1958b). Nuclear structure and mitosis in the Euglenineae. *Arch. Mikrobiol.*, **32**, 32–64.

— (1959a). The time-scale of mitosis in the Euglenineae. *Arch. Mikrobiol.*, **32**, 352–360.

— (1959b). Periodicity of mitosis and cell division in the Euglenineae. *Biol. Bull.*, **116**, 162–174.

— (1959c). Amitosis in three species of *Euglena*. *Cytologia*, **24**, 213–219.

— (1961). Studies on nuclear division in the euglenoid flagellates, with special reference to a possible meiosis in *Hyalophacus ocellatus* Pringsheim. *Proc. 1st Internat. Conf. Protozool., Prague*, pp. 265–266.

— (1962). The evidence for a meiotic process in the Euglenineae. *Arch. Mikrobiol.*, **42**, 237–245.

LEEDALE, G. F., MEEUSE, B. J. D. and PRINGSHEIM, E. G. (1965). Structure and physiology of Euglena spirogyra. I and II. *Arch. Mikrobiol.*, **50**, 68–102.

PRINGSHEIM. E. G. (1946). The biphasic or soil-water culture method for growing algae and flagellata. *J. Ecol.*, **33**, 193–204.

ROBINOW, C. F. (1962). Some observations on the mode of division of somatic nuclei of *Mucor* and *Allomyces*. *Arch. Mikrobiol.*, **42**, 369–377.

SAITO, M. (1961). Studies in the mitosis of *Euglena* I. On the chromosome cycle of *Euglena viridis* Ehrbg. *J. Protozool.*, **8**, 300–307.

SINGH, K. P. (1958). Cytological studies in *Trachelomonas grandis* Singh. *Agra Univ. J. Res. (Sci.)*, **7**, 159–166.

UEDA, K. (1958). Structure of plant cells with special reference to lower plants III. A cytological study of *Euglena gracilis*. *Cytologia*, **23**, 56–67.

3 *The Dinophyceae*

JOHN D. DODGE
B.Sc., Ph.D.
Lecturer, Department of Botany, Birkbeck College,
University of London

INTRODUCTION

The nuclei of some members of the Dinophyceae have been studied, using collections of wild material, since about the year 1880. Most of the early workers looked at the huge nucleus of *Ceratium* but the large number of chromosomes and the unusual mitosis made interpretation very difficult. *Oxyrrhis* was the subject of several studies, that of Hall (1925) being outstanding for its detailed observations. The early work has recently been reviewed (Skoczylas 1958, Dodge 1963a).

With the development, during the last few years, of means of growing dinoflagellates in culture it has become much more easy to study the structure and behaviour of the chromosomes. It is also now possible to carry out experiments, knowing that the material is physiologically uniform. The last ten years have therefore seen an increasing interest in the nuclei of the Dinophyceae, the resultant discoveries are reviewed in this chapter.

CULTURE METHODS FOR DINOPHYCEAE

More than 20 species of marine dinoflagellates have now been successfully grown from single-cell isolates. These are mostly the smaller members of the group, since the large species are difficult to isolate, being more easily damaged. The simplest growth medium consists of sea-water enriched with nitrate, phosphate and with soil extract to supply trace elements and also various undetermined substances. A useful sea-water medium is that known as the Plymouth Erdschreiber Solution which consists of:

1,000 ml. filtered sea-water
50 ml. soil extract
0·2 gm. sodium nitrate (in 10 ml. of water)
0·03 gm. sodium phosphate (in 10 ml. of water)

The components are autoclaved or pasteurised in separate containers allowed to cool and then mixed. Some workers have devised complex mixtures of trace elements and vitamins to replace the soil extract. When it is necessary to know exactly what the medium consists of, as for nutritional and certain physiological experiments, the whole medium can be 'artificial' including the sea-water component. A detailed survey of these more complex media is given by Provasoli, McLaughlin and Droop (1957). Special methods have been devised for culturing the dinoflagellate Zooxanthellae which are normally found as symbionts in many invertebrates (McLaughlin & Zahl 1959).

Fresh-water members of the Dinophyceae have been cultured only with difficulty and hence very little cytological work has been done with them. Some *Peridinium* species will grow in biphasic soil-water tubes and the coccoid *Gleodinium montanum* will grow, very slowly, on soil extract agar.

The simple sea-water cultures can be maintained successfully under fluorescent illumination between 100 and 200 ft.-candles (or in supplemented north-daylight), at a temperature of between 15 and 25°C. Only a few species will survive the higher temperature. Normally light is provided for 12 to 18 hr. per day but continuous light seems not to be deleterious in many cases.

CYTOLOGICAL METHODS

The chromosomes of the Dinophyceae contain much DNA, are sometimes quite large, and are easy to fix and stain. Many fixatives can be used but for convenience absolute methanol has been generally used although Carnoy's 3:1 (absolute alcohol: acetic acid) works equally satisfactorily. Certain species benefit from the addition of a few drops of the mordant, saturated ferric acetate (in acetic acid) to the fixative an hour or so before staining is contemplated. Fixation is carried out in centrifuge tubes, the cells being spun down and the supernatant poured off.

Staining is carried out on a microscope slide. Some fixed material, first washed in water in the centrifuge tube, is pipetted into the centre of a drop of aceto carmine and warmed over a spirit lamp. A cover slip is then placed on the drop and the surplus acetocarmine flushed through with a drop of 45% acetic acid. Aceto-orcein works equally well and the Feulgen stain gives a strong reaction but unfortunately not such a clear picture of the chromosomes.

Examination and photography is best carried out on temporary preparations (ringed with rubber solution) but these can be made permanent by any of the normal methods (wet dish method or dry ice method).

THE CHROMOSOMES AND NUCLEAR DIVISION IN THE DINOPHYCEAE

The structure of the chromosomes and the mode of division in this group differs basically from that found in most other organisms. Whilst it would appear that the fundamental chromosome structure (see later in this chapter) is uniform through the Dinophyceae there is considerable variation in size, in general appearance and in certain details of the mitotic process.

A THE INTERPHASE NUCLEUS

The variety of form shown by the interphase nuclei of the Dinophyceae is rivalled only by the polymorphism among the macronuclei of the Ciliata. A number of species have simple spherical or subspherical nuclei as for example *Katodinium rotundata*, *Oxyrrhis marina* and *Peridinium trochoideum* (Figs. 3.1D, F, G and 3.2E, C). In many species the nucleus is flattened and normally triangular or crescent shaped in side view. Such nuclei are found in *Amphidinium herdmani*, *Prorocentrum micans* and *Exuviaella* spp. (Figs. 3.1E, H and 3.2D, A, G). The most striking interphase nuclei are found in *Gonyaulax* spp. and certain fresh-water *Peridinium* species. Here the nucleus is a deep U-shape normally lying at right angles to the vertical axis of the cell (Figs. 3.1C and 3.2B).

One of the ways in which the interphase of the Dinophyceae is almost unique is that the chromosomes can be fixed and stained without any difficulty throughout that part of the nuclear cycle. This is because they do not lose the metaphase-anaphase condensation of their chromatin. In some species, *Prorocentrum micans* and *Peridinium trochoideum* for example, it has been possible to squash out interphase chromosomes and count their number (Dodge 1963c). Part of a squashed nucleus is shown in Fig. 3.4E where the chromosomes can be seen to be quite distinct. In the example shown the nucleus contained almost 70 chromosomes.

There is a considerable variety in the size of the chromosomes through the group. The largest so far encountered are the long rod-shaped chromosomes of *Prorocentrum micans* which are normally about 15 μ long and 1 μ in diameter. In many species the chromosomes are rod-shaped up to about 7 μ long and 0·5 μ in diameter. Some dinoflagellates have tiny spherical or subspherical chromosomes 1–0·5 μ in diameter (see Fig. 3.1). The interphase chromosomes of *Gonyaulax* and *Oxyrrhis* differ somewhat from the others in that they are relatively long and have an irregular outline.

Structures which appear equivalent to the nucleoli of higher plants, and which will be referred to as nucleoli in the subsequent account, are found in the interphase nuclei of *Oxyrrhis marina* (Fig. 3.2E), *Peridinium trochoideum*, *Katodinium rotundata* (Fig. 3.1D), and various *Gymnodinium* species. *Gonyaulax* (Figs. 3.1C and 3.2B) has a large nucleolus-like body situated between the arms of the nucleus but not surrounded by nuclear material as is usual with nucleoli. In a number of organisms, particularly those belonging to the genera *Prorocentrum* and *Exuviaella* no nucleolus has been clearly demonstrated although one or more hollow spaces are sometimes observed in the interphase nuclei.

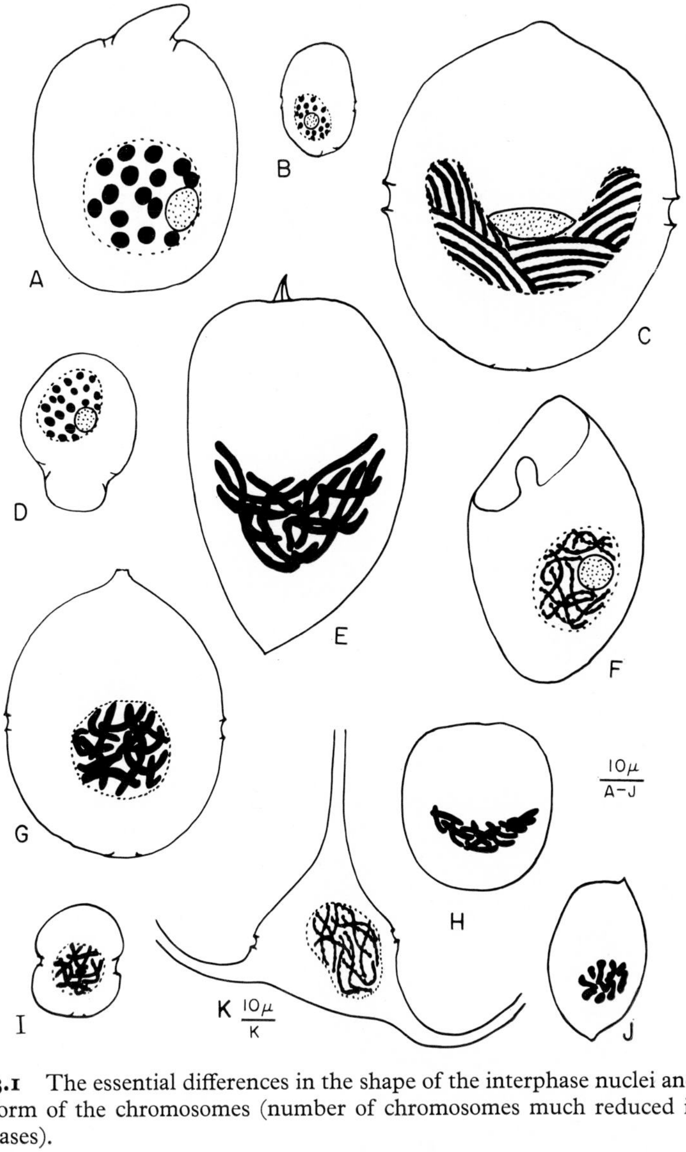

Fig. 3.1 The essential differences in the shape of the interphase nuclei and the form of the chromosomes (number of chromosomes much reduced in all cases).

A *Amphidinium klebsii*
B *Gyrodinium cohnii*
C *Gonyaulax tamarensis*
D *Katodinium rotundata*
E *Prorocentrum micans*
F *Oxyrrhis marina*
G *Peridinium trochoideum*
H *Exuviaella mariae-lebouriae*
I *Gymnodinium vitiligo*
J *Prorocentrum triestinum*
K *Ceratium* sp.

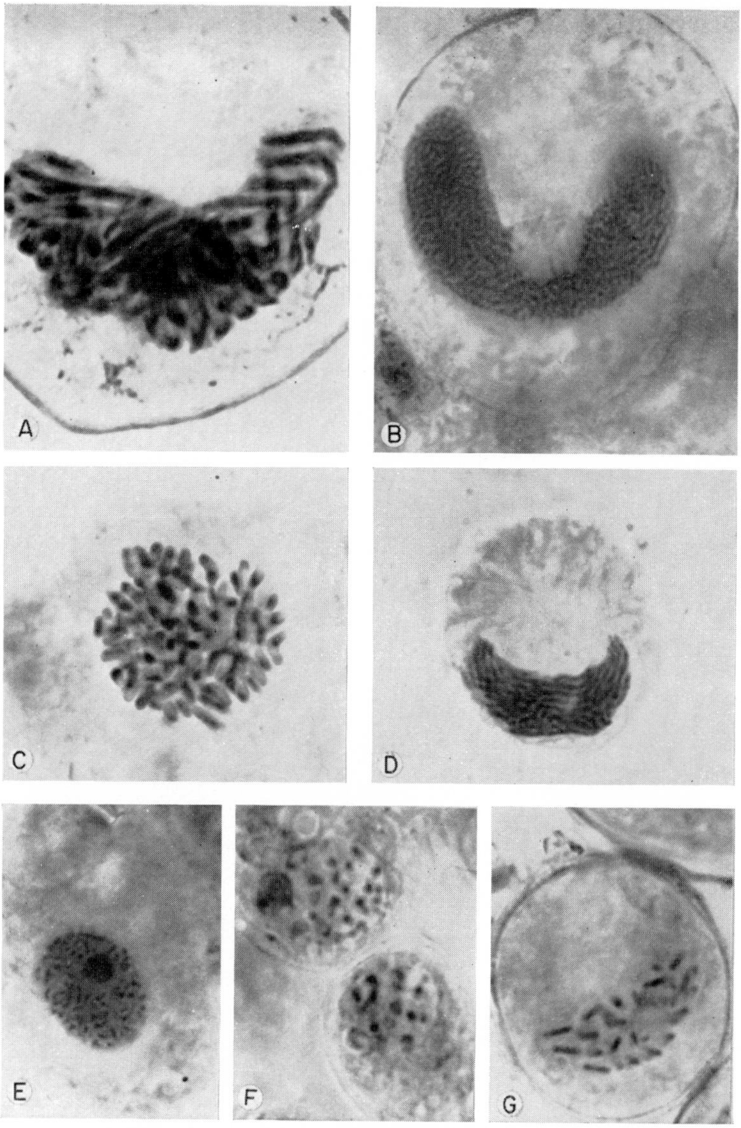

Fig. 3.2 Interphase nuclei in dinoflagellates, stained in aceto-carmine. **A** *Prorocentrum micans.* (x 2,250) **B** *Gonyaulax tamarensis.* Note the large nucleolus between the arms of the nucleus. (x 1,500) **C** *Peridinium trochoideum* partly squashed. (x 2,250) **D** *Amphidinium herdmani.* (x 1,500) **E** *Oxyrrhis marina.* Nucleolus clearly visible. (x 1,500) **F** *Amphidinium klebsii.* (x 2,250) **G** *Exuviaella mariae-lebouriae.* (x 1,500)

A nuclear membrane clearly surrounds the interphase nucleus in *Amphidinium klebsii* (Fig. 3.2F) and *K. rotundata* and a number of other species. These nuclei have a clearly defined outline as seen in the light microscope, and a typical double nuclear envelope is seen in the electron microscope. Many other species have nuclei with a variable or indistinct outline, as *Prorocentrum micans*, and here there was little evidence that a normal nuclear envelope existed. However, recent electron microscopy has shown one to be present.

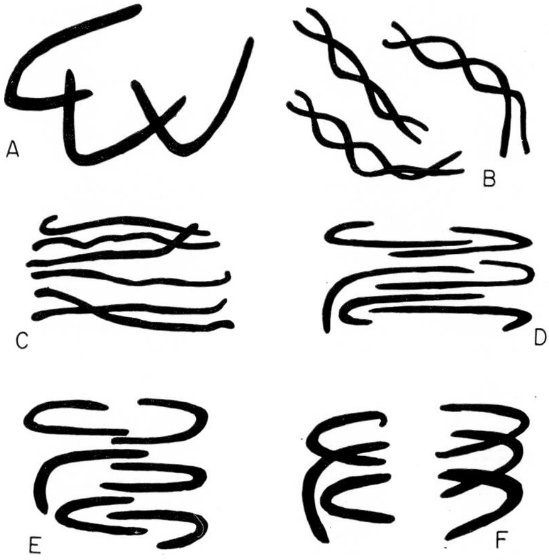

Fig. 3.3 The essential features of the nuclear division in *Prorocentrum micans*. **A** Interphase chromosomes. **B** Prophase pairs of chromatids, relationally coiled together. **C** Metaphase arrangement across the plane of the equator. **D** and **E** Anaphase separation of chromatids. **F** Telophase.

B NUCLEAR DIVISION

This will first be described and illustrated in one species to show the general principles of the process and then the range of behaviour in the other genera will be discussed.

NUCLEAR DIVISION IN *PROROCENTRUM MICANS*

The interphase chromosomes are condensed and clearly visible in the nucleus, so the commencement of mitosis is taken as the point when the chromosomes first appear as double threads (Figs. 3.3B and 3.4A). The pairs of chromatids are relationally coiled together and the three or four turns of this coiling are alone responsible for keeping the pairs together, for there appears to be no centromere joining them. The prophase chromosomes shorten slightly and seem to lose most of their coiling, presumably by a process of rotation of the chromatids, and then become arranged in the metaphase position. This is radically different from the analogous stage in a conventional mitosis as the chromatids lie more or less parallel to each other across the equator (Fig. 3.3C). As the 'equator' in *Prorocentrum* is at right angles to the narrow axis of the cell there is usually insufficient room for the chromatids to lie straight out and their ends bend around. Thus a polar view of metaphase shows a large number of loops of the chromosomes. Such a stage gives way gradually to the anaphase separation, without any clear-cut starting-point like that seen in a normal mitosis. The sister chromatids move towards the opposite poles which in *Prorocentrum*, in spite of some enlargement of the cell, are still kept very close together by the two halves of the cell wall. Thus the separation consists almost entirely of the chromatids, preceded by the end nearest to one pole, gliding in a path of 180° (Figs. 3.3D and E, and 3.4B and C) so that they end up as U-shapes with the open ends facing each other. This separation is by no means simultaneous, as the photographs show, and the time it takes must depend in part on the length of the chromatids. Often odd chromatids are very slow and can be seen crossing the 'equator' long after the majority of chromatids have grouped together at the poles.

The telophase is very simple. Further cell enlargement separates the daughter-nuclei a little (Fig. 3.4D) prior to cell cleavage, and the chromosomes change their orientation through about 90° so that their ends point in the general direction of the anterior end of the cell instead of towards the equator. There is no loss of condensation and mitosis ends with the chromosomes still intact and visible.

The observations on *Prorocentrum* suggested that in this mitosis there was no spindle and the chromosomes did not appear to possess centromeres. Consequently it was necessary to carry out some experiments in an endeavour to prove the absence of these organelles.

Mitotic inhibitors such as colchicine, 8-hydroxy quinoline, acenapthene and α-mercapto ethanol were applied to *Prorocentrum* in various concentrations. No evidence was obtained for the inhibition of mitosis and metaphases did not accumulate. This was taken to indicate that *Prorocentrum* does not have a spindle of the normal type.

Further experiments have involved the use of x-rays (Dodge & Godward 1963). After doses of over 4,000 rads it was found that the chromosomes were broken into a very large number of fragments (Fig. 3.5), the size of which appeared to be inversely proportional to dose, large fragments at 4,000, minute fragments at 8,000 rads. However, many nuclei in this condition were able to carry out anaphase often without leaving any fragments to form micronuclei. The evidence of these experiments clearly seems to indicate the absence of a centromere of the normal type.

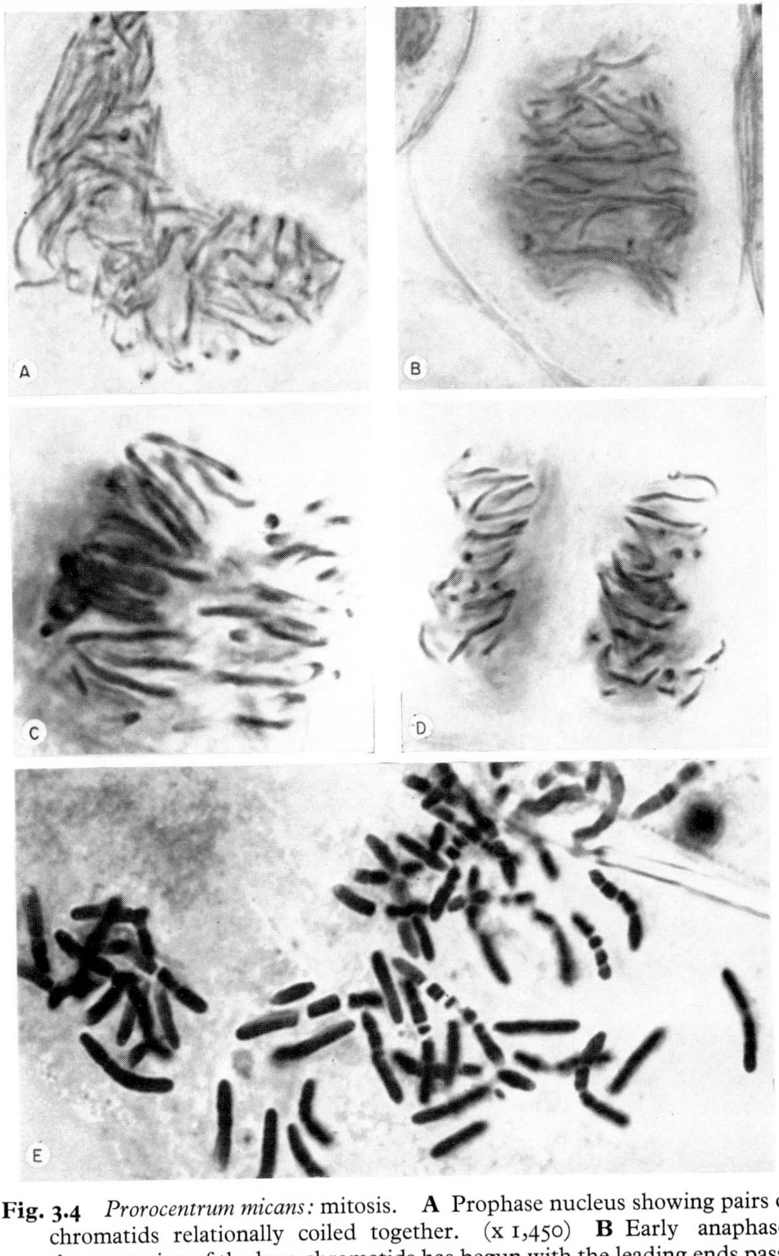

Fig. 3.4 *Prorocentrum micans:* mitosis. **A** Prophase nucleus showing pairs of chromatids relationally coiled together. (x 1,450) **B** Early anaphase, the separation of the long chromatids has begun with the leading ends passing through 180°. (x 1,450). **C** Anaphase nearly complete, U-shaped chromosomes almost all separate. (x 2,150) **D** Late anaphase—telophase with the daughter group of chromosomes clearly established. (x 2,150) **E** Squashed out interphase nucleus showing the distinct chromosomes. In some chromosomes the drastic treatment has separated the gyres of the chromonema. (x 2,900)

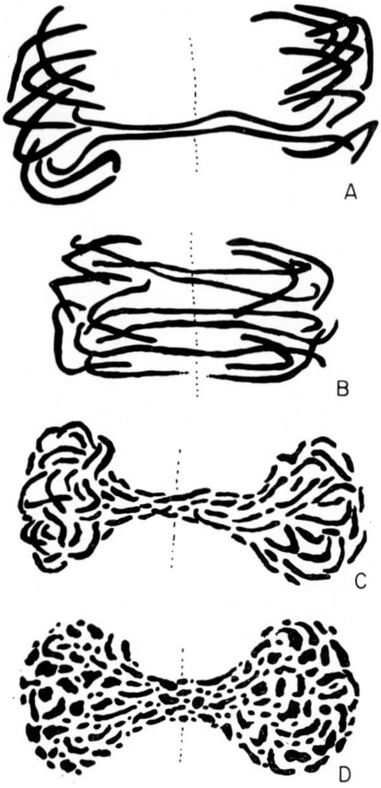

Fig. 3.5 Some types of anaphase bridge found after irradiation of *Prorocentrum* with X-rays of various doses. **A** 2,000 rads. Bridge of two chromosomes. **B** 4,000 rads. Bridge consists of several chromosomes. **C** 6,000 rads. Bridge now composed of large pieces of chromosome. **D** 8,000 rads. Bridge and daughter-nuclei consist of chromosome fragments of varying sizes.

NUCLEAR DIVISION IN OTHER SPECIES

The appearance of the prophase differs considerably in different species as a result of the varying lengths of the chromosomes. Thus in *Gyrodinium fissum* (Fig. 3.6A) the chromosomes are very long and the tangle resulting from each splitting into two is quite remarkable. In species with short chromosomes (e.g. *Gymnodinium* spp., Fig. 3.6B) only one or two coils hold the chromatids together and the individual chromatids are much more distinct. In *Gonyaulax* (Fig. 3.7) a considerable change takes place in the shape of the nucleus before the chromosomes split into pairs of chromatids. The U-shaped interphase nucleus rolls up to form a cylinder around the nucleolus or central body (Fig. 3.7B and C). The pairs of relationally coiled chromatids are then seen lying more or less parallel to the central body.

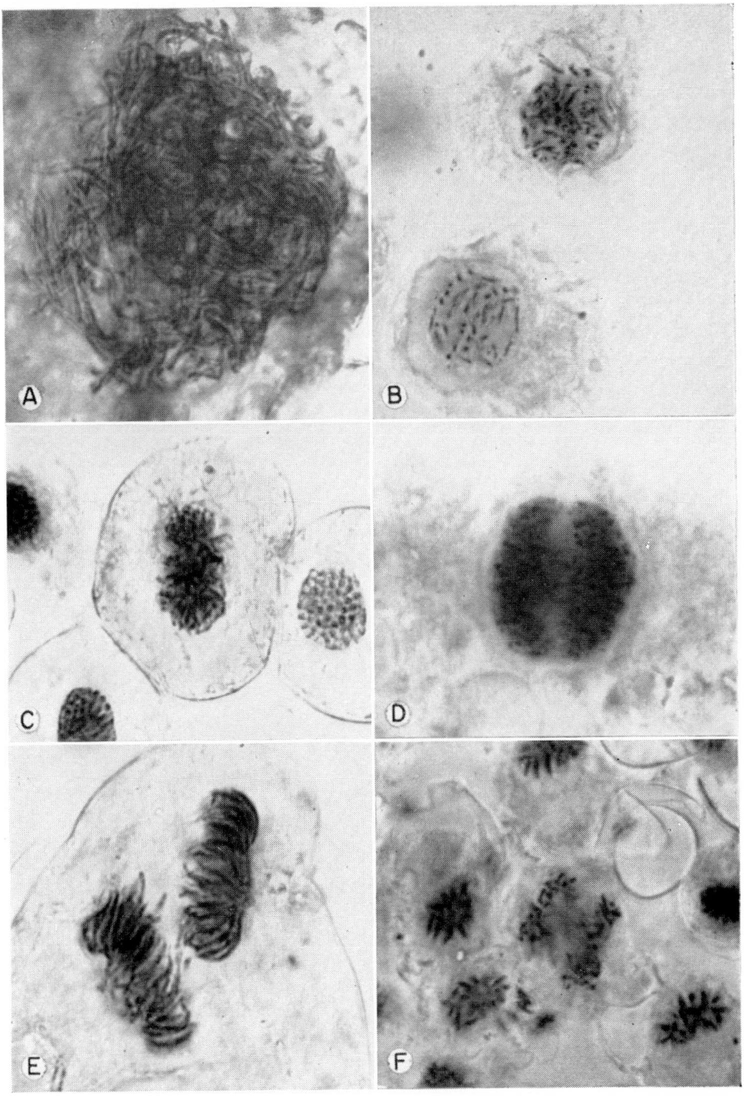

Fig. 3.6 Division stages in various species. (x 1,500) **A** Prophase in *Gyrodinium fissum* a species with very long chromosomes. **B** *Gymnodinium* sp. prophase nucleus with pairs of chromatids (upper) and an interphase nucleus. **C** A metaphase nucleus in *Peridinium trochoideum*. **D** *Oxyrrhis marina* a mid anaphase stage. **E** Late anaphase in *Gonyaulax tamarensis*, the daughter-nuclei have become slightly displaced. **F** *Exuviaella baltica*. An anaphase is seen at the centre, surrounded by several interphase nuclei.

Metaphase seems to differ very little in the species which have been studied. In all cases the pairs of chromatids lie packed close together more or less at right-angles to the equator (Fig. 3.6C). This stage cannot possibly be used for chromosome counting, in the way it normally is in higher plants, as there is never a spread-out metaphase plate.

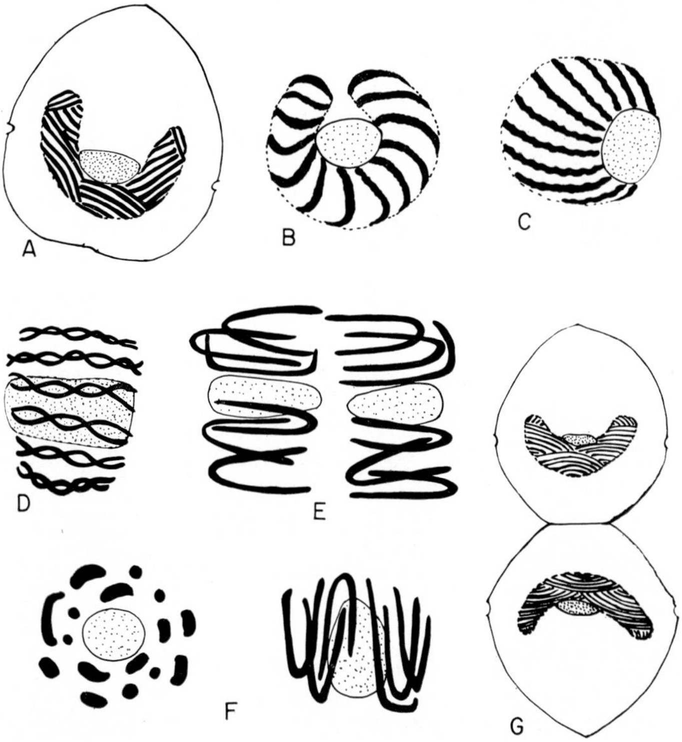

Fig. 3.7 The process of mitosis in *Gonyaulax tamarensis*. **A** Interphase nucleus with central body (dotted). **B** and **C** Early prophase nuclear reorganisation. **D** Metaphase showing chromatids still coiled together. **E** Anaphase nearing completion. **F** Late anaphase with one daughter-nucleus in side view, the other in polar view. **G** End of mitosis, cell cleavage nearly complete. [Reprinted from Dodge 1964c, by permission of Cambridge University Press.]

Anaphase separation in most species follows the same general outline as described for *Prorocentrum* but a group of species differs in having a persistent nucleolus situated at the centre of the chromosomes. As anaphase proceeds this becomes drawn out into two nucleoli, one in each daughter nucleus. This is seen very clearly in *Oxyrrhis marina*, which was well studied by Hall (1925), it also takes place in *Gyrodinium cohnii* and *Gonyaulax tamarensis* (Fig. 3.7E). In *Gonyaulax* there appears to be much variety in the shape taken up by the separating chromatids (Dodge 1964C). A different type of anaphase has been described in *Ceratium* (Skoczylas 1958; von Stosch 1958). Here the mid-point of the pairs of relationally coiled chromatids are the first parts to separate giving rise to V-shaped anaphase daughter-chromosomes. *Ceratium* is also said to possess a persistent nucleolus (or perhaps more than one) but whether this behaves like the examples described above is not clear.

In most species telophase consists simply in the aggregation of the group of chromosomes into daughter-nuclei, followed by cell cleavage. In *Gonyaulax*, however, the particular interphase nuclear shape has also to be re-established. This appears to be accomplished by the group of chromosomes splitting at one side and opening out to give the U-shape (Fig. 2.7F and G). There is a consequent reorientation of the chromosomes and some loss of condensation at this stage.

C MEIOSIS

Recent work by von Stosch (1964) has shown that the 'Knäuelstadium' of Borgert (1910), Schneider (1924) and Skoczylas (1958) is in fact the post-zygotene of meiosis and not a stage of mitosis. This particular nuclear organisation has generally been observed in germinating cysts of *Ceratium* in the spring. Von Stosch has been able to observe the copulation of anisogametes in *Ceratium cornutum* which then gave rise after about 14 days to an encysted zygote. The cyst germinates after several months to give a swarmer in which the first nuclear division is meiotic. Similar anisogamous fusion of gametes has been observed in *C. horridum* and isogamous fusion in *Oyrrhis marina*.

The nuclear fusion following copulation of gametes has been clearly observed in *C. cornutum* and *C. horridum*. The two nuclei, one normally larger than the other, amalgamate with the chromosomes in a contracted and hence stainable state. After fusion the chromosomes decontract and become relatively indistinct. This must be the normal state in the cyst. When meiosis commences the chromosomes again contract or condense and are seen to be in pairs, generally partially twisted together. At the 'Knäuelstadien' they reach their greatest contraction, which is probably why this stage has been most clearly observed. Superficially it resembles the prophase of mitosis in a species with long chromosomes, but the nucleus is rather larger than a mitotic nucleus.

The Anaphase I shows the separating chromosomes to be split longitudinally, and the first meiotic division is followed by a long interphase when the chromosomes are again decontracted. This is presumably followed by the second meiotic division. The fate of the four resulting nuclei would seem not to have been clearly determined.

One outcome of this work is that we can now say with some certainty that meiosis in *Ceratium* (and perhaps in all dinoflagellates) is post-zygotic and that the life-cycle of the organism is of the haplontic type, the vegetative cell having a haploid nucleus.

D THE STRUCTURE OF THE CHROMOSOMES

1 *Light microscopy* The unusual behaviour of Dinophycean chromosomes at mitosis and their condensation throughout the interphase suggests that they might differ structurally from the chromosomes of other organisms. In order to investigate this idea a large number of experiments and tests have been carried out on the nuclei of *Prorocentrum micans.*

The physical structure of the chromosome has been investigated by several methods. The use of desiccation, acid fumes and tension in anaphase bridges has shown that the chromosome consists of a spiral chromonema (Fig. 3.8E). The helix is normally right-handed, and using a standard method of preparation the number of gyres was almost always between five and eight (Dodge 1963b).

Other information which has a bearing both on the physical and the chemical structure of the chromosomes has come from irradiation experiments. At low doses of X-rays (below, 4,000 rads) the chromosomes behaved in a similar manner to normal chromosomes (see Fig. 3.5). Anaphase bridges consisting of one to several chromosomes (Fig. 3.8C) were produced as a result of the chromosome exchanges which had been induced by the X-rays. After doses of ultraviolet light similar bridges were occasionally produced (Dodge 1965), these are very rarely found in higher organisms after U.V. treatment. Higher doses of X-rays produced fragmented chromosome bridges which segregated to the daughter-nuclei in a way which would be impossible in a normal organism. The size of the chromosome fragments was approximately inversely proportional to dose and at 8,000 rads most fragments were very small.

The chemical composition of the chromosomes has been investigated by cytochemical studies of whole cells and of sections of cells embedded in plastic resins (Dodge 1964b, 1964d). The chromosomes very clearly contain a large amount of deoxyribonucleic acid (DNA) as was shown by staining with Feulgen, methyl green and azur B (Fig. 3.8A) using controls treated with deoxyribonuclease enzyme or chemical agents where the chromosomes remained unstained. Normal chromosomes also contain DNA.

No evidence was obtained for the presence of RNA, lipid or, most surprisingly, basic protein (Fig. 3.8B) in the chromosomes. These substances are all normally present in the chromosomes of higher organisms. In certain respects it would appear that dinoflagellate chromosomes are rather similar in chemical structure to the nuclei of bacteria, which they resemble in being composed of fine fibrils when seen in the electron microscope (see later section), as well as in their chemical composition.

Experiments are in progress to ascertain the period of DNA synthesis in

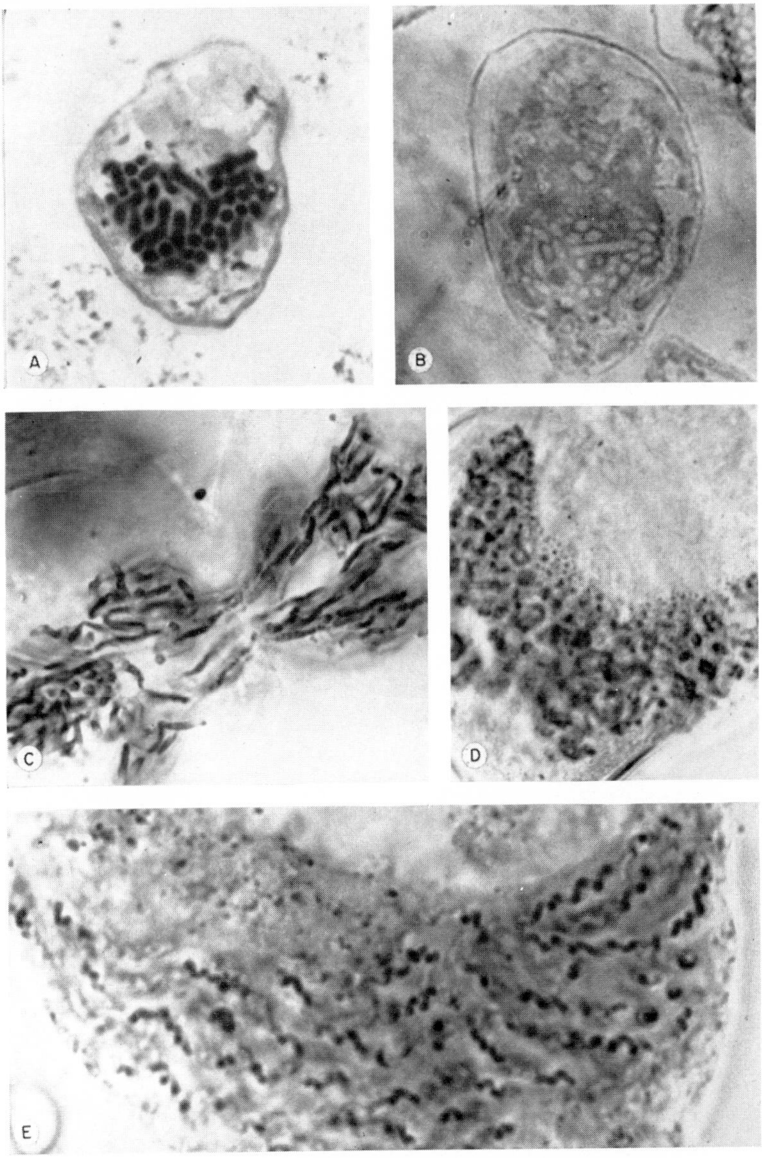

Fig. 3.8 *Prorocentrum micans*, investigations of the chromosome structure. **A** Section of cell stained with azur B to show presence of DNA in the chromosomes. **B** Section of cell stained with alkaline fast green to indicate position of basic protein. The chromosomes are seen to be clear whilst the surrounding cytoplasm is darkly stained. **C** Chromosome bridge at anaphase following treatment with 2,000 rads of X-rays. **D** Nucleus consisting of various sized fragments of chromosomes—small at the top, large at the bottom—following a dose of 5,000 rads. **E** Nucleus treated by desiccation and stained to show the spiral chromonema in the chromosomes. (**A–D**: x 1,450; **E** x 2,900)

the dinoflagellates. It is well known that in higher organisms this is a phased process usually taking place several hours before mitosis. In the bacteria it is said to be continuous and unaffected by division of the nucleus. The early results from labelled nucleotide experiments in *Prorocentrum* suggest that synthesis is a continuous process as it was found to be taking place in every cell which was examined after placing in labelled nucleotide medium.

2 *Electron microscopy of dinophycean chromosomes* The ultrastructure of the chromosomes of higher plants and animals is still a mystery, whilst the fine structure of most cell organelles is now well known. It was shown several years ago (Grassé & Dragesco 1957; Grell & Wohlfarth Bottermann 1957) that the dinoflagellate chromosomes have a fibrillar structure which can be preserved and (as thin sections) examined in the electron microscope. Further studies made by several workers (Giesbrecht 1962; Dodge 1963b, 1964a; de Haller, Kellenberger & Rouiller 1964) have confirmed the essential fibrillar nature of these chromosomes. The diameter of the fibrils is reported by different authors to vary between 40 Å. and 100 Å.

The only thing which can be said with certainty is that the diameter of the chromosome fibrils and the way in which they are aggregated together varies considerably with the type of fixation employed and the physiological state of the organism. As an example of fixation differences (Fig. 3.10B) shows a longitudinal section of a chromosome fixed in glutaraldehyde followed by osmium. The chromosome has a coarse, banded structure. By way of contrast Fig. 3.9C shows material which was fixed in osmic acid followed by uranyl acetate. This shows very fine fibrils and no evidence of coarse banding. It is not uncommon to find several different states of the chromosomes in one fixation. An example is shown in Fig. 3.9A and B where the very condensed chromosomes of *Katodinium* contrast with a nucleus from a similar organism in which the chromosomes are greatly expanded. Both cells were from the same preparation. De Haller *et al.* (1964) have suggested that the degree of condensation is in some measure alterable by changing the conditions of the culture. For example, growth under a diurnal periodicity of 12 hr. light and 12 hr. dark gave rise in *Amphidinium* to a large percentage of cells with expanded chromosomes, whereas keeping cells in continuous light for some days prior to fixation tended to produce condensed chromosomes. They also found that dilution or staling of the medium increased the percentage of cells with highly condensed chromosome.

What can be said with certainty is that in what appears to be the best fixations (i.e. those in which the contents of the chromosomes neatly fill the space available) the chromosomes consist of pairs of fine fibrils (Figs. 3.9C and 3.10A) a large bundle of which is arranged in the form of a helix or compact sinoidal curve to make up the chromosome. There appears to be no other component, no pellicle and no matrix around the fibrils. Electron

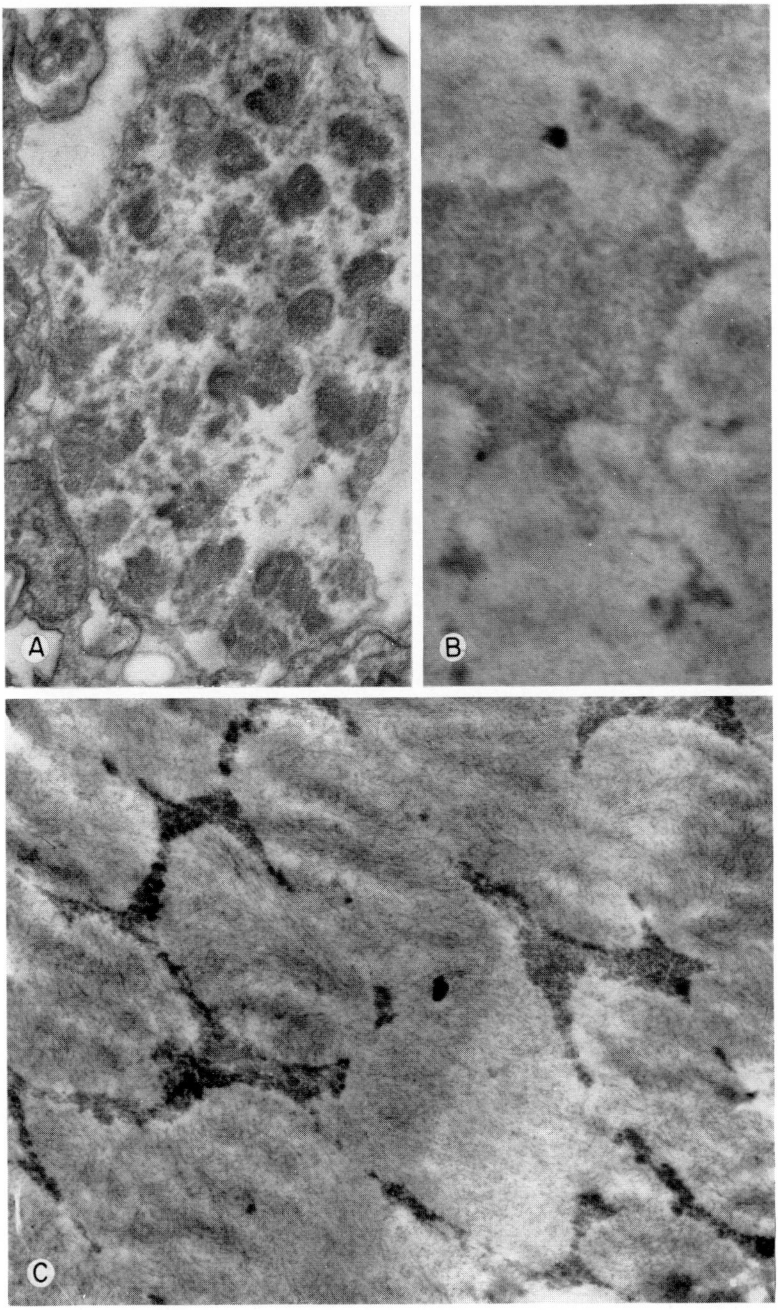

Fig. 3.9 Electron micrographs of dinoflagellate chromosomes. **A** and **B** Sections of *Katodinium rotundata*. In **A** the chromosomes are much condensed whereas in **B** they are expanded. The large granular body in **B** is the nucleolus. (**A**: x 37,500; **B**: x 67,500) **C** Section of nucleus of *Prorocentrum micans*. The chromosomes consist of fine fibrils. (x 37,500) All fixed in osmic acid, uranyl acetate stained, araldite embedded.

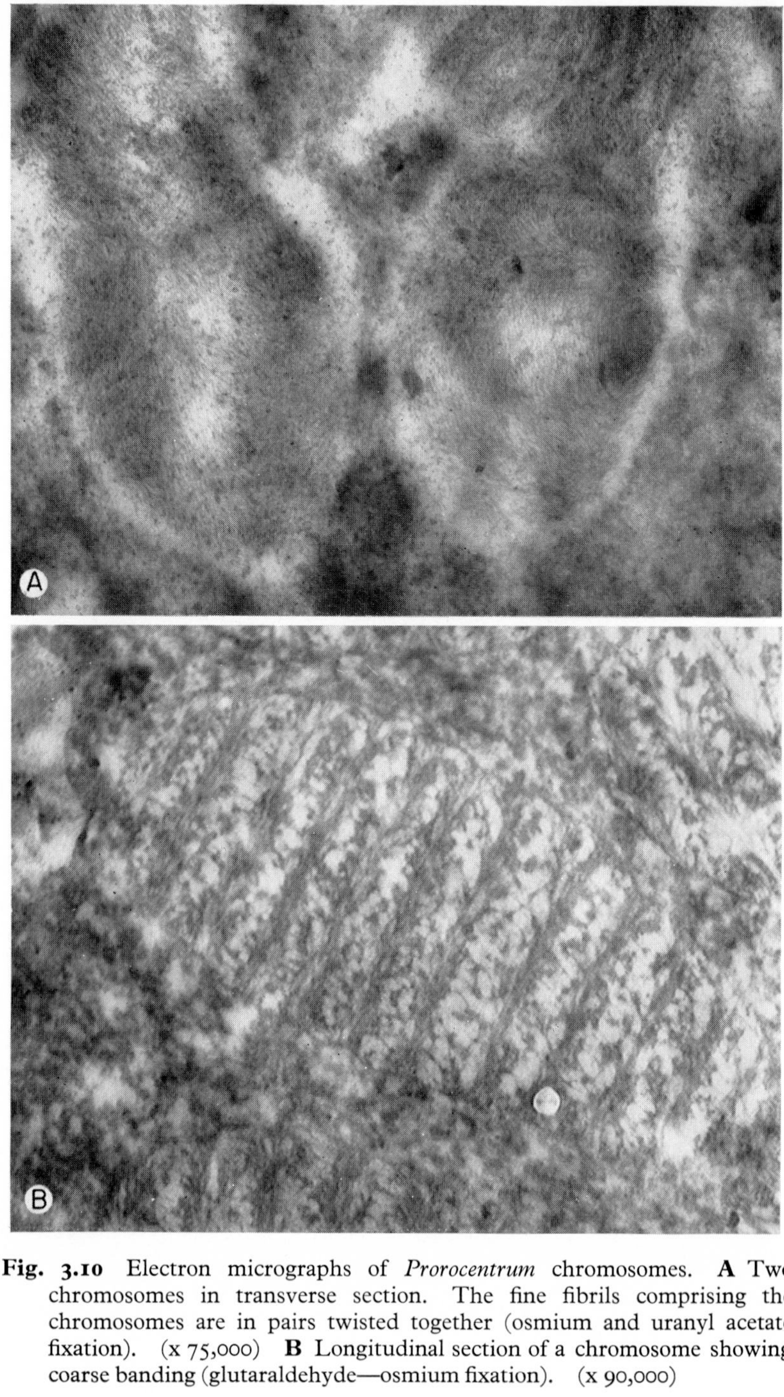

Fig. 3.10 Electron micrographs of *Prorocentrum* chromosomes. **A** Two chromosomes in transverse section. The fine fibrils comprising the chromosomes are in pairs twisted together (osmium and uranyl acetate fixation). (x 75,000) **B** Longitudinal section of a chromosome showing coarse banding (glutaraldehyde—osmium fixation). (x 90,000)

microscopy has shown that the nucleolus consists of large proteinaceous granules (Fig. 3.9B) which appear to be of similar size and staining reaction as the substance scattered through the nucleus around and between the chromosomes (Fig. 3.9A and C). Light microscopical tests have shown this granular material to contain basic protein (Dodge 1964a).

Recently, Grassé *et al.* (1965a, 1965b) have published an interpretation of the fine structure of the dinoflagellate chromosome. In the interphase chromosome each of the many fibrils which make up the chromosome are said to be arranged in the form of a partially flattened helix. During division daughter fibrils separate from each other to give rise to the multifibrillar chromatids. This separation would appear to be possible because the pairs of fibrils are arranged plectonemically and can therefore separate without untwisting being necessary.

SUMMARY AND CONCLUSIONS

In recent years the term Eucaryota has been applied to all the organisms which have a normal nucleus containing several chromosomes and surrounded by a nuclear membrane. This includes all the higher plants and animals and most of the algae and fungi. The term Procaryota is used for the bacteria and blue-green algae which have what appears to be a less well defined nucleus not surrounded by a nuclear envelope and without discrete chromosomes.

When we compare the cytology of the Dinophycean nucleus with these two types we find a considerable area of similarity with both the Eucaryota and Procaryota, as follows:

Characteristics of Eucaryota found in Dinophyceae:

Many chromosomes.
Nuclear membrane.
Mitotic nuclear division.

Characteristics of Procaryota found in Dinophyceae:

No basic protein in nucleus.
Chromosome consists of fine fibrils.
Possibly continuous DNA synthesis.

As the dinoflagellates cannot clearly fit into either of the present two groupings a third should be created for them and probably a number of other unicellular organisms with unusual nuclei, such as the Heliozoa and the Radiolaria. It is proposed that this new group be called the MESOCARYOTA, meaning a group of organisms with an intermediate type of nuclear organisation. Further studies of structure and genetics of the Dinophyceae should show whether this grouping is justified.

CHROMOSOME NUMBERS

Below (Table 3.1) are listed the counts which have been discovered in the literature and the counts recently made (Dodge 1963c) on 11 species. As will be seen from the account of the Dinophycean nuclei earlier in the book, it is exceedingly difficult to make accurate counts in these organisms. Hence the numbers given are only approximate. There is also no evidence that the numbers are constant. The rather disordered mitosis might be thought to give rise to some variation in chromosome number. The recent counts were made mostly on interphase nuclei.

Table 3.1 Chromosome counts in the Dinophyceae

Organism	Range of counts	Mean	Authors
Amphidinium sp.	24–26	25	Grassé & Dragesco 1957
A. klebsii Kofoid & Swezy	28–34	32	Dodge 1963c
Ceratium hirundinella	264–284	274	Entz 1921
C. tripos var. *subsala*		c. 200	Borgert 1910
Gonyaulax polygramma		c. 100	Entz 1921
G. tamarensis Lebour	134–152	144	Dodge 1963c
Gymnodinium vitiligo Ballantine		44	,, ,,
G. zachariasi		64	Entz 1921
Exuviaella baltica Lohmann	18–22	20	Dodge 1963c
E. mariae-lebouriae Parke & B.	30–34	32	,, ,,
E. pusilla Schiller	20–25	24	,, ,,
Katodinium rotundata (Lohm) Fott	64–70	68	,, ,,
Oxyrrhis marina Dujardin		c. 40	Hall 1925
O. marina Dujardin		c. 55	Dodge 1963c
Peridinium trochoideum (Stein) Lem.		44	,, ,,
Prorocentrum micans Ehrenberg	65–69	68	,, ,,
P. triestinum Schiller	20–27	24	,, ,,

REFERENCES

BORGERT, A. (1910). Kern und Zellteilung bei marinen *Ceratium*-Arten. *Arch. Protistenk.*, **20**, 1–46.

DODGE, J. D. (1963a). The nucleus and nuclear division in the Dinophyceae. *Arch. Protistenk.*, **106**, 442–452.

— (1963b). Chromosome structure in the Dinophyceae. I. The spiral chromonema. *Arch. Mikrobiol.*, **45**, 46–57.

— (1963c). Chromosome numbers in some marine dinoflagellates. *Botanica Marina*, **5**, 121–127.

— (1964a). Some effects of maleic hydrozide and other mutagens on the nucleus of a dinoflagellate. *Protoplasma*, **58**, 312–317.

DODGE, J. D. (1964b). Chromosome structure in the Dinophyceae. II. Cytochemical studies. *Arch. Microbiol.*, **48**, 66–80.

— (1964c). Nuclear division in the dinoflagellate *Gonyaulax tamarensis*. *J. gen. Microbiol.*, **36**, 269–276.

— (1964d). Cytochemical staining of sections from plastic-embedded flagellates. *Stain Techn.*, **39**, 381–386.

— (1965). Effects of ultra-violet light on the survival and nuclear division of a dinoflagellate. *Protoplasma*, **59**, 485–493.

DODGE, J. D. and GODWARD, M. B. E. (1963). Some effects of X-rays on the nucleus of a dinoflagellate. *Rad. Bot.*, **3**, 99–104.

ENTZ, G. (1921). Uber die mitotische Teiling von *Ceratium hirundinella*. *Arch. Protistenk.*, **43**, 415–430.

GIESBRECHT, P. (1962). Vergleichende Untersuchungen an den Chromosomen des Dinoflagellaten *Amphidinium elegans* und denen der Bakterien. *Zbl. Bakt., 1. Abt. orig.*, **187**, 452–492.

GRASSÉ, P-P. and DRAGESCO, J. (1957). L'ultrastructure du chromosome des Péridinians et ses conséquence génétiques. *C. R. Acad. Sci., Paris*, **245**, 2447–2452.

GRASSÉ, P-P., HOLLANDE, A., CACHON, J., and CACHON-ENJUMET, M. (1965a). Nouvelle interprétation de l'ultrastructure du chromosome de certains Péridiniens. *C. R. Acad. Sci., Paris*, **260**, 1743–47.

— (1965b). Interprétation de quelques aspects infrastructuraux des chromosomes de Péridiniens en division. *C. R. Acad. Sci., Paris*, **260**, 6975–78.

GRELL, K. und WOHLFARTH-BOTTERMAN, K. E. (1957). Licht- und elektronenmikroskopische Untersuchungen an dem Dinoflagellaten *Amphidinium elegans* n.sp. *Z. Zellforsch.*, **47**, 7–17.

HALL, R. P. (1925). Binary fission in *Oxyrrhis marina* Dujardin. *Univ. Calif. Pub. Zool.*, **26**, 281–324.

HALLER, G. DE, KELLENBERGER, E. and ROUILLER, C. (1964). Variations ultrastructurales des chromosomes *d'Amphidinium*. *J. Microscopie*, **3**, 627–42.

MCLAUGHLIN, J. J. A. and ZAHL, P. A. (1959). Axenic zooxanthellae from various invertebrate hosts. *Ann. N.Y. Acad. Sci.*, **77**, 55–72.

PROVASOLI, L., MCLAUGHLIN, J. J. A. and DROOP, M. R. (1957). The development of artificial media for marine algae. *Arch. Mikrobiol.*, **25**, 392–428.

SCHNEIDER, H. (1924). Kern und Kernteilung bei *Ceratium tripos*. *Arch. Protistenk.*, **48**, 302–315.

SKOCZYLAS, O. (1958). Über die Mitose von *Ceratium cornutum* und einigen anderen Peridineen. *Arch. Protistenk.*, **103**, 193–228.

STOSCH, H. A. VON (1958). Züm Chromosomenformwechsel der Dinophyten sowie zur Mechanik und Terminologie von Schrauben. *Arch. Protistenk.*, **103**, 229–240.

— (1964). Züm Problem der sexuellen Fortgflanzung in der Peridineeen gattung *Ceratium*. *Helgoländer wiss Meeresunters*, **10**, 140–155.

A recent paper by Giesbrecht (1965, *Zbl. Bact. 1. Orig.*, **196**, 516–519) has another model of the ultrastructure of the dinoflagellate chromosome which appears to differ in certain respects from the model of Grassé *et al.* (1965). Grell and Schwalbach (1965, *Chromosoma Berl.*, **17**, 230–245) has published electron-micrographs of the chromosomes of various dinoflagellates.

4 The Cryptophyceae

MAUD B. E. GODWARD
M.Sc., Ph.D.
Professor, Department of Botany, Queen Mary College,
University of London

CRYPTOPHYCEAE

Fifteen chromosome counts, nearly all approximate, are due to Thakur (1965). Contrary to the previous accounts (Hollande 1942, 1954) numerous small chromosomes, sometimes very numerous, are found in four genera. The older accounts mistook the metaphase plate, which lies parallel with the long axis of the cell, for a single long chromosome.

Only *Cynophora paradoxa* has a chromosome number as low as 10. In

Table 4.1 Chromosome numbers in the Cryptophyceae

Species	Chromosome numbers
A FRESHWATER SPECIES	
Cryptomonas ovata var. *palustris*	86 ± 6
Cryptomonas-4	109 ± 5
Cryptomonas-11	108 ± 11
Cryptomonas-16	145 ± 5
Cryptomonas-17	164 ± 4
Cryptomonas-37	209 ± 7
Cryptomonas sp. (supplied by Pringsheim)	83 ± 6
Cryptomonas sp. *nov.* (collected from Epping)	42 ± 2
Cyanophora paradoxa	10
Chilomonas paramecium	35 ± 2
B MARINE SPECIES	
Cryptomonas appendiculata	61 ± 6
C. biplastida	53 ± 3
C. suberosa	34 ± 4
Chroomonas salina	42 ± 4
C. mesostigmatica	24 ± 2

other genera, species have a range of numbers suggesting possible polyploidy. The highest numbers are found in material long cultured and may be the consequence of mitotic irregularities.

REFERENCES

HOLLANDE, A. (1942). Etude cytologique et biologique de quelques flagellees libres. *Arch. Zool. Exp. Gen.*, **83**, 1–268.

— (1954). Classe des *Cryptomonadineae. Traite de Zoologie*, **1**, GRASSE, P., Ed., 285–308.

THAKUR, M. (1965). Ph.D. thesis, London University.

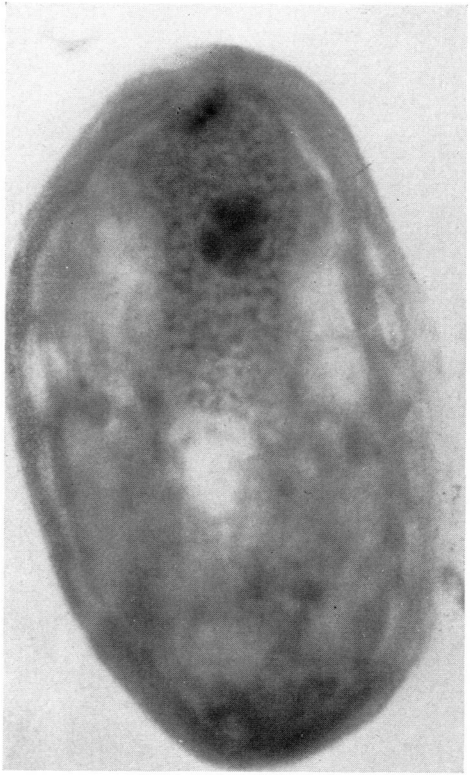

Fig. 4.1 *Cryptomonas*-17. Interphase nucleus showing internal differentiation of the nucleolus. (x 3,000)

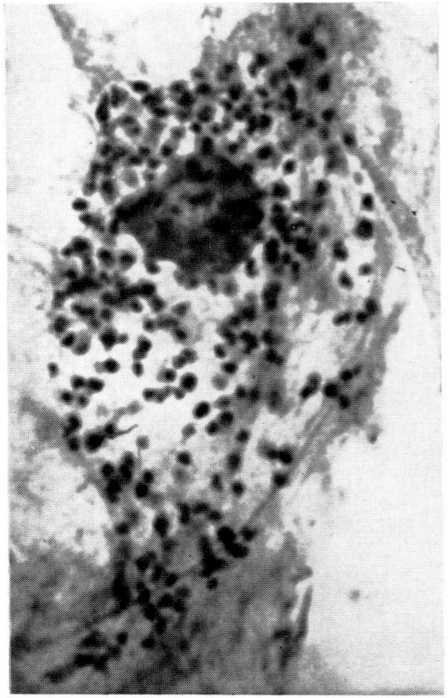

Fig. 4.2 *Cryptomonas*-37. Prophase showing well separated chromosomes, numerous and small. (x 3,000)

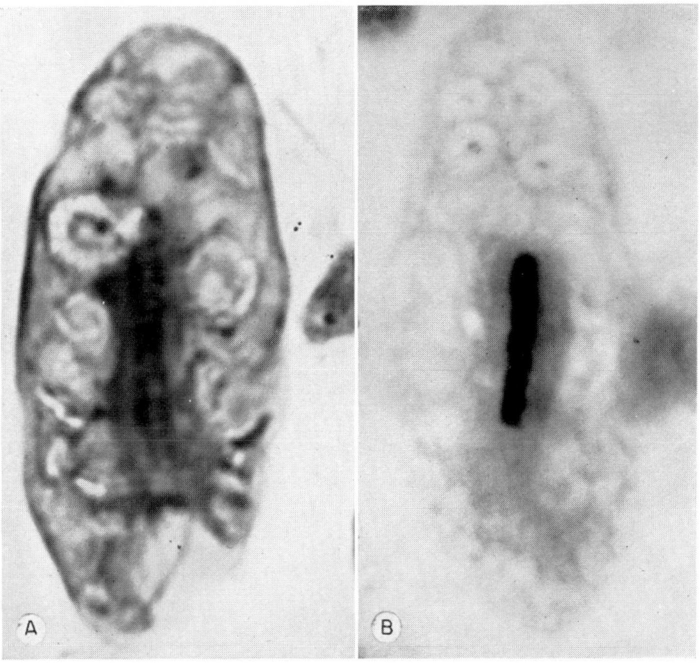

Fig. 4.3 *Chilomonas paramecium.* **A** Early anaphase. **B** Metaphase, showing contraction of chromosomes and compact metaphase plate. (x 3,650)

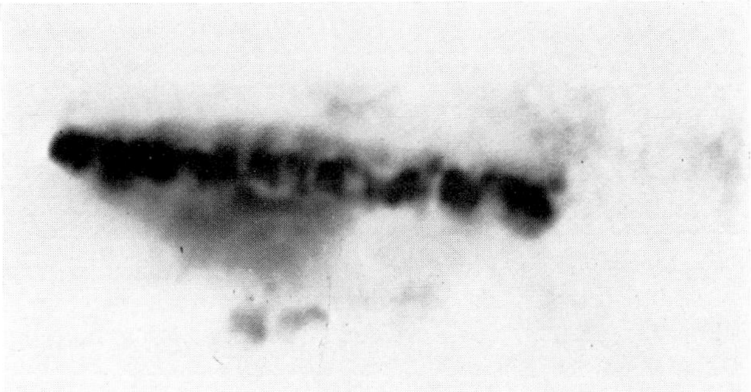

Fig. 4.4 *Cryptomonas*-16. Metaphase plate in lateral view, showing individual chromosomes.

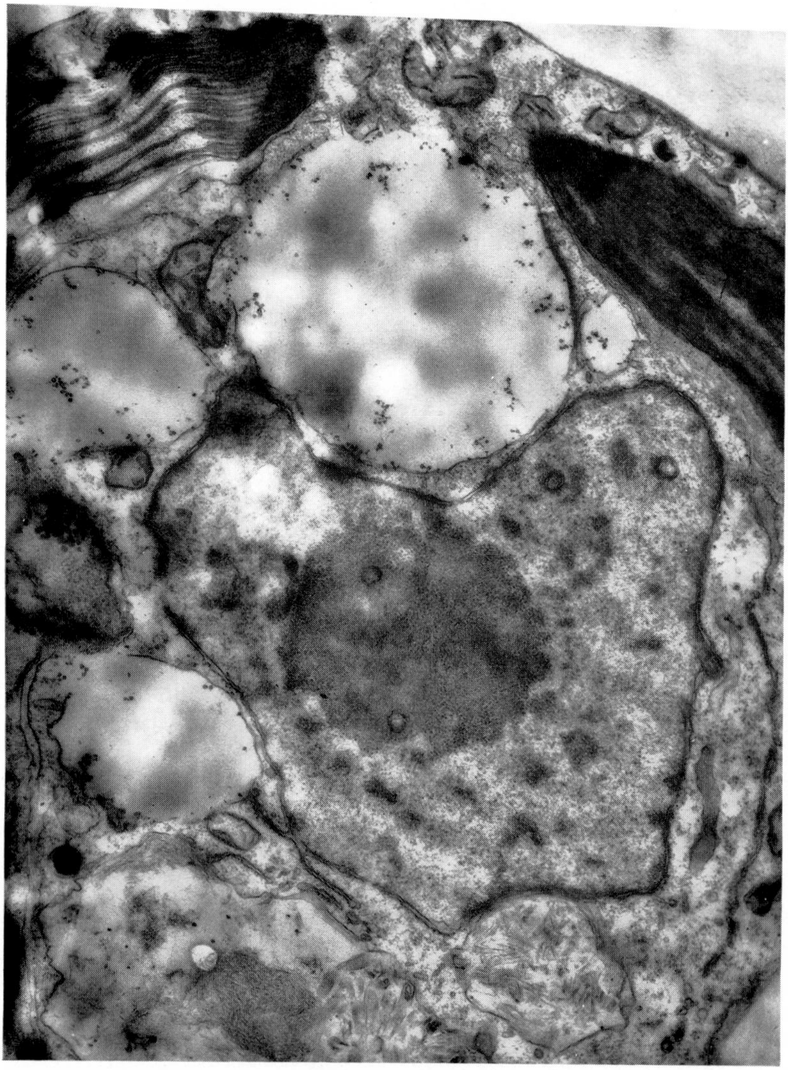

Fig. 4.5 *Cryptomonas ovata* var. *palustris*. Section, showing nucleus with nucleolus and protrusions from the nuclear membrane; top left, plastid with apparent granum. (Specialised structures not yet investigated.)

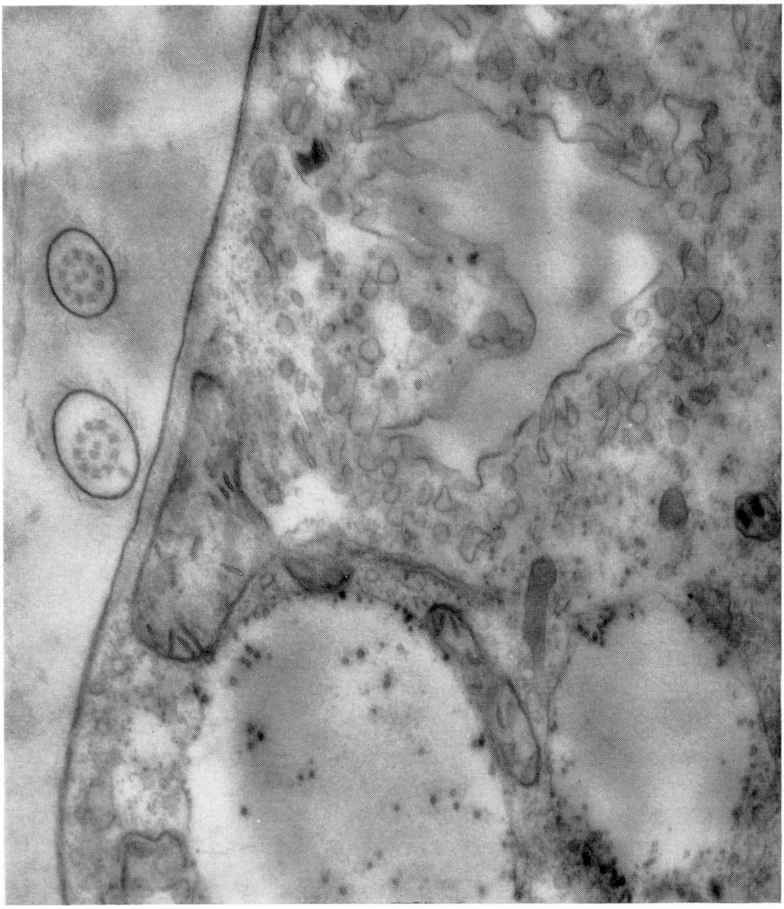

Fig. 4.6 *Cryptomonas oavata.* Section, with sections of the two flagella. Both have flimmer.

5 The Phaeophyceae

Part I

LEONARD V. EVANS
M.Sc., Ph.D.
Lecturer, The Department of Botany, University of Leeds

CYTOLOGY OF THE GENUS FUCUS (*WITH SOME REFERENCE TO OTHER GENERA OF THE FUCALES*)

1 VEGETATIVE CELLS OF *FUCUS SPIRALIS* L., *F. VESICULOSUS* L., *F. SERRATUS* L., AND *F. CERANOIDES* L.

(a) *Interphase nuclei*

Such nuclei can be seen to be slightly granular in appearance and lightly staining. They vary from 3 to 11 μ in diameter depending on the position of the cell in the thallus, when prepared by an acetocarmine squash method. There are one or two nucleoli, best seen after fixation with Karpenchenko fixative. Apart from the nucleoli, staining bodies known as chromocentres have been recorded in resting nuclei of somatic cells and gametangial initials of certain members. These include *Halidrys siliquosa* (L.) Lyngb. (le Touzé 1912; Roy 1938; Naylor 1958), and *Cystoseira tamariscifolia* (Huds.) Papenfuss. (Roy 1938; Naylor unpub.). (See also pp. 155–160.)

(b) *Dividing nuclei* (*mitosis*)

The best source of somatic nuclei undergoing mitosis is found to be the paraphyses and clavate hairs in young conceptacles (Fig. 5.1A). The granular appearance of the nuclei becomes more apparent with the onset of prophase. In those members with chromocentres, these can be seen to be linearly arranged as if on the chromosomes at prophase, but they become increasingly indistinguishable with the contraction of the chromosomes approaching metaphase, to reappear at the next interphase and prophase. As mitosis proceeds the thread-like chromosomes become shortened rods. They take up the stain more intensely at late prophase and early metaphase when they average 0·5–0·8 μ, but sometimes up to 1·2 μ, across their greatest length. At metaphase (Fig. 5.1A), the nuclei have a diameter of 4–9 μ, when seen in polar

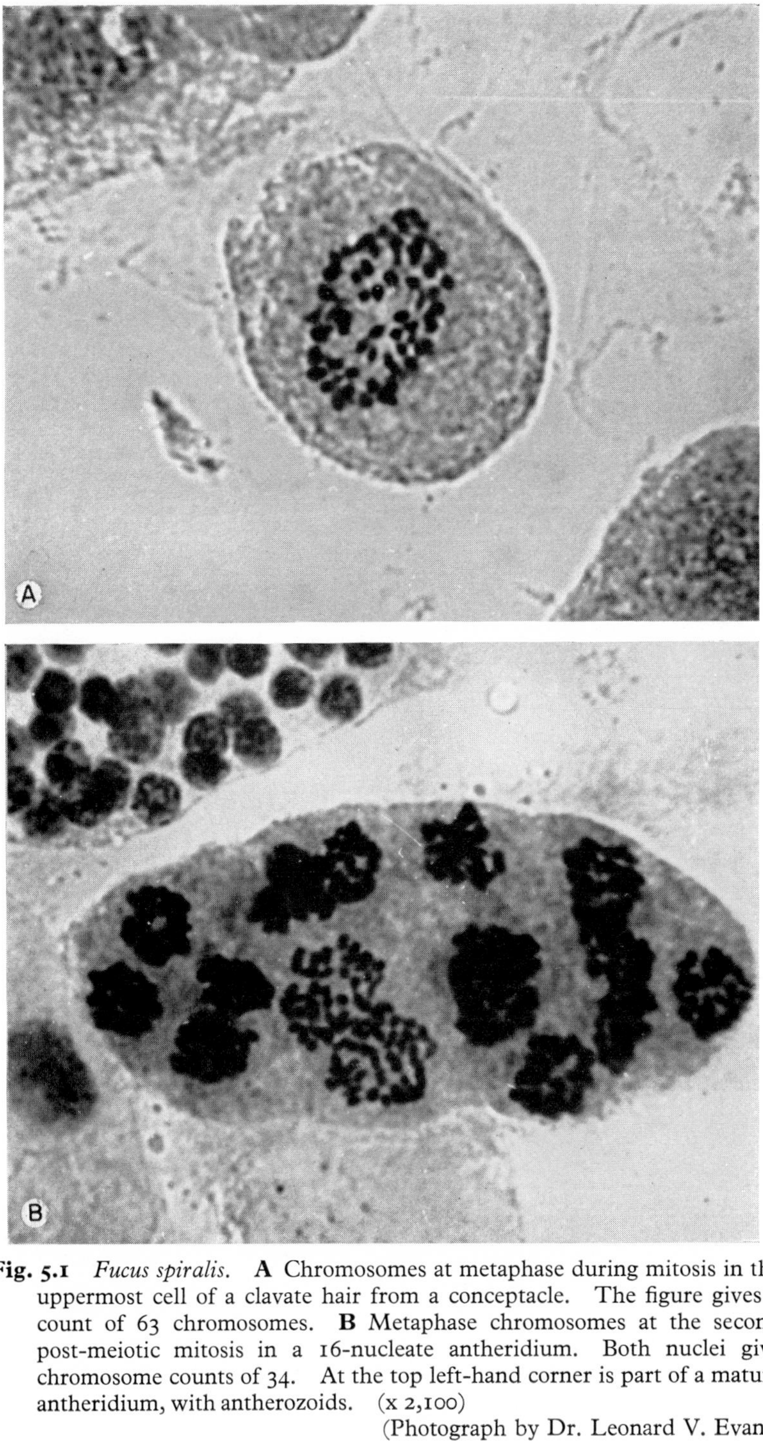

Fig. 5.1 *Fucus spiralis.* **A** Chromosomes at metaphase during mitosis in the uppermost cell of a clavate hair from a conceptacle. The figure gives a count of 63 chromosomes. **B** Metaphase chromosomes at the second post-meiotic mitosis in a 16-nucleate antheridium. Both nuclei give chromosome counts of 34. At the top left-hand corner is part of a mature antheridium, with antherozoids. (x 2,100)

(Photograph by Dr. Leonard V. Evans)

view. According to Yamanouchi (1909) the nuclear membrane probably persists up to late metaphase, and according to Farmer and Williams (1896) the spindle is therefore intranuclear. Yamanouchi (1909) observed the centrosomes in *Fucus* and also the spindle and astral rays. Anaphase and telophase proceed in the usual way. No difference in morphology can be seen between chromosomes of the species, and no constancy in the size of one or more chromosomes throughout one species, or between the species, appears to occur.

2 ANTHERIDIA AND OOGONIA OF THE FOUR SPECIES

(a) *Interphase nuclei*

These resemble vegetative nuclei, in being speckled in appearance at this stage. Non-dividing oogonial nuclei vary from 6 to 13 μ in diameter and occasionally evidence of delicate 'chromatin' threads can be seen. Antheridial nuclei have an average diameter of 10 μ in the early stages but by the 32- and 64-nucleate stage their diameters have decreased to 3–5 μ.

(b) *Dividing nuclei of antheridia (post meiotic)*

Again these appear much like those of somatic cells. The fine thread-like chromosomes shorten into spherical or rod-shaped bodies with increase in staining intensity. The nuclear membrane disappears at an earlier stage than that of vegetative nuclei. Metaphase chromosomes (Fig. 5.1B) range between 0·4 and 1·4 μ in length or diameter, and are arranged, closely packed, on equatorial spindles. Divisions of all the nuclei of an atheridium occur simultaneously. No difference can be seen in the morphology of antheridial chromosomes of the four *Fucus* species.

A reduction division was found to occur during the first division of the nucleus of the antheridial initial although no direct observation of it was made. When plates of 2-nucleate antheridia at later stages are examined, the haploid chromosome number is always found. The second division of meiosis must follow quickly after the first and four further mitoses take place to give 64 nuclei.

(c) *Dividing nuclei of oogonia (post-meiotic)*

Prophase nuclei have a diameter of 6–12 μ. "A black staining body associated with a nucleolus", now known as the chromophilous spherule, was figured in young oogonia of *F. vesiculosus* by Yamanouchi (1909, Fig. 44 a). It was not seen in any species of *Fucus* by the present author, but it has been seen during prophase in the oogonial initial cell of *Halidrys siliquosa* by Naylor (1958). Though it has not been seen to divide, a similar body has been recorded by Naylor as appearing in each of the daughter-nuclei during the second and third prophases in oogonia of *H. siliquosa*. Other Fucales in

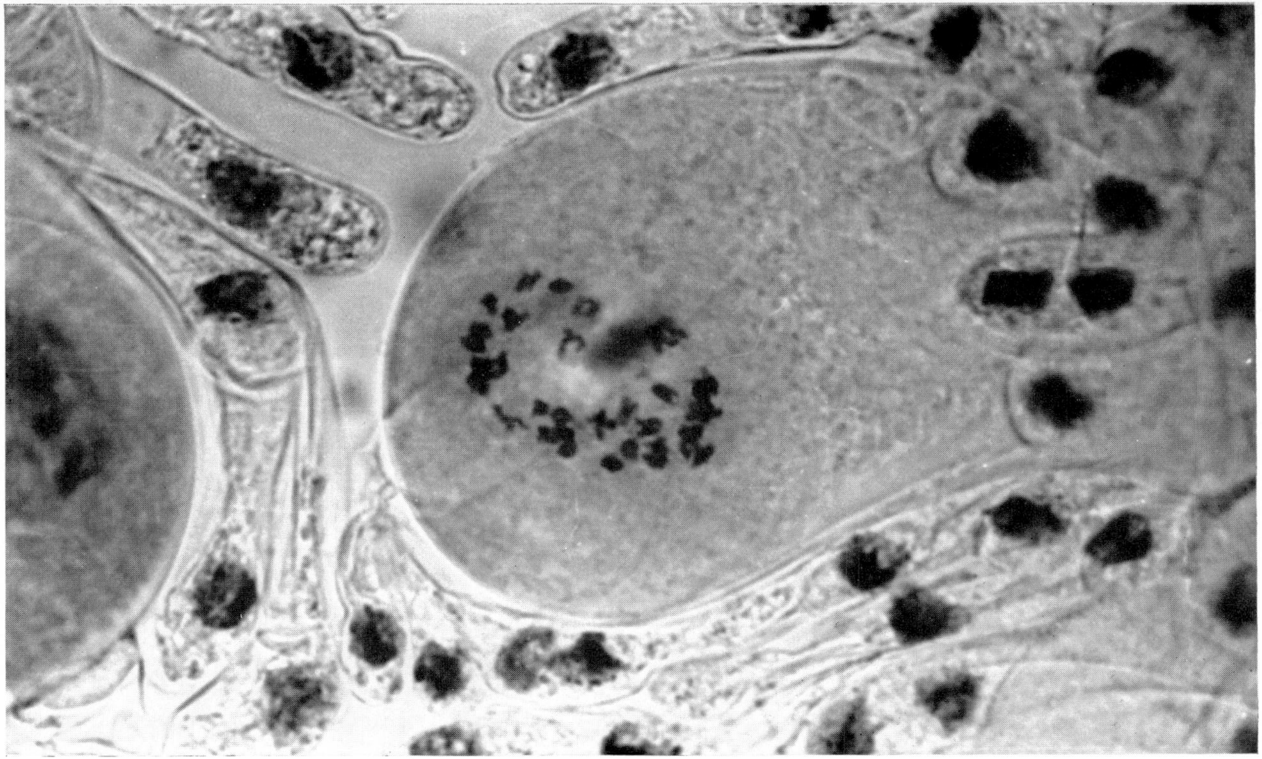

Fig. 5.2 *Fucus vesiculosus.* Diakinesis during the first division of meiosis in an oogonium. (The latter is surrounded by paraphyses, with nuclei at interphase.) The nucleus gives a count of 33 ± 1. (x 2,100)
(Photograph by Dr. Leonard V. Evans)

which a similar body has been recorded include *Sargassum horneri* (Okabe 1929) (oogonia); *S. piluliferum* (Inoh & Hiroe 1954) (antheridia); *S. tortile* (Inoh & Hiroe 1956) (antheridia); *Carpophyllum flexuosum* (Dawson 1940) (oogonia); and *Coccophora landsdorfi* (Tahara 1929) (oogonia). For other brown algae where this body has been recorded, see p. 155. All of these are non-British. This body is similar in appearance to the *Nebenkörper* of Geitler and other authors. It may well be simply a small 'droplet' of nuclear material which has failed to become incorporated in the nucleolus (Godward personal communication).

The appearance of the chromosomes becomes changed from thin threads to round masses as in somatic cells and antheridia, as prophase proceeds. Polar views of metaphase plates are only rarely seen because the axis of the spindle usually coincides with the longitudinal axis of the oogonium, and oogonia often take up a position with their longitudinal axes parallel with the slide, giving side views of plates when squashed. Oogonial metaphase plates when seen in polar view measure from 6 to 12 μ across, during the first and second division of meiosis. The chromosomes are 0·6–1·8 μ in diameter at this stage.

The first division of the oogonial nucleus has been found to be meiotic. During this process, the diploid number of chromosomes come together in pairs to form the haploid number of bivalents with clear evidence of chiasmata between homologous chromosomes (Fig. 5.2). Meiosis then proceeds normally, giving daughter-nuclei, after which there is a period of rest. Many oogonia can be seen with the four nuclei lying in close association in the centre. Yamanouchi (1909) states there is a rapid growth of the oogonium which almost reaches its full size before its third and last division, to give eight nuclei, takes place.

As for antheridia and vegetative cells, no constancy in size of one or more chromosomes throughout one species or between the species, can be seen to occur.

For chromosome counts see Table 5.1.

Table 5.1 Chromosome counts recorded for Fucus species (1940–1965)

Alga	*n*	2*n*	Author
Fucus spiralis L.	32	64	Evans 1962
F. vesiculosus L.	32	—	Lewis 1956
	32	64	Evans 1962
F. serratus L.	32	64	,, ,,
F. ceranoides L.	32	64	,, ,,
F. evanescens Ag.	32	—	Yabu & Imai 1957

CULTURE OF LAMINARIALES

Over the past hundred years many studies on the life-histories of members of the order Laminariales have been made. Germination of zoospores was first observed by Thuret in *Saccorhiza polyschides* and *Laminaria saccharina* in 1850. However it was not until 1915 that it was shown by Sauvageau that there is a definite alternation of generations with antheridia and oogonia on dioecious gametophytes of *S. polyschides* and *Alaria esculenta*. Since then a large number of workers have confirmed the findings of Sauvageau and added to our knowledge, so that alternation of generations throughout the order is now a firmly established fact.

The three most important factors which must be considered when culturing the gametophytes of these algae are nutrient requirements, temperature and light. Earlier workers like Drew (1910), Killian (1911) and Kylin (1916), all enriched the sea-water used for culturing *Laminaria* spp. with nitrate and phosphate as also did Kylin (1918), and Miyake (1928) for *Chorda filum*. Schreiber (1930) and Harries (1932) carried out more detailed studies of the nutrient requirements of *Laminaria* spp. in culture and the solution recommended by Schreiber has been used by other workers since. In some cases the solution has been modified slightly by the inclusion of soil extract, and is then called Erdschreiber solution, as used by Naylor (1956), etc. Harries found that zoospores grown in sea-water alone, passed out germ tubes and rested temporarily, increasing in size only when sufficient nutrient was added. The maximum growth she found occurred in cultures to which nutrient had been added in relatively large quantities at definite intervals, e.g. 0·25–0·6 ml. of a 0·01 M solution of KH_2PO_4 together with 0·25–0·75 ml. of a 0·01 M solution of KNO_3, and 0·1 ml. of a 0·01 M solution of KI per 25 ml. of filtered sea-water, added at intervals of 10 days.

Most investigators have found a temperature of approximately 10–16°C to be the optimum for culturing the gametophytes of Laminariales. At lower temperatures development is generally found to be slower and less vigorous whilst at higher temperatures, vegetative growth occurs more readily but production of reproductive organs and gametes is suppressed. Only Harries (1932) has performed controlled light experiments. She found that *L. digitata* and *L. saccharina* grew normally in wave-lengths at the blue end of the spectrum but when the red portion only is available, growth is less, antheridia mature but not the oogonia, and the female gametophytes are definitely retarded. She also recorded that with low light intensities growth and antheridial production were retarded but a few oogonia developed. Although this did not happen at higher intensities, sporophyte formation was slightly inhibited. Broadly speaking a light intensity of 50–300 ft.-candles is suitable, this light being produced artificially or from a window with a northerly aspect so that the plants are never subjected to direct sunlight.

Fertile plants of all four *Laminaria* species, and *Alaria* can be collected at low water of a spring tide during the late autumn, winter and early spring months, and of *Saccorhiza* and *Chorda* during the summer and into autumn. Such plants can be distinguished by the dark brown patches or sori which appear on the laminae in *Laminaria* spp., on the wings of the flattened stipe and sometimes on the lamina and attaching bell also of *Saccorhiza*; and on the sporophylls at the base of the *Alaria* plant. The sporangia are embedded in the surface layer of the cylindrical thallus of *Chorda*, and can therefore be detected only by cutting a moderately thin hand-section.

Well-washed fertile pieces blotted to remove most of the water, and kept in a polythene bag in a dark, cool place overnight will usually liberate varying quantities of zoospores, when they are put in a dish of sea-water under a bright light the following morning. These biflagellate zoospores will swim vigorously for some time, and those with eye-spots, viz. *Chorda* and *Saccorhiza*, will congregate at the meniscus on the side of the dish which is most brightly illuminated. During this period of activity, zoospores can be pipetted off on to coverslips or slides standing in petri dishes. The spores should then be allowed to settle overnight, after which 25 ml. of filtered sea-water should be added, or else the coverslips transferred to small tanks containing 1 or 2 litres of filtered sea-water. It has been found that gametophytes of each species have preferences in regard to nutrients, temperature and light, within the broad limits given earlier. Each species will be considered in turn and the optimum culture conditions, where sporophytes appear first and where they are biggest and most numerous, given for each:

Two simple nutrients can be used, one being weaker than the other. In the absence of any added nutrients, very little development occurs.

Nutrient A 0·01 M solution of KH_2PO_4
0·01 M " " KNO_3
0·5 ml. of each of these is added per 25 ml. of sea-water; every 14 days.

Nutrient B 10^{-5} M solution of KH_2PO_4 (i.e. above stock solution diluted x 20)
5×10^{-5} M " " KNO_3 (i.e. above stock solution diluted x 4)
0·5 ml. of each of these is added per 25 ml. of sea-water every 14 days.

A third more complex solution, ASP2 (Provasoli, McLaughlin & Droop 1957) is an excellent medium and maturity of gametophytes of all species is reached most rapidly in this. Also, a far greater abundance of eggs are produced in ASP2, and subsequent growth of the abundant young sporophytes far exceeds that in the simple nutrients. If gametophytes are grown in ASP2, however, they are very reduced in cell number, the females often consisting of one cell only, this cell acting directly as an oogonium (Fig. 5.3A). Gametophytes grown in nutrients A or B are far more filamentous, i.e. more vegetative growth occurs.

In the event of running sea-water being available, gametophytes can be grown in this but because of contamination by epiphytic diatoms, etc., they are not very satisfactory subjects for cytological purposes. When grown in running sea-water, the gametophytes tend to be of the reduced type seen in medium ASP2.

When culturing in petri dishes of nutrients A or B or ASP2 at 4°–18°C, a light intensity of 20–100 ft.-candles for 12 hr. a day is adequate, but when using ASP2 in tanks at 10° a light intensity of 200-250 ft.-candles is desirable and for an 18-hr. period daily.

Recommended conditions for each species are:

Laminaria digitata Nutrient B or ASP2 at 16–18°C or ASP2 (in tank) at 10°C.

L. saccharina and *L. ochroleuca* Nutrient A or ASP2 at 16–18°C, or ASP2 (in tank) at 10°C.

L. hyperborea Nutrients A or B or ASP2 at 16–18°C, or ASP2 (tank) at 10°C.

Alaria esculenta Nutrient A or ASP2 at 10°C, or ASP2 (tank) at 10°C.

Saccorhiza polyschides Nutrients A or B or ASP2 at 16°C, or at 10°C with a light of 200–250 ft.-candles for 18 hr.

Under these conditions gametes and young sporophytes appear in 12–15 days.

Chorda filum Nutrient A or ASP2, both in tanks or petri dishes, at 10°C with 18 hr. light of 200–250 ft.-candles. Sporophytes will appear in about 30 days. Sporophytes which are more uniform in age and size, through many eggs being liberated simultaneously, can be obtained by culturing in petri dishes of nutrient A at 4°C for about 20 days and then transferring to ASP2. Young sporophytes will be seen after 45–60 days.

Young sporophytes grow well in culture (Fig. 5.3B) and will reach lengths of up to 6 mm. in dishes containing 25–100 ml. of nutrient. The time taken to achieve this size depends on the nutrient medium, growth occurring very much more quickly in ASP2 than in nutrients A and B. In order to get the plants to grow beyond this size they have to be transferred to very much larger tanks of ASP2 (Burrows 1958) or into tanks of running sea-water (Evans 1965) (Fig. 5.3C and E). No plant of *Laminaria* spp. or *Saccorhiza* will become digitate under laboratory conditions—in order that this can happen the plants must be transferred to positions of water currents in the open sea.

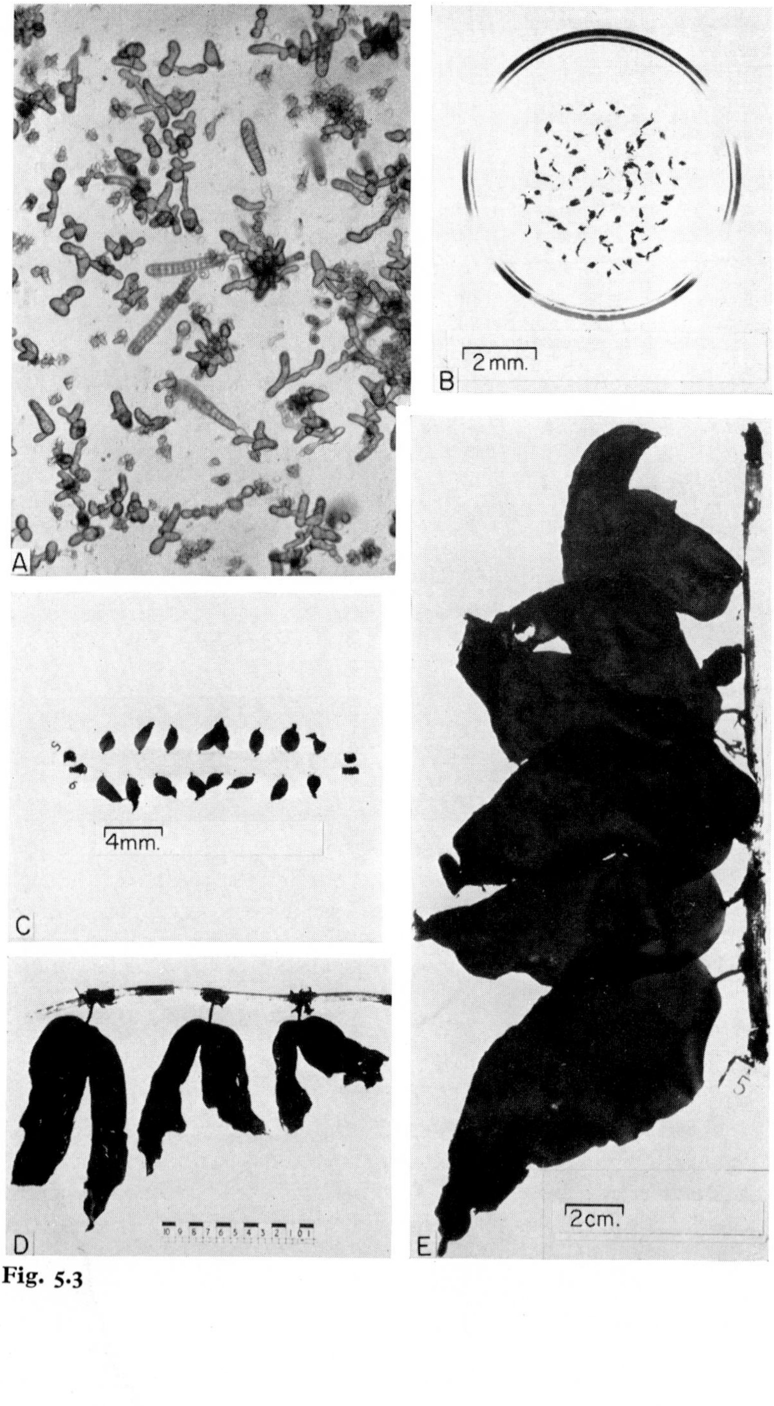

Fig. 5.3

Sundene (1962) and Evans (1965) found that fronds of *L. digitata* and *L. hyperborea*, respectively, split once longitudinally within eight weeks of being transferred from culture conditions to the sea (Fig. 5.3D).

CYTOLOGICAL TECHNIQUES

For examining the chromosomes of Brown algae, a squash technique is best used, as sectioned material can lead to many inaccuracies. The acetocarmine squash technique devised by Schneider in 1880, adapted as a standard method for chromosome work by Belling (1926) and further modified for algae by Godward (1948), etc., is still the technique principally used, in a further adapted state, for brown algae. This further change of technique has been necessary in order that a softening pretreatment may be included, brown algal material being very tough and resilient and not amenable to maceration and spreading by squashing in a fixed but otherwise untreated state. The only other technique which is used is the Feulgen technique (Naylor 1959; Evans 1965), but as this is a critical and more lengthy method it is not used as often as acetocarmine. It has the advantage however that no cytoplasmic staining at all occurs. Details of the schedule are given on p. 133.

Two softening pretreatments are currently used, as preliminaries to the basic acetocarmine method. The first is that of Naylor (1959) where material is pretreated with sodium carbonate (p. 153). The second is a less drastic treatment than the first and is used by Evans (1962, 1963a, 1965) for *Fucus* and for sporophyte material of Laminariales. Filamentous material, e.g. Laminarian gametophytes, does not require a softening treatment. The schedule is as follows, stages three and four being omitted for material of a filamentous nature:

1 Fix material in a mixture of one part glacial acetic acid to three parts industrial ethyl alcohol until it is bleached and is no longer mucilaginous, i.e. 12–18 hr.

2 Wash well in several changes of tap water or in running tap water.

Fig. 5.3 *Laminaria hyperborea.* **A** Male and female gametophytes and young sporophytes, grown in culture (ASP2 medium at 10°C with 18 hr. light). **B** Young sporophytes 211 days after liberation of zoospores. Ready for transference from culture vessels to running sea-water. **C** Some of the young sporophytes from **B** attached by placing their haptera in little slits in polythene tubes. They are 300 days old and growing in running sea-water. **D** Showing a longitudinal splitting of the laminae, eight weeks after transplantation from laboratory tanks to the Menai Straits. **E** Some of the sporophytes in *c*, eight weeks after attachment to polythene tubes (360 days old). They are growing in aquarium tanks with running sea-water, and receiving a light intensity of 300 ft.-candles for 18 hr. out of 24. (x 65) (Photograph by Dr. Leonard V. Evans)

3 Immerse in excess of a 1 M solution of a salt of a monovalent metal of low atomic weight such as lithium chloride, for 15 min. (Evans 1963a).

4 Transfer to tap water and leave for 15 min. No change is necessary.

5 Dissect the material out of the meristoderm or outer layer, if this is present as for example in vegetative tips of Fucoids; place on a slide under a coverslip, and squash lightly and evenly, if possible with a firm chizel-shaped bone or plastic instrument.

6 When spread of the material is judged to be sufficient, a few drops of acetocarmine solution are put around the edge of the coverslip. Acetocarmine is not allowed to come into contact with the material earlier, because of its inimical effect on spreading. The stain should contain one drop of saturated ferric acetate solution (in acetic acid) per 25 ml. and it should be made up, and the acetate added, as long as possible before using. Not all batches of stain are good and a number should be made up using carmine from various sources. No separate mordanting in a solution of ferric alum is required for adequate staining, and indeed, is to be avoided because the mordant as well as the acetocarmine is inimical to spreading. If the stain does not penetrate it can be helped by raising the coverslip gently from each side in turn, whilst holding it in place with the fingers of the other hand.

7 When the stain is evenly spread apply heat with a spirit lamp, continuing to do so over a period of about 30 sec. the slide being withdrawn from the flame at 3- or 4-sec. intervals and allowed to cool by placing on the bench or a piece of glass for a few seconds before reheating. On no account should the acetocarmine be allowed to boil. The heating–cooling sequence is carried out three or four times.

8 Squash the coverslip again, and take up excess stain with a piece of filter paper.

9 Temporary preparations should be ringed with glycerine jelly (or rubber solution) to prevent drying out.

10 If the material is judged to be overstained before ringing, or a preparation kept in a temporary stain for some time requires redifferentiation, destaining of the cytoplasm should be carried out. To do this, flood with a mixture of one part acetocarmine solution to five parts of glacial acetic acid, and heat gently for 15 sec. or so. The need for destaining the cytoplasm has been found to be greatest in gametophytes and zoosporangial material which has been left in 1:3 acetic alcohol for longer than 18–24 hr. The best method of

storage is in 70% alcohol at 2°C, the material being washed very thoroughly in tap water after fixation. This reduces cytoplasmic staining, but undoubtedly the best preparations are those made immediately after a short period of fixation (i.e. until the material is bleached) and without storage.

Good preparations should be made permanent in the following way.

11 Remove the glycerine jelly seal by scraping with a razor blade, or rubber solution by lifting with a mounting needle.

12 With a diamond marker, outline the four corners of the coverslip on the glass of the slide. A small piece from one corner (e.g. the top right) or the coverslip should always be cut off, so that the coverslip be returned to the same position later.

13 Flood the slide with the destaining solution above, if required, and with acetocarmine if no destaining is required. Lift the coverslip very gently to allow the liquid to penetrate. Penetration of destainer in particular is very rapid if a little heat is applied.

14 As soon as the coverslip is loose, lift off and put it and the slide into a dish of 95% alcohol.

15 After 5 min. transfer to absolute alcohol (two changes after 5 min.) and then into euparal essence.

16 Replace the coverslip on the slide in its original position, in a drop of euparal, and allow to harden overnight on a hot plate.

The Feulgen method (adapted from Naylor 1959). The procedure which is most successful for gametophyte material of Laminariales can be summarised as follows: Coverslips on which gametophytes are growing are fixed in 1:3 acetic alcohol, washed thoroughly in tap water, and hydrolysed in NHCl at 60°C for 8–10 min. After this time, hydrolysis is stopped by placing them in cold water. Then the coverslips are transferred to decolourised Schiffs reagent and left for 8 hr. at room temperature. After this they are bleached in three changes of recently made sulphur dioxide water, and then squashed in this liquid, before being dehydrated by immersion for 10 min. in 30%, 50%, 70%, 95% and absolute alcohol. Following this they are put into euparal essence and finally into a drop of euparal on a slide. The euparal must then be allowed to harden. Considerable care should be taken when flooding with 30% alcohol after squashing in sulphur dioxide water or much of the material will become dislodged and lost.

Two other techniques worthy of mention, though not in wide use on algal material at present, are those of Lewis (1956). The present writer did not find these methods particularly helpful but repeated application and persistency might have led to greater success.

1. *Oxalate/peroxide treatment.* This is a method of isolating and softening conceptacles of the Fucaceae following fixation. The following steps are involved:

(i) Split the receptacles longitudinally, removing as much of the mucilage as possible, and fix for 12 hr. in an alcoholic fixative (e.g. 1:3 acetic alcohol, but not a formalin-containing fixative).

(ii) Transfer to a solution made up of equal parts of saturated ammonium oxalate solution, and 20-volume hydrogen peroxide. They should be left here for 20 min., preferably in an illuminated position.

(iii) Wash, over 15 min., in two or three changes of distilled water.

After this, the cortex and medulla are softened and the conceptacles can be dissected away from the receptacles, either for storage or immediate staining. The method is recommended for oogonial material, and is not regarded by Lewis as suitable for antheridia.

2. *A fixation/maceration technique.* This method is primarily designed for cytological investigations of male material, but it appears to be applicable to female material also. Its main advantages are said by Lewis to be as follows: improved fixation, effective and rapid removal of cell pigments and cytoplasmic inclusions, and in facilitating cell separation thus permitting better spreading and staining. The following is the recommended procedure:

(i) Macerate 30 gm. of receptacle material for 4 min., in 150 ml. of fixative, such as 1:3 acetic alcohol, in a Waring Blendor.

(ii) Transfer to a graduated cylinder; after a few minutes three distinct layers will have formed. The middle of these, consisting mainly of sex organs from ruptured conceptacles, should be pipetted off, and a normal squash:staining procedure carried out.

It is important to use the weight of receptacles, volume of fixative, and maceration time given, otherwise decreased efficiency will result.

INCREASING CELL DIVISION

It was found that nuclear divisions in the Fucaceae and Laminariales appear to occur rather infrequently, and large numbers of slides normally had to be made to encounter a few high-quality polar views of metaphase chromosomes. Treatments carried out to explore the possibility of increasing the incidence of divisions included: sampling over various periods and states of the tide; cold and light treatments; use of colchicine, paradichlorobenzene, and indo-3-acetic acid; wounding so as to cause production of a callus; and introduction of plants into water the salinity of which was progressively decreased (Evans 1962). None of these gave any startling improvement, with the possible exception of the last, and most results were suspected to have been obtained from naturally occurring divisions.

In Laminarian gametophytes the natural frequency of divisions per coverslip varied from none to some three dozen, suggesting a possible inherent rhythm. It is therefore preferable to fix a batch of coverslips a few at a time over intervals of one or two days. The problem was most acute in zoosporangial material, where treatments on the same lines as those carried out for *Fucus* species had no appreciable effect (Evans 1965). One method which gave a modicum of success, however, was to store pieces of fertile thallus of *Chorda filum* for at least 4 days in static sea water in darkness at 10°C, and then subject to rapidly running sea water in bright sunlight. Fixations made 45–60 min. later showed many sporangial nuclei in some stage of division, whilst untreated material remained at interphase. Unfortunately the method can only be applied to *Chorda* as the other members of the order cannot survive the dark period necessary.

CYTOLOGY OF THE LAMINARIALES

1 CELLS OF GAMETOPHYTES AND YOUNG SPOROPHYTES

(a) *Interphase nuclei*

Nuclei of non-dividing cells appear as speckled or granular bodies with one prominent nucleolus. Nuclei of female gametophytes vary from 4–5 μ in diameter when prepared by squash methods in all species except *Saccorhiza polyschides* where their diameter is 8–14 μ, with nucleoli of 3–4 μ in size. Male gametophyte nuclei have a diameter of 2·5–3·5 μ but in *Saccorhiza*, the range is 2·5–4·2 μ, when stained with acetocarmine or Schiffs reagent. The interphase nuclei of male gametophytes take up the stain most intensely, those of young sporophytes are less deeply coloured whilst nuclei of female gametophytes only stain very lightly indeed (Naylor 1956; Evans 1965).

(b) *Dividing nuclei (mitosis)*

In early prophase the diameter of the nucleus is found to increase somewhat, this being most obvious in young sporophytes and in the division prior to egg formation in the female gametophytes—oogonial nuclei of *Saccorhiza* having a diameter of 18 μ are not uncommon at this stage. As prophase proceeds the chromosomes begin to appear as fine, beaded threads occasionally with small clumps of darker staining 'chromatin'. These increase in size and become short, thick threads. Apparent connecting fibres become less and less obvious. The threads contract further to give rod-shaped chromosomes, by which stage (prometaphase) the nuclear membrane has broken down. Slight shortening of the chromosomes gives the typical appearance shown in

Figs. 5.4, 5.5 and 5.7. At this stage chromatids can be seen in many of the chromosomes. Anaphase and telophase proceed in the usual way.

2 UNILOCULAR SPORANGIA

The size range here is considerable. Sporangia of *Chorda filum* vary from about 19 μ long and 7 μ wide in the uninucleate stage, to 37 μ long and 17 μ wide in the 16-nucleate stage. In *Laminaria* spp. and in *Alaria esculenta* and the uninucleate sporangia are of the same order of size as those of *Chorda*, but 32-nucleate sporangia are up to approximately 5 μ long and 15 μ wide in the one nucleate stage, to 124 μ long and 13–20 μ wide in the 128-nucleate stage.

Thirty-two zoospores are produced in each sporangium of the four species of *Laminaria* and in *Alaria*. In *Saccorhiza* 128 are produced in each, and in *Chorda* 16.

(a) *Interphase nuclei*

These resemble their counterparts in the cells of gametophytes and young sporophytes. They have a diameter of 4–5 μ in all species. Their size decreases at first as their number in a sporangium increases, e.g. in 2-nucleate sporangia to about 4·2 μ and in 4-nucleate sporangia to about 3·5 μ, etc. Beyond the 4- to 8-nucleate stage the decrease in nuclear size is not so apparent, and in sporangia containing over this number of nuclei, their size appears to remain in the range of 2–3 μ. A prominent nucleolus is present in the interphase nucleus.

(b) *Dividing nuclei (meiosis)*

The first sign of division is the enlargement of the nucleus to a diameter of up to 8 μ and the appearance of an increasingly conspicuous web of thin threads, which gradually thicken, occasionally congregating on one side of the nuclear membrane. The threads at this stage present a beaded or knobbly appearance, and the chromosomes apparently differentiate from these 'knots'. No doubt the 'knots' are chromocentres or centres of contraction. By diakinesis the threads have shortened to a length and the bivalents are widely dispersed in the nucleus. Bivalents at diakinesis show both terminal and interstitial chiasmata; sometimes only one interstitial, more usually one interstitial and one terminal, or one interstitial and two terminal, occasionally two terminal only. Diakinesis stages are exceedingly rare, and this could be indicative of their short duration. By this stage the nucleolus is no longer visible, but the nuclear membrane can sometimes be seen to persist at metaphase. Further condensation results in smaller, often spherical bivalents which become arranged on a compact equatorial plate (Fig. 5.6). Anaphase I and telophase proceed in the usual manner, details being difficult to observe. The scarcity of 2-nucleate sporangia may indicate that they exist for only a short period before the onset of the second division. Further divisions of the four products of meiosis follow to give 16, 32 or 128 nuclei, according to the species. Changes of the sporangial cytoplasm occur to form the zoospores, each containing a nucleus together with a chromatophore. The zoospores are released by the breakdown of the hyaline sporangial cap.

3 A POSSIBLE SEX CHROMOSOME AND CHROMOSOME MORPHOLOGY IN *LAMINARIA* SPP. *C. FILUM* AND *A. ESCULENTA*

The chromosomes of these species vary in size and shape as seen during mitotic metaphases. Their size ranges between 0·4 μ and 1·7 μ across their greatest dimension when prepared by the acetocarmine squash method. In nuclei of female gametophytes (Fig. 5.4A) of these species there are at least two chromosomes at the lower end of this scale being between 0·4 and 0·7 μ in size. At the other end of the scale is one chromosome, which is 1·3–1·7 μ along its greatest length (Evans 1963b). Due to its varying orientation from preparation to preparation it is not always distinguishable from the largest of the others, which are 0·7 μ–1·2 μ in greatest length, but it usually appears as in Figs. 5.4A and 5.5.

It is difficult to obtain reliable information from nuclei of male gametophytes because of their small size, but metaphase stages, of these nuclei which can be observed with some accuracy, whilst showing variation in size of the chromosomes, show that there does not appear to be a chromosome in the 1·3–1·7 μ size range present. Good metaphase figures from young sporophytes show the presence of only one large chromosome (Fig. 5.4B) and this further supports the evidence that only the female nucleus contributes a chromosome of this size. As stated previously high-quality diakineses are very rare. The occasional good one seen, though not providing a definite answer shows that there is one bivalent which seems slightly larger than the others (Fig. 5.6). Careful microscopic examination shows that one chromosome of the bivalent appears larger than the other, one being thin and the other wider and more bulky.

4 SEX CHROMOSOME AND CHROMOSOME MORPHOLOGY IN *SACCORHIZA POLYSCHIDES*

In this plant, the large chromosome is very much bigger than that of the other Laminariales. Due to its size it can never fail to be recognised, and is invariably present, at the periphery of metaphase nuclei of female gametophytes and young sporophytes (Fig. 5.7A and C). This chromosome has been designated the *x*-chromosome by analogy with an identical body present in many mosses and liverworts including *Sphaerocarpos donnellii* where its presence was first found by Allen (1917). The *x*-chromosome was absent from nuclei of male gametophytes (Fig. 5.7B) and its homologue here is a much smaller body, the *y*-chromosome.

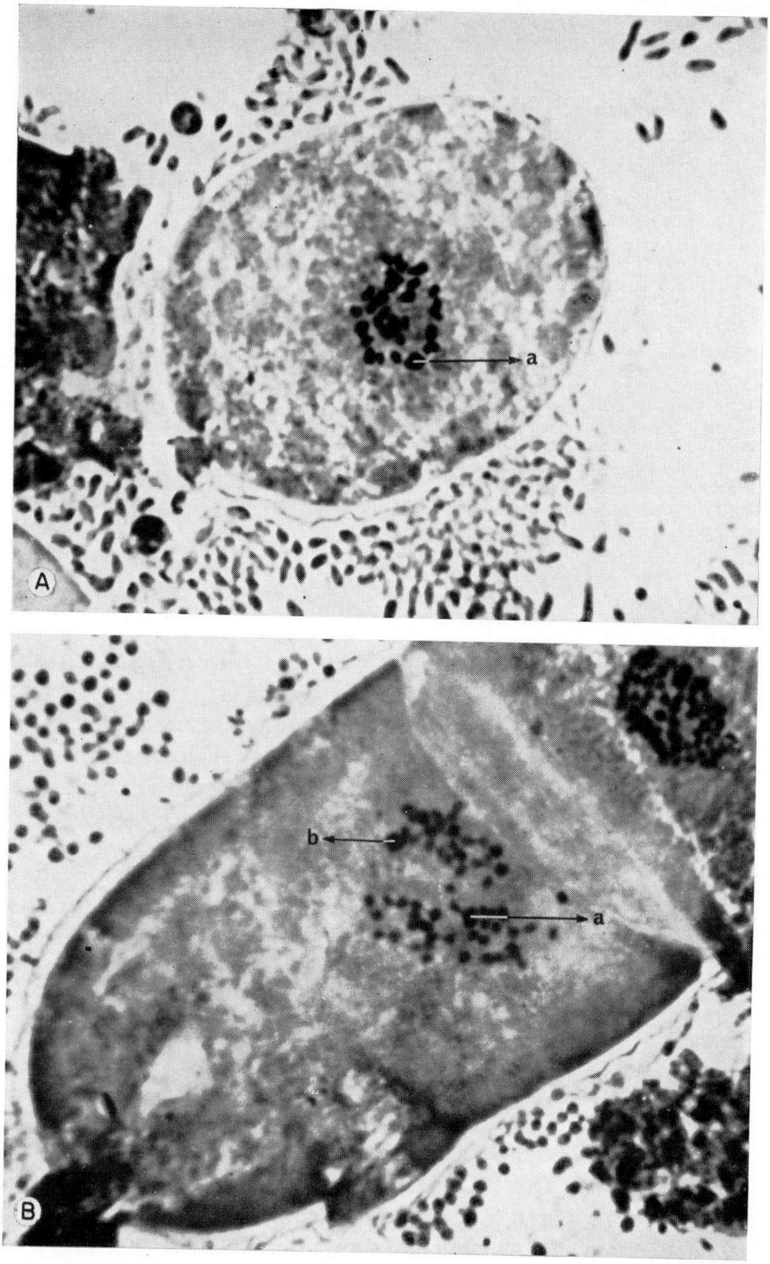

Fig. 5.4 *Laminaria digitata.* **A** Chromosomes at metaphase in a one-celled female gametophyte. The large chromosome is labelled *a*, and the count is 31 chromosomes. **B** Chromosomes at metaphase during mitosis in a two-celled sporophyte. (The second nucleus, also at metaphase, can be seen in the top right-hand corner of the photograph.) The large chromosome is labelled *a*, whilst the body *b* is two chromosomes partially overlapping. The figure gives a count of 62 chromosomes. (x 2,100)

(Photograph by Dr. Leonard V. Evans)

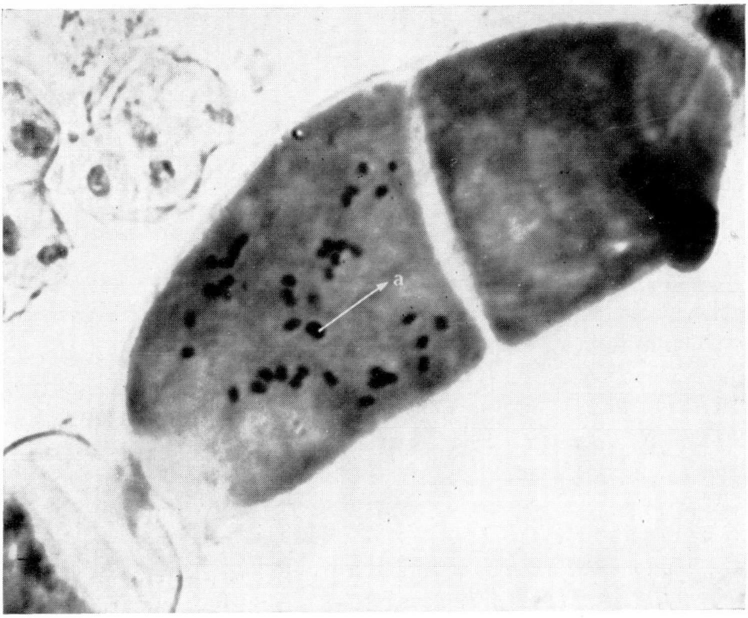

Fig. 5.5 *Laminaria hyperborea.* Chromosomes at metaphase during mitosis in an unfertilised, two-celled, sporophyte. *a* is the large chromosome. The count is c. 36. (x 2,100) (Photograph by Dr. Leonard V. Evans)

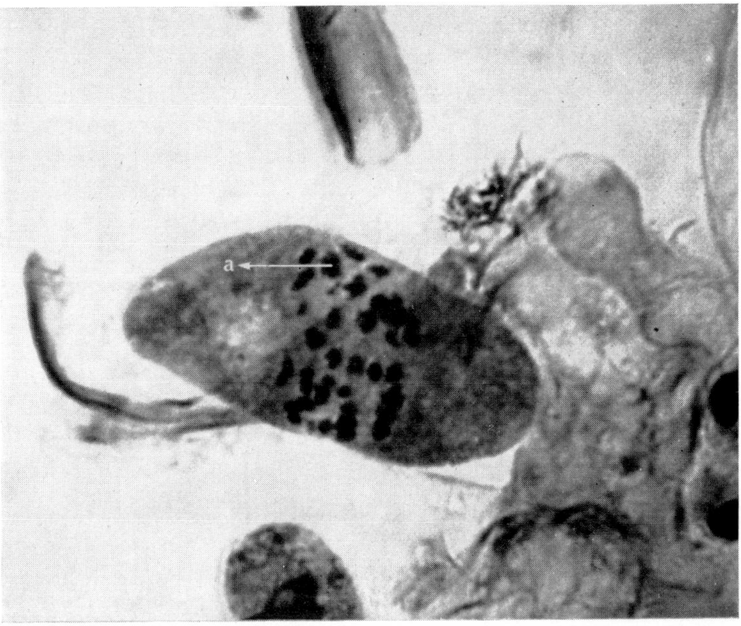

Fig. 5.6 *Laminaria saccharina.* Late prophase/early metaphase chromosomes showing at the first (meiotic) division in the zoosporangium. *a* is the bivalent which is slightly larger than the others, and the chromosome count is c. 32. (x 2,100) (Photograph by Dr. Leonard V. Evans)

The other chromosomes of female gametophytes of *S. polyschides*, as seen at metaphase, can also be grouped according to size (Fig. 5.7A). There are at least three chromosomes which are markedly smaller than the rest, being from 0·4 to 0·7 μ long. The majority are between 0·8 and 1·0 μ across their greatest dimension, but three of these are larger being from 1·1 to 2·6 μ (*u*, *v* and *w* in Fig. 5.7A). The largest chromosome of all, the *x*-chromosome, varies between 4 and 6 μ in length. The nuclei of male gametophytes also show that the chromosomes vary in size, and that three of them are larger than the others, being in the 1–1·4 μ size range (*r*, *s*, *t*, Fig. 5.7B). The three larger chromosomes from the female nucleus and at least two of the three larger chromosomes from the male nucleus can be seen in most young sporophyte nuclei (*u*, *v*, *w* and *s*, *t*, respectively, in Fig. 5.7C), together of course with the *x*-chromosome from the female nucleus.

Although the *y*-chromosome from the male cannot be pinpointed in the sporophyte nucleus, it was found, pairing with the large *x*-chromosome, during meiosis in a sporangium (Fig. 5.8A). At the end of the first division of meiosis, the *x*-chromosome can be seen to have passed to one of the two daughter-nuclei only, and the other must have received the *y*-chromosome (Fig. 5.8B). Products of division of the nucleus containing the *x*-chromosome will therefore give rise to female gametophytes (one-half of the total number of zoospores), and products of the nucleus containing the *y*-chromosome will give rise to male gametophytes, on germination. Segregation of sex takes place therefore during the first division of meiosis. This evidence together with that from Fig. 5.8A strongly supports the idea of an *x*/*y* sex determining mechanism in *S. polyschides*. In *Laminaria* spp. *Chorda filum* and *Alaria esculenta* the difference in size is very much less, but it is likely that further work will show the definite existence of such a mechanism in these genera also.

This is the first group of algae in which sex chromosomes have definitely been seen and *S. polyschides* is easily the clearest example in which a large *x*-chromosome has been demonstrated. It is of interest to note that Allen (1919) who first recorded definite sex chromosomes in *Sphaerocarpos don-*

Fig. 5.7 *Saccorhiza polyschides.* **A** Metaphase chromosomes during mitosis in a newly-extruded egg. The large *x*-chromosome can be seen, and also the two chromosomes *v* and *w*, which are next in size to the sex chromosome. The chromosome *u*, which is larger than all the others, but smaller than *v* and *w*, is also visible. The count is 31 chromosomes. **B** Chromosomes at metaphase of a mitosis in a male gametophyte. The chromosome *x* is absent but three chromosomes (*r*, *s*, and *t*), which are larger than all the others, can be seen. The figure gives a chromosome count of 28–29. **C** Metaphase chromosomes during mitosis in a one-celled sporophyte. The *x*-chromosome can be seen at the periphery of the nucleus, and the figure also shows the three larger chromosomes from the female nucleus (*u*, *v* and *w*), and two of the larger ones from the male (*s* and *t*). The count is 59 chromosomes. (x 2,100) (Photograph by Dr. Leonard V. Evans)

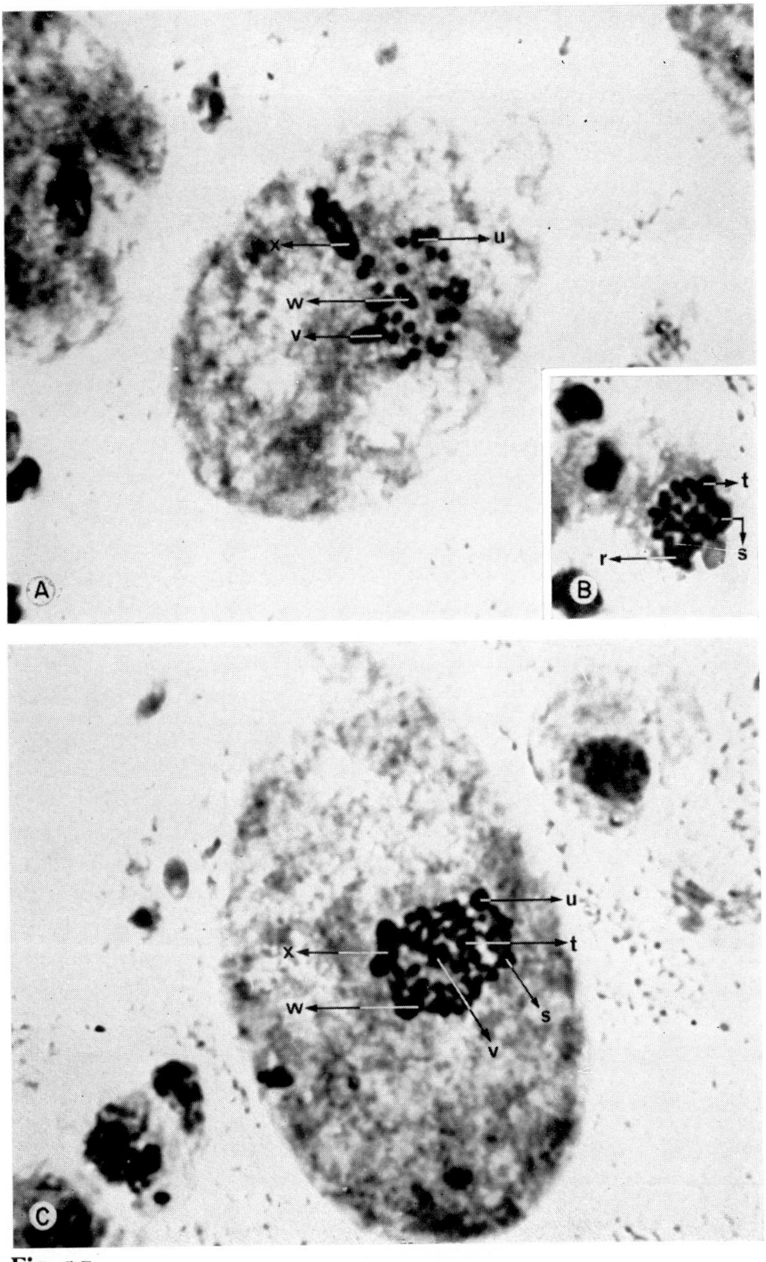

Fig. 5·7

nellii, stated his belief that similar bodies would be found in other plants the most promising being other dioecious bryophytes 'and next would come perhaps some of the dioecious algae'.

In mosses and liverworts many cases have been reported of sex chromosomes, and it appears that only species with well differentiated dioecious gametophytes show the presence of a well marked *x/y* mechanism; monoecious forms do not appear to have this mechanism. Moreover a number of workers have shown that the size of the *x*-chromosome differs amongst species of the genus *Sphaerocarpos* (e.g. Lorbeer 1934), and that some although dioecious do not possess a very well-marked *x/y* system, e.g. *Marchantia polymorpha* L. (Haupt 1935). This state, where the difference between *x* and *y* chromosomes ranges from very great to much less marked, could well be the same in British Laminariales.

It will be of great interest to find out whether an *x/y* mechanism will be found in all brown algae with marked sexual dimorphism among their gametophytes, e.g. in the uninvestigated Sporochnales, Desmarestiales, etc. The condition of monoecious species in predominantly dioecious genera is also of considerable interest—e.g. *Chorda tomentosa* Lyngb. (Sundene 1963) and *Desmarestia viridis* (O.F. Mull.) Lamour being hermaphrodite (Kornmann) (1962)) should lack any *x/y* mechanism.

CHROMOSOME NUMBERS OF THE LAMINARIALES

Most haploid counts are obtained from dividing cells of female gametophytes, including oogonia and recently-extruded, unfertilised, eggs. Cells of male gametophytes are too small to give reliable information in this respect. Occasionally halpoid counts are obtained from mitoses, diakineses, and meiotic metaphases in sporangia, and from two or four-celled sporophytes, where the nuclei are large as opposed to those of somatic cells of the older sporophyte plant.

Some differences in individual counts for the same species do occur, and these are partly due to the difficulty of distinguishing between larger chromatids and the smaller chromosomes, as separation of chromatids is often quite

---

Fig. 5.8 *Saccorhiza polyschides.* **A** A late diakinesis in a zoosporangium, showing pairing of the *x*-chromosomes from the female nucleus with the very much smaller *y*-chromosome from the male nucleus. **B** Metaphase chromosomes during the second division of meiosis in a zoosporangium. The left-hand nucleus contains the *x*-chromosome (one of the larger chromosomes, *u*, from the female nucleus can also be seen in it), whilst the nucleus on the right lacks the *x*-chromosome. The latter must therefore carry the *y*-chromosome, as well the chromosomes *r*, *s*, and *t*, characteristic of a male nucleus. (x 2,100) (Photograph by Dr. Leonard V. Evans)

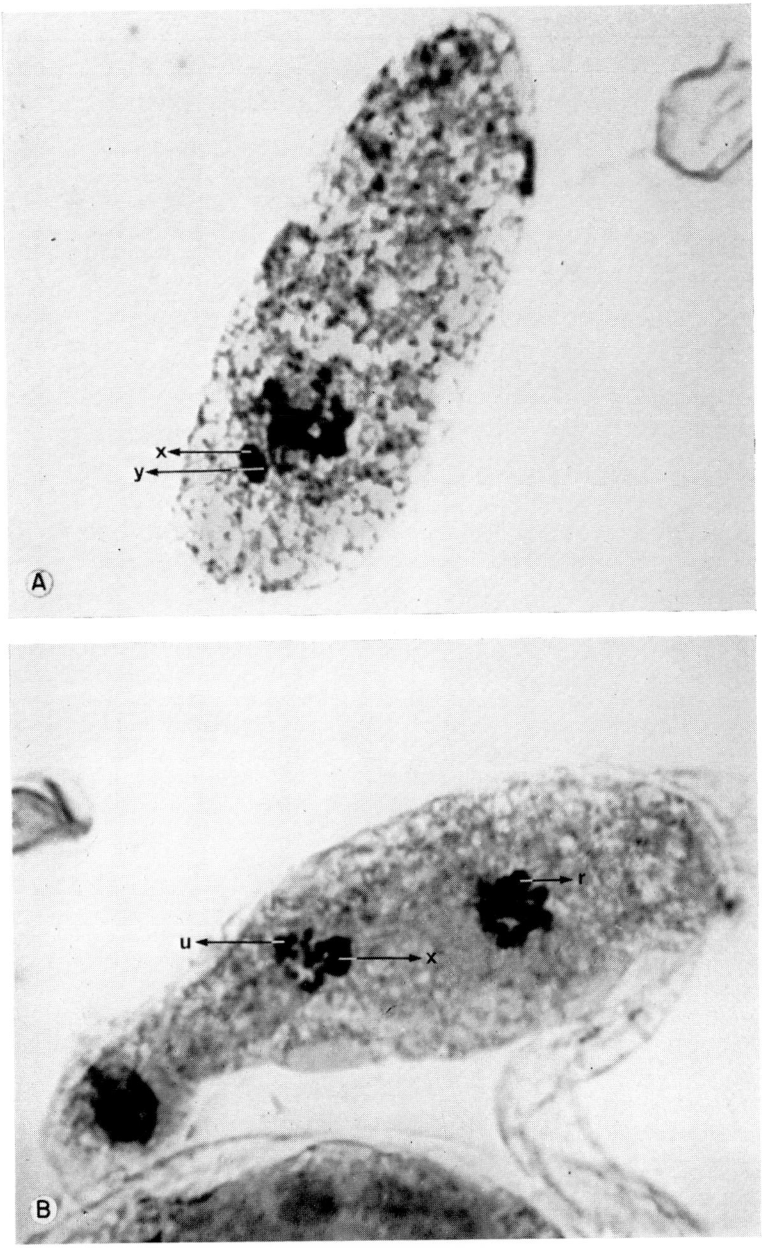

Fig. 5.8

Table 5.2 Chromosome numbers for the Laminariales investigated (1940–1965)

Alga	n	2n	Author
CHORDACEAE			
Chorda filum (L.) Stack.	c. 30★•		Nishibayashi & Inoh 1961a, 1961b
	c. 28★†	c. 56†	Evans 1965
LAMINARIACEAE			
Laminaria angustata Kjellm.	22★•		Nishibayashi & Inoh 1956
L. diabolica Miayabe	22★•		Yabu 1958
L. digitata (Huds.) Lamour	13★•		Magne 1953
	8†	16†	Walker 1954
	27–31†		Naylor 1956
	31†	62†	Evans 1965
L. hyperborea (Gunn.) Foslie		22†	Walker unpubl.
	31†	62†	Evans 1965
L. ochroleuca La Pylaie	27–31†		Naylor 1956
	31†	62†	Evans 1965
L. saccharina (L.) Lamour	13★•	26†•	Magne 1953
	27–31†		Naylor 1956
	31†★	62†	Evans 1965
Sacchoriza polyschides (Lightf.) Batt.	31†	62†	,, ,,
Costaria costata (Turn.) Saund.	c.30★•		Nishibayashi & Inoh 1957
Arthrothamnus bifidus (Gmel.) J. Ag.	22★•		Yabu & Tokido 1963
Agarum cribrosum (Mert.) Bory	22★•		Yabu 1964
Kjellmaniella gyrata (Kjellm.) Miyabe.	22★•		Yabu 1965
LESSONIACEAE			
Nereocystis luetkeana Mertens Post. & Rupr.	c.31★•†		Kemp & Cole 1961
Macrocystis integrifolia Bory.	16†	32†	Walker 1952
ALARIACEAE			
Alaria crassifolia Kjell.	22★•		Yabu 1957
A. praelonga Kjellm.	22★•		,, 1964
A. esculenta (L.) Grev.	28★†	56†	Evans 1965
Undaria pinnatifida (Harv.) Sur.	22★•		Inoh & Nishibayashi 1954, 1955
	c. 30★•		Inoh & Nishibayashi 1960
Ecklonia stolonifera Okamura	c. 31★•	c. 62	Ohmori 1965
E. cava Kjellman	c. 30★•		,, 1965
U. undarioides (Yendo) Okam.	c. 30★•		Nishibayashi & Inoh 1960a, 1960b

★ = from meiotic cells; † = from mitotic cells; • = results from sectioned material (of the type shown by the symbol immediately to the left of •).

advanced by metaphase. The size difference between the largest and smallest chromosomes also introduces the possibility that occasionally a small chromosome may be concealed behind a larger one. In spite of these difficulties, two or three dozen good chromosome figures, of the type selected for reproduction here, usually reveal a commonly recurring number, which can be taken as representing the true count for that species, with reasonable confidence.

As can be seen from Table 5.2 of chromosome counts, all the *Laminaria* spp. and *Saccorhiza polyschides* almost certainly have a haploid chromosome number of 31 and a diploid number of 62. *A. esculenta* has a haploid number of 28 and a diploid number of 56, and *C. filum* is likely to have these numbers also. These figures agree with those of Naylor (1956) for *L. digitata*, *L. saccharina*, and *L. ochroleuca*, and with those of Nishibayashi and Inoh (1961a and b) for *C. filum*. The counts of Walker (1954, 1952) should be disregarded as it appears from the photographs and figures that the objects he illustrates differ very markedly from normal chromosomes. The conclusiveness of most of the earlier counts recorded, in particular from non-British species, is also disputable, as many have been obtained by sectioning techniques on sporangial material, a method which experience has shown to be unreliable and inaccurate when applied to algae.

It is obvious that a considerable amount of reinvestigation is required for most genera, using squash techniques. As has been shown previously, careful restudy of the cytology of members of the genus *Fucus* (Evans 1962) revealed the incorrectness of a number of past records. Again Naylor (1958) on re-examination by squash methods showed the inaccuracies previously recorded by sectioning techniques of the cytology of *Halidrys siliquosa* (L.) Lyngb. Not until confirmation of past results obtained from sections is obtained, and many more new members investigated by squash methods, can taxomic relationships within and between orders of Phaeophyta be put forward with much confidence.

REFERENCES

ALLEN, C. E. (1917). A chromosome difference between the sexes of *Sphaerocarpos*. *Science*, **46**, 466–467.

— (1919). The basis of sex inheritance in *Sphaeocarpos*. *Proc. Amer. phil. Soc.*, **58**, 289–316.

BELLING, J. (1926). The iron-acetocarmine method of fixing and staining chromosomes. *Biol. Bull.*, **50**, 160–162.

BURROWS, E. M. (1958). Sublittoral algal population in Port Erin Bay, Isle of Man. *J. mar. biol. Ass. U.K.*, **37**, 687–703.

DAWSON, A. E. E. (1940). Studies in the Fucales of New Zealand. 2. Observations on the female frond of *Carpophyllum flexuosum* (Esp.) Grev. *New Phytol.*, **39**, 283–302.

DREW, G. H. (1910). The reproduction and early development of *Laminaria digitata* and *L. saccharina*. *Ann. Bot., Lond.*, **24**, 177–190.

EVANS, L. V. (1962). Cytological studies in the genus *Fucus*. *Ann. Bot., Lond.*, **26**, 345–360.

— (1963a). The use of lithium chloride as a pretreatment to an acetocarmine technique on *Fucus*. *Phycologia*, **2** (4), 187–195.

— (1963b). A large chromosome in the Laminarian nucleus. *Nature, Lond.*, **198**, 215.

— (1963c). Cytological studies in the Laminariales. Ph.D. thesis, University of Wales.

— (1965). Cytological studies in the Laminariales. *Ann. Bot., Lond.* 29, no. 116, 541–562.

FARMER, J. B. and WILLIAMS, J. L. (1896). On fertilisation and the segmentation of the spore in *Fucus*. *Ann. Bot., Lond.*, **10**, 479–481.

GODWARD, M. B. E. (1948). The iron alum acetocarmine method for algae. *Nature, Lond.*, **161**, 203.

HARRIES, R. (1932). An investigation by cultural methods of some of the factors influencing the development of the gametophytes and the early stages of the sporophytes of *Laminaria digitata*, *L. saccharina*, and *L. Cloustoni*. *Ann. Bot., Lond.*, **46**, 893–928.

HAUPT, G. (1932). Beiträge zur Zytologie der Gattung *Marchantia* (L.). *I.Z. indukt. Abstamm. -u. VerebLehre*, **62**, 367–428.

INOH, S. and HIROE, M. (1954). Cytological studies on Fucaceous plants. III. On the meiotic division in the antheridium of *Sargassum piluliferum* C. Ag. *La Kromosomo*, **21**, 767–769.

— — (1956). Cytological studies on Fucaceous plants. VI. On the meiotic division in the embryo of *Sargassum tortile* C. Ag. *La Kromosomo*, **27–28**, 942–947.

INOH, S. and NISHIBAYASHI, T. (1954). On the mitosis in the sporangium of *Undaria pinnatifida* (Harv.) Sur. *Biol. J. Okayama Univ.*, **1**, 217–225.

— — (1955). On the mitosis in the sporangium of *Undaria pinnatifida* (Harv.) Sur. *La Kromosomo*, **22–24**, 788–93 (in Japanese).

— — (1960). On the mitosis in the sporangium of *Undaria pinnatifida* (Harv.) Sur. *La Kromosomo*, **44–45**, 1498–1499 (in Japanese).

KEMP, L. and COLE, K. (1961). Chromosomal alternation of generations in *Nereocystis Luetkeana* (Mertens) Postels and Ruprecht. *Can. J. Bot.*, **39**, 1711–1724.

KILLIAN, C. (1911). Beiträge zur Kenntnis der Laminarien. *Z. Bot.*, **3**, 433–494.

KORNMANN, P. (1962). Der Lebenszyklus von *Desmarestia viridis*. *Helgoländ wiss. Meeresunters*, **8** (3), 287–292.

KYLIN, H. (1916). Üeber den Generationswechsel bei *Laminaria digitata*. *Svensk. bot. Tidskr.*, **10**, 551–561.

— (1918). Studien über die Entwicklungsgeschichte der Phaeophyceen. *Svensk. bot. Tidskr.*, **12**, 1–64.

LE TOUZÉ, M. H. (1912). Contribution à l'etude histologique des Fucacées. *Rev. gén. Bot.*, **24**, 33–47.

LEWIS, K. R. (1956). A cytological survey of some lower organisms with particular reference to the use of modern techniques. Ph.D. thesis, University of Wales.

LORBEER, G. (1934). Zytologie der Lebermoosen mit besonderer Berucksichtigung allgemeiner Chromosomenfragen. *Jb. wiss Bot.*, **80**, 567–817.

MAGNE, F. (1953). Méiose et nombre chromosomique chez les Laminariaceae. *C. R. Acad. Sci., Paris*, **236**, 515–517.

MOSS, B. L. and ELLIOT, E. (1957). Observations on the cytology of *Halidrys siliquosa* (L.) Lyngb. *Ann. Bot., Lond.*, N.S., **21**, 143–151.

MIYAKE, K. (1928). On the sexual generation of Japanese Laminariaceae. *Proc. 3rd Pan-Pacif. sci. Congress, Tokyo*, 1926, **2**, 1922–1923.

NAYLOR, M. (1956). Cytological observations on three British species of *Laminaria*. A preliminary report. *Ann. Bot., Lond.*, N.S., **20**, 431–437.

— (1958). The cytology of *Halidrys siliquosa* (L.) Lyngb. *Ann. Bot., Lond.*, **22**, 205–217.

— (1959). Feulgen reaction in Fucales. *Nature, Lond.*, **183**, 627.

NISHIBAYASHI, T. and INOH, S. (1956). Morphogenetical studies in the Laminariales. I. The development of zoosporangia and the formation of zoospores in *Laminaria angustata* Kjell. *Biol. J. Okayama Univ.*, **2**, 147–158.

— — (1957). Morphogenetical studies in the Laminariales. II. The development of zoosporangia and the formation of zoospores in *Costaria costata* (Turn.) Saunders. *Biol. J. Okayama Univ.*, **3**, 169–181.

— — (1960a). Morphogenetical studies on Laminariales. V. The formation of zoospores in *Undaria undarioides* (Yendo) Okamura. *Biol. J. Okayama Univ.*, **6**, 83–90.

— — (1960b). The formation of zoospores in Undaria undarioides (Yendo) Okamura. *Bot. Mag., Tokyo*, **73**, 494–496 (in Japanese).

— — (1961a). Morphogenetical studies on Laminariales. VI. The formation of zoospores in *Chorda filum* (L.) Lamour. *Biol. J. Okayama Univ.*, **7**, 126–132.

— — (1961b). The formation of zoospores in *Chorda filum* (L.) Lamour. *Bot. Mag., Tokyo*, **74**, 195–197 (in Japanese).

OKABE, S. (1929). Meiosis im Oogonium von *Sargassum horneri* (Turn). *Ag. Sci. Rep. Tôhuku Univ.*, ser. 4, **4**, 661–669.

OHMORI, T. (1965). Morphogenetical studies on Laminariales VIII. The formation of zoospores in *Ecklonia stolonifera* Okamura and *Ecklonia cava* Kjellman. *Biol. J. Okayama Univ.*, **11**, 1–18.

PROVASOLI, L., MCLAUGHLIN, J. J. A. and DROOP, M. R. (1957). The development of artificial media for marine algae. *Arch. Microbiol.*, Bd. 12, Heft **3**, 392–428 (p. 408 especially).

ROY, K. (1938). Recherches sur la structure du noyau quiescent et sur les mitoses somatiques de quelques Fucacées. *Rev. Algol.*, **11**, 101–188.

SAUVAGEAU, C. (1915). Sur le développement et la biologie d'une Laminaire (*Saccorhiza bulbosa*). *C. R. Acad. Sci., Paris*, **160**, 445–448.

SCHNEIDER, A. (1880). Über Befruchtung. *Zool. Anz.*, **3**, 252–7.

SCHREIBER, E. (1930). Untersuchungen über Parthenogenesis, Geschlechtsbestimmung und Bastardierungsvermögen bei Laminarien. *Planta*, **12**, 331–353.

SUNDENE, O. (1962). Growth in the sea of *Laminaria digitata* sporophytes from culture. *Nyt. Mag. Bot.*, **9**, 5–24.

— (1963). Reproduction and ecology of *Chorda tomentosa*. *Nyt. Mag. Bot.*, **10**, 159–167.

TAHARA, M. (1929). Oogenesis in *Coccophora langsdorfii* (Turn.) Grev. *Sci. Rep. Tôhuku Univ.*, ser 4, **1**, 551–556.

THURET, G. (1850). Recherches sur les zoospores des Algues et les anthéridies des Cryptogames. I. *Ann. Sci. Nat. Bot. III*, **14**, 214–260.

WALKER, F. T. (1952). Chromosome number of *Macrocystis intergrifolia* Bory. *Ann. Bot., Lond.*, **16**, 23–26.

— (1954). Chromosome number of *Laminaria digitata* Lamour. *Ann. Bot., Lond.*, **18**, 112–118.

YABU, H. (1957). Nuclear division in the sporangium of *Alaria crassifolia* Kjell. *Bull. Fac. Fish. Hokkaido Univ.*, **8** (3), 185–189 (in Japanese).

— (1958). On the nuclear division in the zoosporangium of *Laminaria diabolica* Miyabe. *Bull. Jap. Soc. Phycol.*, **6**, 57–60 (in Japanese).

— (1964). Mitosis in the sporangium of *Agarum cribrosum* Bory and *Alaria praelonga* Kjellman. *Bull. Fac. Fish. Hokkaido Univ.*, **15** (1), 1–4.

— (1965). Nuclear division in the zoosporangium of *Laminaria angustata* var. *longissima* Miyabe, and *Kjellmaniella gyrata* (Kjellm.) Miyabe. *Bull. Fac. Fish. Hokkaido* Univ., **15** (4), 205–206.

YABU, H. and IMAI, A. (1957). On the nuclear division in the antheridium of *Fucus evanescens* and *Pelvetia wrightii* and on the four-egged oogonium of *Pelvetia wrightii*. *Bull. Jap. Soc. Phycol.*, **5**, 44–49 (in Japanese).

YABU, H. and TOKIDA, J. (1963). On the nuclear division in the sporangium of *Arthrothamnus bifidus* (Gmel.) J. Ag. *Bull. Fac. Fish. Hokkaido Univ.*, **14**, 37–9.

YAMANOUCHI, S. (1909). Mitosis in *Fucus*. *Bot. Gaz.*, **47**, 173–197.

5 The Phaeophyceae

Part II

MARGARET ROBERTS
M.Sc., Ph.D.
Hon. Research Associate, Department of Botany,
University of Hull

I CULTURE METHODS

I have used the same culture technique on a variety of species, namely *Stictyosiphon tortilis* (Rupr.) Reinke, *Laminaria digitata* (Huds.) Lamour., *L. saccharina* (L.) Lamour., *L. ochroleuca* Pyl., *Chorda filum* (L.) Stackh., *Scytosiphon lomentarius* (Lyngb.) Link, *Petalonia fascia* (O. F. Müller) Kuntze, *Adenocystis utricularis* (Bory) H. et H., *Scytothamnus australis* H. et H., *Splachnidium rugosum* (L.) Grev., *Chordaria flagelliformis* (O. F. Müller) C. Ag. and *Dictyosiphon foeniculaceus* (Huds.) Grev.

Wherever practicable, whole plants including attachment are collected, or where this is impossible, large portions of the fruiting region. This is done as soon as possible after the plants are uncovered by the ebb tide, and the material carried back to the laboratory wrapped in blotting paper or newspaper slightly dampened with sea-water and enclosed in a polythene bag. The time in transit has varied from 20 min. to about 3 hr.

To remove as much surface impurity as possible, the plants are then washed several times in a jet of boiled sea-water, or shaken vigorously in a stoppered bottle of boiled sea-water, blotting between washings. This process should take only a few minutes. After the final washing the plants are left for about 10 min. wrapped in slightly damp blotting paper and then immersed in a beaker of boiled sea-water when the zoids are usually released. Sometimes the plants have been left in the refrigerator overnight, and successful release obtained the following morning.

When the zoid suspension is of a suitable concentration, it is poured into a covered flat dish on the bottom of which have been placed the sterilised slides or coverslips on which the zoids are to germinate. The zoids usually settle on the bottom within half an hour, when the slides or coverslips are removed with forceps, washed with a jet of boiled sea-water to remove surface debris and placed in the culture vessels. It is not advisable to leave the slides longer than half an hour, otherwise the cultures may become heavily contaminated.

One method is to use coverslips and to grow them in Petri dishes containing the culture medium. I have preferred to 'seed' cultures on slides and grow paired slides, back to back, in cellophane covered, 4-oz. glass pots. This method has several advantages. Large numbers of spores can be handled simultaneously, the slides are less fragile than coverslips, they can be more easily marked for identification on fixation, handling during staining can be easily done in vertical Coplin dishes and cooling carried out by standing the culture pots in trays through which water circulates. Further, when it is necessary to establish cultures near the coast and then transport them considerable distances for further growth and examination, the paired slides can be readily carried in 1-in. specimen tubes, either thin glass ones with a pad of foam rubber in the bottom, or in hard ones made from Nessler tubing.

In order to obtain as rapid a growth rate as possible, it is desirable at least to extend the hours of daylight, if not to give permanent illumination. I have usually used a battery of three 80-watt fluorescent tubes, two daylight and one warm white, about 4 ft. above the culture trays. Under these conditions there is virtually no growth gradient between top and bottom of the slides. I have also used a single tube at bench level with the slides facing it at varying distances. Cultures have been maintained at temperatures of as near 15°C as possible: great fluctuations in temperature should be avoided.

I have usually used 'Erdschreiber' culture medium, using John Innes Compost No. 3 to provide the soil extract.

With this technique I have been able to maintain actively growing cultures of all the species listed, fixing at intervals up to about 10 days to obtain vegetative divisions. Gametophytes of the three species of Laminaria listed become fertile at 9–14 days, and *Dictyosiphon foeniculaceus* (Huds.) Grev. has produced plurilocular sporangia at four weeks.

II *CYTOLOGICAL PREPARATION*

PHAEOPHYTA

Acetocarmine and Feulgen squash techniques are now being successfully used in investigations on the Phaeophyta, both for small filamentous plants and for bulky parenchymatous ones.

Filamentous forms

For small filamentous genera such as *Ectocarpus*, and for adelophycean phases or stages of genera such as *Scytosiphon*, *Stictyosiphon* and *Laminaria*, the acetocarmine method first used by Godward (1948) on *Spirogyra* has been applied without significant modification (Naylor 1956; Naylor 1958). Ideally plants growing in culture are used on slides or coverslips for easy handling.

Similarly, the Feulgen technique is readily applicable to such filamentous stages and phases.

Two schedules as used by Naylor

Acetocarmine

Fix 3:1, alcohol:acetic acid for 24 hr., preferably changing fixative after first hour.

Add a few drops of saturated solution of ferric acetate in 45% acetic acid, until fixative is a pale amber colour.

Rinse material in 3:1, alcohol:acetic acid.

Add acetocarmine:cover:boil gently:exert pressure, rolling with pith if necessary.

Invert slide in smearing dish of 45% acetic acid until coverslip drops off.

Pass slide through acetic acid:alcohol series, viz.:—3:1, 1:1, 95% alcohol.

Pass through Euparal Essence and mount in Euparal.

Feulgen (1959)

Fix 3:1, alcohol: acetic acid for at least 24 hr.

Transfer to distilled water.

Bring slide up to 60°C in distilled water.

Hydrolyse with N.HCl at 60°C for 15 min.

Stop hydrolysis by transferring to cold water.

Transfer to Schiff's reagent for 6 hr.

Wash in running water 10 min.

Bleach in three changes of freshly made SO_2 water,* 10 min. in each.

Transfer to distilled water.

Cover and squash in distilled water, rolling with pith.

Invert slide in smearing dish of 95% alcohol until coverslip falls off.

Transfer to Euparal Essence.

Mount in Euparal.

Large parenchymatous plants

In larger parenchymatous forms such as members of the Laminariales and Fucales, it has been necessary to incorporate certain modifications. The chief difficulty here is the nature of the cell walls which does not permit adequate spreading of the preparations unless a softening agent is used. Naylor (1957) used sodium carbonate following a chrom-acetic-formalin fixative; Evans (1963) used lithium chloride following acetic-ethyl alcohol fixation.

* SO_2 water: N.HCl—5 ml.: 10% $K_2S_2O_5$—5 ml.: distilled water—100 ml.

The presence in many tissues of abundant plastids which darken and mask or obscure the staining reaction if fixatives containing chromic or osmic acid are used, is a further difficulty. If acetic alcohol or propionic alcohol fixatives are used, the pigments gradually dissolve, and if fixation is continued for 24 hr. decolorisation is usually complete. This type of fixative has proved satisfactory for all filamentous stages and phases investigated by Naylor and Evans, and by Evans for fixation of small portions of apices and receptacles of Fucus and of sori of Laminaria. Naylor, however, has sometimes obtained inconsistent results with this type of fixative for parenchymatous material and has preferred to use Karpechenko fixative (Langlet 1932) followed by bleaching with H_2O_2.

Karpechenko fixative followed by bleaching

In this method, pieces of tissue not more than 1 cm. square are fixed 12–24 hr. in Karpechenko fixative and then washed under a running tap for *at least* 10 *min.* This washing is particularly important if the material is to be examined by means of the Feulgen reaction, when any remaining traces of formalin from the fixative cause a red colour to develop in the walls and cytoplasm and obscure the nuclear reaction. After washing, bleaching is carried out for 3–4 hr. in 20% H_2O_2 (i.e. two parts 100-volume solution to one part distilled water), delicate structures such as receptacles of *Cystoseira* requiring shorter periods than vegetative apices. The H_2O_2 must, in turn, be completely removed by washing in running water otherwise bleaching continues and the material is ruined.

Feulgen staining

This fixation and bleaching procedure may be followed either by the Feulgen or acetocarmine squash technique. In the case of a Feulgen reaction, the portions of material are heated to 60°C in distilled water and then hydrolysed in N.HCl at 60°C for about $7\frac{1}{2}$–10 min. If the bleaching has been omitted, then the hydrolysis time needs to be extended, probably within the range of 15–30 min. A perfectly good reaction is obtained without the bleaching, but the material may prove difficult to spread. Hydrolysis is stopped by transference to cold distilled water, and after washing for 10 min. in running water the material is bleached in freshly made SO_2 water. At this stage, hand sections are cut and mounted in SO_2 and squashed by firm pressure on the coverslip, assisted by rolling with pith. If permanent preparations are required, the coverslip is allowed to drop off in SO_2 water and the preparation dehydrated and mounted in Euparal. The method has been successfully applied to both vegetative apices and developing receptacles of all the British members of the Fucales except *Pelvetia canaliculata* which has not been investigated.

Acetocarmine staining

If an acetocarmine technique is used, a softening agent is needed to assist in spreading the tissues. After bleaching and washing the material is transferred to 1:3, glacial acetic acid: ethyl alcohol to which has been added a few drops of a saturated solution of ferric acetate in 45% acetic acid, in which it may be stored satisfactorily for up to a year. The material is washed in 70% alcohol to remove excess acetate and hand sections are cut, washed in water and mounted in 6% Na_2CO_3. The preparation is then warmed gently, using a slide as a hot-plate, and the weight of the coverslip gradually spreads the section: manual pressure may be applied if further spreading is required. After irrigation with distilled water to remove excess carbonate, the preparation is irrigated with acetocarmine and gently boiled. Differentiation, dehydration and mounting follows the same procedure as given for filamentous forms.

Another difficulty frequently encountered is the scarcity of dividing nuclei in preparations, and various claims have been made as to the most favourable times of day or state of the tide at which to make fixations. Yamanouchi (1909) claimed that figures were abundant in *Fucus* after one to two hours' immersion by the incoming tide, and a similar claim was made by Roy (1938). However, I have found abundant figures in young and actively growing material of a variety of members of the Fucales fixed immediately after exposure by the ebbing tide.

There appears to be synchronisation of vegetative divisions at least in the early stages of growth in culture of filamentous stages and phases, when growth from the spore to the two-, three- and four-celled filament at least, appears to take place simultaneously throughout cultures of thousands of plants. *Dictyosiphon foeniculaceus* (Huds.) Grev., *Stictyosiphon tortilis* (Rupr.) Reinke, *Chordaria flagelliformis* (O.F. Müller) C.Ag., *Scytosiphon lomentarius* (Lyngb.) Link, *Adenocystis utricularis* (Bory) H. et H., *Scytothamnus australis* H. et H. and *Splachnidium rugosum* (L.) Grev. have all been observed in this respect. Yet fixation at 30 min. intervals over a period of 30 hr. during this phase of growth has consistently failed to reveal any time of day or night when significantly larger numbers of dividing nuclei are present.

Similarly, the periodic simultaneous discharge of reproductive bodies is a well known phenomenon of the Dictyotales and the submerged members of the Fucales, particularly those in which the oogonia are retained on the receptacles by mucilaginous stalks. This discharge appears to be associated with mass nuclear maturation of the products, but I was again unable to find any preparations with large numbers of meiotic divisions using *Marginariella urvilliana* (Ach. Rich) Tandy kept in large tanks and fixed at 30-min. intervals, although the oogonia matured and discharged their contents during the period of observation. Some workers have claimed that in these totally submerged species meiotic divisions occur in the early hours of the morning, a time lag which could possibly be associated with utilisation of metabolic products synthesised during the hours of daylight.

Probably the divisions are too rapid for the time interval used to detect any rhythm. However, *in all the species mentioned, divisions can always be found,* though not necessarily in large numbers, provided that the cultures used are young and active (I find 7–10 days yield good results) and that portions of the larger plants are cut from healthy and actively growing apices or reproductive regions.

Various attempts have been made artificially to increase the number of divisions, but with doubtful success. These have included:

(i) *Application of colchicine* I have placed actively growing cultures in solutions varying in concentration from 0·01% to 1% for an hour before fixation. In all instances I have found that the 1% solution has certainly produced a large number of inhibited metaphases, but so contracted that individual chromosomes cannot be detected. This appears to be the experience of most other workers, although Levan and Levring (1942) found little effect produced on the members of the Phaeophyceae they studied.

(ii) *Refrigeration* I have had some success with this method, and although the results have been neither spectacular nor reliable, have adopted it as standard pretreatment in older cultures. Material to be fixed is placed in mild (domestic) refrigeration for 15 to 18 hr. and then fixed at intervals after exposure for 1 hr. to bright light and a temperature of about 15°C.

(iii) *Wounding* The rapid formation of proliferations as a response to wounding in the Fucales is well known, and suggests a method of artificially stimulating vegetative growth. It has been tried by Evans on *Fucus*, but he found the cells produced so full of dark contents as to be useless.

(iv) *Indole-acetic acid* This was reported by Davidson (1950) to stimulate growth in *Fucus* sporelings. This suggests a possible application in this field, but Evans was unable to obtain any increase in divisions.

Several other methods are discussed in detail by Evans (1962, pp. 346–349).

III *CYTOLOGY*

Recent investigations show that the nuclei of the Phaeophyta resemble those of the Angiosperms both in structure and behaviour. The principal difference is one of size. The metaphase plate is often of the order of 5 μ in diameter (vegetative cells; first division of antheridia and oogonia of *Halidrys*: gametophyte of *Laminaria* spp: unilocular sporangia of *Stictyosiphon tortilis*) whilst the chromosomes contract so drastically during prophase that the metaphase chromosomes are completely spherical (dot chromosomes) and of the order of 0·1 μ in diameter. This gives a characteristic appearance to the metaphase plate, both in polar and in side view, an unmistakable dumb-bell shape to the chromosomes as they divide by a hemispherical constriction into daughter chromatids, and a characteristic anaphase separation of two flat plates of chromatids which frequently arch over as they reach the poles.

A feature peculiar to the Phaeophyta is a staining body associated with the nucleolus ('chromophilous spherule' of some writers), occasionally found at meiosis. It has been recorded at tetraspore formation in *Dictyota dichotoma* (Williams 1904), *Dictyopteris divaricata* (Yabu 1958), *Padina pavonia* (Georgevitch 1918; Carter 1927) and *Padina japonica* (Kumagae, Inoh & Nishibayashi 1960; Kumagae & Inoh 1960), in developing oogonia of *Halidrys siliquosa* (Naylor 1958), *Cystoseira granulata* (Naylor, unpublished), *Fucus vesiculosus* (Yamanouchi 1909), *Carpophyllum flexuosum* (Dawson 1940) and *Sargassum horneri* (Okabe 1929) and in developing antheridia of *Hizikia fusiformis* (Inoh & Hiroe 1954a), *Sargassum piluliferum* (Inoh & Hiroe 1954b) and *S. tortile* (Inoh & Hiroe 1956).

It is probably not an important structure as its appearance is by no means invariable in these species. It is the opinion of Godward (unpublished) that it is the *Nebenkorper* of Geitler and other authors, also found sporadically at mitosis in a variety of organisms, and that it represents a droplet of nucleolar material which has failed to be organised into the main nucleolus.

Halidrys siliquosa (L.) Lyngb.

(FUCALES: Cystoseiraceae)

The nuclei of *H. siliquosa* vary considerably in size from tissue to tissue, their average diameter ranging from 3 μ in the meristoderm, through 4–5 μ in the cortex to 10 μ or more in the medulla. In the resting stage they are characterised by the presence of a nucleolus and 2–9 Feulgen positive bodies (chromocentres) of about 0·75 μ–1·5 μ in diameter (Fig. 5.9A). Fine 'chromatin' threads bearing large numbers of much smaller granules (Naylor 1958a, Plate 1c) can also be seen.

MITOSIS

Dividing somatic nuclei are readily found in the apical groove. During the prophase enlargement the chromocentres, now clearly seen to be arranged at intervals along the 'chromatin' threads, gradually lose their capacity to stain. Simultaneously the fine threads contract, for a time still retaining their bead-like appearance, until in late prophase they are so contracted as to be almost spherical and evenly distributed throughout the nucleus which is now about 8 μ in diameter (Fig. 5.9B). Because of the extreme contraction it is impossible to say whether the chromocentres are represented at metaphase by un-

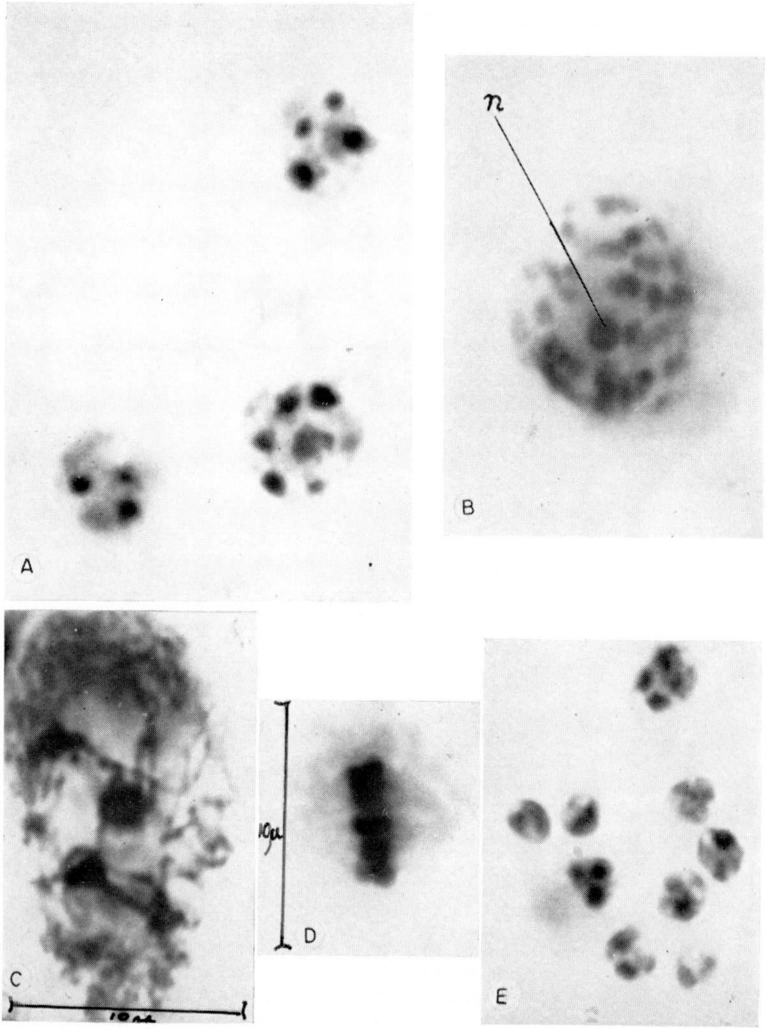

Fig. 5.9 **A** Resting nuclei from cortex of *Halidrys siliquosa* (L.) Lyngb., showing a varying number of chromocentres. Feulgen. **B** Prophase of vegetative nucleus from apical groove of *H. siliquosa*: nucleus fully enlarged with chromosomes differentiated and dispersed throughout; nucleolus still present. Acetocarmine. **C** Prophase in antheridial initial: chromosomes visible as long threads with chromocentres along them. Acetocarmine. **D** Metaphase I in antheridial initial showing bivalents. Acetocarmine. **E** Fully differentiated sperm nuclei showing varying numbers of chromocentres, as in A. (x 3,500)

(Photograph by Dr. Margaret Roberts)

stained portions of chromosome. Nucleolus and nuclear membrane now disappear. The ensuing metaphase plate is very compact, about 5 μ in diameter and crowded with such large numbers of very small chromosomes that a count is only possible if the plate is absolutely flat (Naylor 1958a, Pl. I, 1-m). There is no well spaced pro-metaphase permitting a count in this species. I have only been able to count 55 chromosomes.

A well defined intranuclear spindle is established (seen very clearly with acetocarmine following sodium carbonate pretreatment) and separation of chromatids occurs by means of an equatorial constriction. The daughter chromatids separate as two flat plates which later curve over as they reach the poles.

MEIOSIS

As in *Fucus*, meiosis occurs at the first division of the developing oogonia and antheridia.

Antheridia

The nucleus of the antheridial initial is about 5–6 μ in diameter, and is usually large relative to the size of the cell. In its initial resting stage, it resembles a nucleus of a somatic cell in the possession of a conspicuous nucleolus and five or six chromocentres.

Prophase is prolonged and the early stages resemble those in the somatic cells, except that the enlargement of the nucleus is considerably greater—to a diameter of 10 μ or more—and in these larger nuclei the stages can be seen more clearly. The chromosomes differentiate earlier relative to the disappearance of the chromocentres so that these can be clearly seen at intervals along the threads (Fig. 5.9C). As the chromosomes differentiate, traces of spiral coiling can be seen (Naylor 1958a, Plate II, f) and polarisation towards one end of the nucleus is usually visible. Interpretable diakinesis stages, permitting observation of chiasmata, were not found.

During the final stages of prophase the chromosomes become fully contracted into spheres. The nucleolus and nuclear membrane disappear and a clear intranuclear spindle is organised.

As in mitosis, there is no well spread pro-metaphase, and the chromosomes quickly become arranged in a regular flat plate. This is slightly smaller than in the somatic cells, about 4 μ in diameter, the chromosomes themselves appearing much the same size in polar view. Three plates counted at this stage (two Feulgen, one acetocarmine) gave counts of 30, 32 and 34 respectively (Naylor 1958a, Plate II, j–l). In side view (Fig. 5.9D) the plate clearly shows a double row of spheres, presumably the bivalents, as the number counted approximates to half the chromosomes counted at mitosis. It would be very difficult to distinguish visually between this appearance and that seen in mitosis when the equatorial constriction divides the chromosomes, but on separation the two plates seem to be free of the attenuated 'waists' sometimes seen at mitosis, and of consequent bridges.

Anaphase and telophase follow the same course as in mitosis with separation of two flat plates which curve and crowd together at opposite ends of the cell before losing their capacity to stain and passing into a resting stage.

During a brief interphase before the second division, the chromocentres briefly reappear, then again lose their staining capacity as prophase proceeds. Differentiation and contraction of the chromosomes follows and two compact metaphase plates are organised. These plates are similar in size to that formed at the first division, and counts at this division also give values of about 30. Again a clear intranuclear spindle can be seen, and anaphase and telophase follow as before.

Usually four more divisions follow, simultaneously, and accompanied by progressive diminution in the size of the plate and chromosomes until at the final division the plate is about 3 μ across. During each interphase the chromocentres reappear, and at each stage show the same range in number, i.e. 2–9, as in the diploid vegetative nuclei.

After the final division cytoplasmic cleavage occurs, and the sperm nucleus, about 2 μ in diameter, passes into a resting stage. In this condition they are liberated (Fig. 5.9E).

Oogonia

After the formation of the oogonial initial, the nucleus undergoes a resting phase lasting several months. The prophase of the first division may also be prolonged as the preliminary enlargement was found in January but no divisions until February, two and four weeks later.

Prophase resembles that in the antheridial initials, except that the enlargement is very much greater, to a diameter of 17–25 μ, and the chromocentres disappear earlier relative to the differentiation of the chromosomes. These do not differentiate until enlargement is completed, whilst the chromocentres appear to lose their capacity to stain during the prolonged resting stage preceding division, although occasionally they may be seen (Naylor 1958, Plate IVa). Consequently, the enlarging nucleus appears clear and non-staining and the chromocentres are never seen on the differentiating chromosomes as in the antheridia. The nucleolus enlarges correspondingly to a diameter of 6–7 μ and sometimes, though by no means always, a spherical or discoid body staining with acetocarmine is seen close beside it. This reappears after the metaphase plate is established in this and the two ensuing divisions.

After enlargement is completed, the chromosomes differentiate as slender, coiled threads which condense and become localised at one end of the nucleus as a small peripheral cap, and the nucleolus then disappears. No clear diakinesis stage permitting observation of bivalents with chiasmata was found.

The metaphase plate is small and compact, about 5 μ in diameter as in the antheridium, despite the large size of the nucleus. At this stage 28 bivalents have been counted. An intra-nuclear spindle occupying only a small portion of the enlarged nucleus is organised, often placed asymmetrically relative to the nucleus as a whole. Separation of two flat plates of chromosomes follows, a clumped telophase and then a resting stage during which deeply staining chromocentres reappear.

Prophase of the second division rapidly follows, and during this phase the nucleus enlarges to 10 μ and the chromocentres disappear so that it becomes clear and non-staining, as in the preceding division. The two nuclei divide simultaneously and the two metaphase plates are organised within the boundaries of the original nucleus, each with a conspicuous spindle. Anaphase with separation of flat plates and a clumped telophase follow and four small daughter-nuclei with deeply staining chromocentres are organised.

The four nuclei usually lie close together well within the boundary of the initial nucleus. These also quickly divide, again enlarging during prophase to 10 μ, the chromocentres disappearing and giving the cytoplasm a clear, non-staining appearance before the chromosomes differentiate. Four small metaphase plates are organised, each with a conspicuous spindle and associated staining body.

The eight daughter-nuclei are small with prominent chromocentres. Seven nuclei are extruded, and these retain their chromocentres and lie between the cytoplasm and oogonium wall as curved, flattened discs. The eighth takes up a central position, enlarges to about 15 μ, loses its chromocentres and passes into prophase with differentiation of long, slender chromosomes. It is in this state when the oosphere is released, in contrast to the resting condition of the sperm nucleus. The egg nucleus is usually surrounded by a region of cytoplasm, stellate in outline, which is finely granular and deeply staining with acetocarmine, in contrast with the bulk of the oogonial cytoplasm which contains large, clear and lightly staining granules of reserve food materials.

Meiosis thus follows the same course in antheridia and oogonia, with prolonged prophase, polarisation of differentiating chromosomes, reduction in chromosome number and in both is followed by a number of vegetative divisions, one in oogonia, four in antheridia. The principal differences lie in the relatively earlier disappearance of chromocentres and later differentiation of chromosomes in the oogonia, and in the sporadic occurrence in the oogonia of the staining body associated with the nucleolus.

There can be no doubt that this is meiosis since the chromosome number is halved, but extreme contraction renders it impossible to observe clearly both the chromatids and also the homologous chromosomes forming the bivalents. No bivalents as such can therefore be described, and that the apparent 'chromosomes' of Metaphase I are bivalents is just an inference from their reduced number.

Chromocentres such as just described in *Halidrys siliquosa* are not a usual feature of the nucleus of the Phaeophyta. They have only been recorded to date in *Bifurcaria rotunda* (Huds.) Papenfuss and in a few species of *Cystoseira* (Roy 1938; Roberts 1964). Those in *H. siliquosa* vary in number, usually between two and nine being present, whether in the diploid nuclei of the thallus or in the haploid nuclei of the developing antheridia. In this respect, as also in their distribution throughout the resting nucleus and in their arrangement at intervals along the chromosomes, they resemble the chromocentres of *Trillium* (Darlington & La Cour 1940). Godward, however, has demonstrated in *Spirogyra* (Godward 1950, 1954) a definite number of chromocentres per chromosome, progressively reduced during prophase until they coalesce through final contraction of the chromosome. This is seen particularly clearly in *S. subechinata* (Godward 1950).

Stictyosiphon tortilis (Ruprecht) Reinke

(DICTYOSIPHONALES: Striariaceae)

Stictyosiphon tortilis (Ruprecht) Reinke is a species in which the thallus is only seasonally obvious on the shore. On the North Yorkshire coast (Naylor 1958b) this period lies within the range of January to August. In autumn the vegetative fronds die back leaving the basal regions of the axis as a perennating organ which proliferates to give new growth in the following spring. The vegetative thallus produces unilocular sporangia, the germlings from which have been grown in culture when they have produced microscopic creeping filaments. This stage or phase reproduced by means of plurilocular sporangia whose zoids produced a further similar phase. The relationship of this microscopic phase to the life-history as a whole is not yet fully understood, but cytologically it appears to be haploid whilst the macroscopic thallus is diploid.

MITOSIS

This has been followed in the macroscopic thallus and in the germling.

The germling

The resting nucleus of the germling is about 2 μ in diameter, deeply staining with acetocarmine to show a prominent nucleolus and a finely granular appearance similar to that in *Fucus*. During prophase the nucleus enlarges to about 4 μ in diameter and the chromosomes differentiate as long, fine threads rapidly undergoing drastic shortening to short rods and ultimately to spheres not more than 0·5 μ in diameter. When the nuclear membrane disappears there is usually a well spaced prometaphase before the metaphase plate is organised. Several counts have been made at this stage yielding figures ranging from 21 to 26. The one illustrated (Fig. 5.10D) gave a count of 26.

This was a particularly clear count and may well represent the correct value.

The metaphase plate which follows is very small (Fig. 5.10E), not much more than 2·5 μ in diameter, and the chromosomes too small and crowded to be counted. As in *Laminaria* (Naylor 1956), the side view of the plate shows the

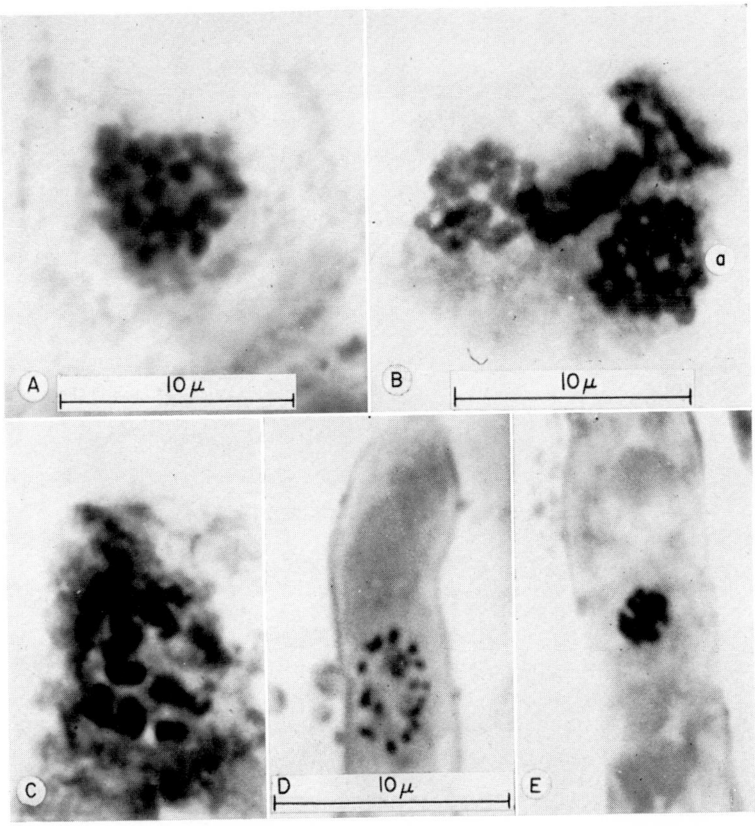

Fig. 5.10 **A** Polar view of Metaphase I in sporangial initial of *Stictyosiphon tortilis* (Ruprecht) Reinke. **B** Metaphase of third division in sporangial initial of *S. tortilis* showing two plates in polar view, two in side view: the plate at (a) gave a firm count of 26, and shows only slight diminution in size compared with Metaphase I. **C** Diakinesis at first division in sporangial initial of *S. tortilis*. **D** Prometaphase in vegetative nucleus of germling of *S. tortilis*; this gave a firm count of 26 (three planes). **E** Metaphase plate in vegetative nucleus of germling of *S. tortilis* showing small size and crowded chromosomes. All stained acetocarmine. (x 3,500)

(Photograph by Dr. Margaret Roberts)

chromosomes to be slightly elongated in the direction of the spindle. The chromatids separate on the development of an equatorial cleft and the whole has a characteristic dumb-bell-like shape.

The spindle is conspicuous and intranuclear, as in *Fucus* and *Halidrys*, and anaphase separation occurs as two regular flat plates with an occasional chromosome lagging.

The macroscopic thallus

These observations were nearly all made on plants grown in culture. *Scytosiphon tortilis* propagates very easily by vegetative means and the cultures were established by isolating portions about six cells long from the terminal uniseriate region of the thallus and transferring to Erdschreiber where they grew rapidly and yielded many dividing nuclei.

Mitosis follows the same course as in the germling, the main difference being one of scale. The resting nuclei are about 5 μ in diameter in the non-active surface cells, and about 8 μ in the meristematic cells at the thallus tip and at the bases of the ectocarpoid hairs.

During prophase the nucleus enlarges to 8 μ and the chromosomes differentiate and shorten as in the germling. A prometaphase, where the chromosomes are often still visible as short rods, is followed by a compact metaphase plate about 4–5 μ in diameter.

Counting is very difficult at both these stages, during the prometaphase on account of confusion caused by depth of focus and at metaphase because of the very crowded nature of the plate. So far only three counts have been made, and the highest count obtained was 45, but in all three instances a number of chromosomes remained uncounted.

Once more a conspicuous intranuclear spindle is established and separation of two nearly flat plates occur. These are considerably larger than in the germling, appearing about 4 μ in diameter in optical section. Telophase and constitution of two daughter-nuclei follow.

Despite the lack of a firm count of the macroscopic plant, it is clear that the nuclei concerned represent the haploid and diploid phases.

MEIOSIS

These observations were made on plants collected from the shore in May and June and fixed on collection.

Meiosis occurs in the unilocular sporangia, and the groups of sporangial initials can be readily distinguished from the surrounding vegetative cells. The vegetative cells contain a relatively small nucleus and numerous plastids and pyrenoids. The sporangial initials contain a large nucleus relative to the size of the cell, whilst the cytoplasmic contents are clear and homogeneous and stain deeply with acetocarmine. This feature makes the initials conspicuous, but unfortunately lessens the contrast between chromosomes and cytoplasm. Divisions are not synchronous and usually all stages can be found within a single sorus.

Prophase is prolonged, and involves enlargement of the nucleus to 8 μ and the differentiation of long, coiled chromosomes which later become localised to one end of the nucleus. After a while, drastic shortening to short rods occurs and occasional diakinesis stages have been seen. The deep-staining cytoplasm has made this stage difficult to observe and photograph, but usually one or two terminal chiasmata per bivalent appear to occur (Fig. 5.10C).

Still further contraction occurs till the bivalents resemble two closely apposed spheres, when they become arranged on the metaphase plate. The plate is compact, 5 μ in diameter, only slightly larger than in the vegetative cells, but the components are of slightly greater diameter in polar view, and a little easier to distinguish. Six plates were counted at this stage (Fig. 5.10A), giving figures ranging from 20 to 26, as in mitosis in the germling.

Anaphase and telophase follow the usual course and result in the production of a faintly staining nucleus.

A second division follows before there is any cytoplasmic cleavage, the four daughter-nuclei again staining only very lightly and lying within the limits of the original nucleus. This disposition of the products seems to be a feature of meiosis in the Phaeophyta.

This division is often followed immediately by a third (Fig. 5.10B) resulting in an 8-nucleate condition. Cleavage of cytoplasm and formation of septa follow. Subsequent divisions, accompanied by cleavage and septum formation, occur within these walled compartments.

There is no appreciable diminution in the size of the metaphase plate in the first three divisions. The plate illustrated (Fig. 5.10B (a)) gave a count of 26. This was a very clear count, and supports the view that the count of 26 on the germling represents the haploid number.

After this division the plates and nuclei rapidly diminish in size until by the 32-nucleate stage they are the same size as in the germling.

IV CHROMOSOME COUNTS SINCE 1940

Table 5.3 Chromosome numbers in the Phaeophyceae.

	n	*2n*	Author
ECTOCARPALES			
Hapterophycus canaliculatus. S & G.	c. 12	c. 24	Hollenburg 1947
DICTYOSIPHONALES			
Dictyosiphon foeniculaceus (Huds.) Grev.	18	—	Abe 1940
Stictyosiphon tortilis (Rupr.) Reinke	c. 26	c. 45	Naylor 1958b
SPOROCHNALES			
Sporochnus pedunculatus (Huds.) Ag.	20	—	Magne 1953

Table 5.3 (*cont.*)

	n	*2n*	Author
LAMINARIALES, see p. 144			
DICTYOTALES			
Dictyota dichotoma (Huds.) Lamour.	14–16	26–32	Giraud 1956
	32	—	Yabu 1958; Kumagae, Inoh & Nishibayashi 1960
Dictyopteris divaricata (Okamura) Okamura	16	—	Yabu 1958
D. membranacea (Stackh.) Batt.	14–16	26–32	Giraud 1956
Padina japonica Yamada	32		Kumagae, Inoh & Nishibayashi 1960
FUCALES			
Ascophyllum nodosum (L.) le Jol.	32	—	Lewis 1956
Fucus evanescens C.Ag.	32	—	Yabu & Imai 1957
Fucus sp., see p. 126			Evans 1962
Pelvetia canaliculata (L.) Dcne. & Thuret	22	44	Subrahmanyan 1956, 1957a, 1957b
P. wrightii Yendo	32	—	Yabu & Imai 1957
Himanthalia elongata (L.) S. F. Gray	—	c. 60	Naylor 1957
	24, 26	—	Moss 1958
Bifurcaria rotunda (Huds.) Papenfuss	28, 34	64	Giraud 1956
Cystophyllum crassipes (Mert.) C.Ag.	—	64	Inoh 1944
Halidrys siliquosa (L.) Lyngb.	8	—	Moss & Elliott 1957
	c. 30	c. 55	Naylor 1958b
Hormosira banksii (Turn.) Dcne.	24	12	Osborn 1949
Hizikia fusiformis Okamura	32	—	Inoh & Hiroe 1954b
Sargassum borneri (Turn.) Ag.	32	—	Inoh & Hiroe 1954d
S. patens Ag.	—	64	Inoh & Hiroe 1954e
S. piluliferum Ag.	32	—	Inoh & Hiroe 1954c
	—	64	Inoh & Hiroe 1954a
ADDITIONAL CHROMOSOME NUMBERS			
Asperococcus fistulosus (Huds.) Hook.	8	16	Blackler (personal communication)
Herponema velutinum (Grev.) J. Ag.	8	16	,, (personal communication)

REFERENCES

ABE, K. (1940). Meiotische Teilung von *Dictyosiphon foeniculaceus*. *Sci. Repr. Tôhoku Univ.*, 4 Ser., **15**, 317–320.

BELLING, J. (1926). The iron-aceto-carmine method of fixing and staining chromosomes. *Biol. Bull.*, **50**, 160–162.

CARTER, P. W. (1927). The life history of *Padina pavonia*. I. The structure and cytology of the tetrasporangial plant. *Ann. Bot. Lond.*, **41**, 146–159.

DARLINGTON, C. D. and LA COUR, L. F. (1940). Nucleic acid starvation of chromosomes in *Trillium*. *J. Genetics*, **40**, 185–212.

DAVIDSON, F. F. (1950). The effects of auxins on the growth of marine algae. *Amer. J. Bot.*, **37**, 502–510.

DAWSON, A. E. E. (1940). Studies in the Fucales of New Zealand. II. Observations on the female frond of *Carpophyllum flexuosum* (Esp.) Grev. *New Phytol.*, **39**, 283–302.

EVANS, L. V. (1962). Cytological studies in the genus *Fucus*. *Ann. Bot., Lond.*, N.S., **26**, 345–360.

— (1963). The use of lithium chloride as a pretreatment to an acetocarmine technique on *Fucus*. *Phycologia*, **2** (4), 187–195.

GEORGEVITCH, M. P. (1918). Génération asexuée du *Padina pavonia*. *C.R. Acad. Sci., Paris*, **167**, 536–537.

GIRAUD, G. (1956). Recherches sur l'action de substances mitoclasiques sur quelques algues marines. *Rev. Gen. Bot.*, **63**, 202–236.

GODWARD, M. B. E. (1948). The iron acetocarmine method for Algae. *Nature, Lond.*, **161**, 203.

— (1950). On the nucleolus and nucleolar organising chromosomes in Spirogyra. *Ann. Bot., Lond.*, N.S., **14**, 39–54.

— (1954). The 'diffuse' centromere or polycentric chromosomes in *Spirogyra*. *Ann. Bot., Lond.*, N.S., **18**, 143–156.

GROSS, F. (1937). Notes on the culture of some marine plankton organisms. *J. mar. biol. Ass., U.K.*, **21**, 753–768.

HOLLENBURG, G. J. (1947). Culture studies of marine algae. II. *Hapterophycus canaliculatus* S. & G. *Amer. J. Bot.*, **28**, 677–683.

INOH, S. (1944). Embryological studies on *Turbinaria* and *Cystophyllum*. *J. Fac. Sci. Hokkaido Univ.*, 5 ser., **5**, 199–214.

INOH, S. and HIROE, M. (1954a). Cytological studies on the Fucaceous plants. II. On the meiotic division in the antheridium of *Hizikia fusiformis* Okamura. *La Kromosomo*, **21**, 764–766.

— — (1954b). Cytological studies on the Fucaceous plants. I. On the somatic mitosis in the embryo of *Sargassum piluliferum* C.Ag. *La Kromosomo*, **21**, 760–763.

— — (1954c). Cytological studies on the Fucaceous plants. III. On the meiotic division in the antheridium of *Sargassum piluliferum* C.Ag. *La Kromosomo*, **21**, 767–769.

— — (1954d). Cytological studies on the Fucaceous plants. IV. On the meiotic division in the antheridium of *Sargassum horneri* (Turn.) Ag. *Bot. Mag. Tokyo*, **47**, 190–192.

— — (1954e). Cytological studies on the Fucaceous plants. V. On the mitotic division in the embryo of *Sargassum patens* C.Ag. *Biol. J. Okayama Univ.*, **2**, 1–6.

— — (1956). Cytological studies on the Fucaceous plants. VI. On the meiotic division in the antheridium of *Sargassum tortile* C.Ag. *La Kromosomo*, **27–28**, 942–947.

KUMAGAE, N. and INOH, S. (1960). Morphogenesis in Dictyotales. II. On the meiosis of the tetraspore mother cell in *Dictyota dichotoma* (Huds.) Lamour. and *Padina japonica* Yamada. *La Kromosomo*, **46–47**, 1521–1530.

KUMAGAE, N., INOH, S. and NISHIBAYASHI, T. (1960). Morphogenesis in Dictyotales. II. On the meiosis of the tetraspore mother cell in *Dictyota dichotoma* (Huds.) Lamour. and *Padina japonica* Yamada. *Biol. J. Okayama Univ.*, **6**, 91–102.

LANGLET, O. (1932). Über Chromosomenverhältnisse und Systematik der Ranunculaceae. *Svensk Bot. Tidskrift*, **26**, 381–400.

LEVAN, A. and LEVRING, T. (1942). Some experiments on c-mitotic reactions within Chlorophyceae and Phaeophyceae. *Hereditas*, **28**, 400–408.

LEWIS, K. R. (1956). A cytological study of some lower organisms with particular reference to the use of modern techniques. Ph.D. thesis, University of Wales.

MAGNE, F. (1953). La méiose chez les *Sporochnus pedunculatus* C.Ag. *C.R. Acad. Sci., Paris*, **236**, 1596–1598.

MATHIAS, W. T. (1935). The life history and cytology of *Phloeospora brachiata*. *Publ. Hartley Bot. Labs.*, **13**, 1–24.

MOSS, B. (1958). Observations on the development and cytology of *Himanthalia elongata* (L.) S. F. Gray. *Brit. phycol. Bull.*, **1** (6), 31–32.

MOSS, B. L. and ELLIOT, E. (1957). Observations on the cytology of *Halidrys siliquosa* (L.) Lyngb. *Ann. Bot., Lond.*, N.S., **21**, 143–151.

NAYLOR, M. (1956). Cytological observations on three British species of *Laminaria*: a preliminary report. *Ann. Bot., Lond.*, N.S., **20**, 431–437.

— (1957). An acetocarmine squash technique for the Fucales. *Nature, Lond.*, **180**, 46.

— (1958a). The cytology of *Halidrys siliquosa* (L.) Lyngb. *Ann. Bot., Lond.*, N.S., **22**, 205–217.

— (1958b). Some aspects of the life history and cytology of *Stictyosiphon tortilis* (Rupr.) Reinke. *Acta Adriatica*, **8**, 3–22.

— (1958c). Chromosome numbers in the algae. Phaeophyta. *Brit. phycol. Bull.*, **1** (6), 34–37.

— (1959). Feulgen reaction in the Fucales. *Nature, Lond.*, **183**, 627.

OKABE, S. (1929). Meiosis im Oogonium von *Sargassum horneri* (Turn.) Ag. *Sci. Repr., Tôhoku Imp. Univ.*, 4 Ser., **4**, 661–669.

OSBORN, J. E. M. (1949). The structure and life history of *Hormosira banksii* (Turn.) Decaisne. *Trans. Roy. Soc. N.Z.*, **77**, 47–71.

PAPENFUSS, G. F. (1935). Alternation of generations in *Ectocarpus siliculosus*. *Bot. Gaz.*, 96, 421–446.

ROBERTS, M. (1962). Chromosome numbers in the algae. Phaeophyta II. *Brit. phycol. Bull.*, **2** (3), 165–166.

ROBERTS, M. (1964). The cytology of the Phaeophyta—a review of recent developments, current problems, and techniques. In *Algae and Man*. Ed. Daniel F. Jackson. New York. Plenum Press. 65–76.

ROY, K. (1938). Recherches sur la structure du noyau quiescent et sur les mitoses somatiques de quelques Fucacées. *Rev. Algol.*, **11**, 101–188.

SUBRAHMANYAN, R. (1956). Observations on the anatomy, cytology, development of the reproductive structures, fertilisation and embryology of *Pelvetia canaliculata* Dcne. and Thur. Part I. Anatomy of thallus and somatic mitosis. *J. Indian Bot. Soc.*, **35**, 374–390.

— (1957a). Observations on the anatomy, cytology, development of the reproductive structures, fertilisation and embryology of *Pelvetia canaliculata* Dcne. and Thur. Part II. Development of the conceptacles, reproductive structures and meiotic division of the nucleus during gametogenesis. *J. Indian Bot. Soc.*, **36**, 12–34.

SUBRAHMANYAN, R. (1957b). Observations on the anatomy, cytology, development of the reproductive structures, fertilisation and embryology of *Pelvetia canaliculata* Dcne. and Thur. Part III. The liberation of reproductive bodies, fertilisation and embryology. *J. Indian Bot. Soc.*, **36**, 373–395.

WILLIAMS, J. LLOYD (1904). Studies in the Dictyotaceae. I.: Cytology of the tetrasporangium and germination of the tetraspore. *Ann. Bot., Lond.*, **18**, 141–160.

YABU, H. (1958). On the nuclear division in tetrasporangia of *Dictyopteris divaricata* (Okamura) Okamura and *Dictyota dichotoma* Lamour. *Bull. Fac. Fish. Hokkaido Univ.*, **8** (4), 290–296.

YABU, H. and IMAI, A. (1957). On nuclear division in the antheridium of *Fucus evanescens* and *Pelvetia wrightii*. *Bull. Jap. Soc. Phycol.*, **5**, 44–49.

YAMANOUCHI, S. (1909). Mitosis in *Fucus*. *Bot. Gaz.*, **47**, 173–196.

6 *The Rhodophyceae*

PETER S. DIXON
M.Sc., Ph.D.
Senior Lecturer, Department of Botany,
University of Liverpool

INTRODUCTION

Interest in the cytology of the Rhodophyta over the last 60 years has been largely concerned with investigations aimed at elucidating the complex life histories in this group of organisms.* Because of this, these investigations tend to give a fragmentary account of meiosis or mitosis in a particular species, or at worst, little more than the numbers of chromosomes alleged to have been found in different parts of the plant. The classical researches of Yamanouchi (1906a, b), Svedelius (1915, 1933, 1937, 1942) and Kylin (1914, 1916, 1916a, b, c, 1917, 1923, 1928) provided a much-needed basis for the understanding of life-histories, although in terms of comparative cytology the data are extremely scanty. Westbrook (1935) gave the first detailed survey of nuclear organisation in the Florideophycidae using the Feulgen technique, whilst the various papers by Drew (1934, 1937, 1939, 1943, 1944) gave additional information, despite the fact that the principal aim of her investigations was the life-history of the organism. Further brief surveys by Celan (1941) and Rao (1960) were followed by the recent major treatment by Magne (1964a) who has given the only detailed treatment of the cytology of the Florideophyceae. The position with regard to the Bangiophyceae is still far from satisfactory in that only rare cytological investigations have been undertaken, the results of these are often contradictory, and there is no detailed survey of the cytology of the group as a whole.

There are certain morphological peculiarities of the Rhodophyta, particularly in members of the Florideophyceae, which make technical demands not met with in representatives of other groups. First, cell division in the Florideophyceae is restricted to apical cells except in a few genera of the Corallinaceae and Delesseriaceae where intercalary cell division of specialised type occurs. The apical cells of the Florideophyceae are of two types, those of the filaments of unlimited growth which occur at the apex of axes, and those of the filaments of limited growth. The filaments of limited growth compact to

* For a full bibliography, see Magne (1964a), pp. 7–11.

form the cortical tissues so that their apical cells occur as the outer layer of the thallus which is thus a potentially meristematic layer and not merely an inert epidermis. Secondly, fertilisation results in the formation of a carposporophyte which is partially or completely parasitic on the female gametophyte, the tissues of the two phases often becoming intermingled in the most intimate manner. For this reason it is often essential to be able to identify the cell whose nucleus or nuclei are under investigation.

METHODS

The techniques listed below contain a general survey of the methods which have been applied in cytological investigations of the Rhodophyta. It must be borne in mind that there is considerable variation in response to fixatives and stains, not only between different genera and species, but also between different parts of the same plant. The often violent differences of opinion as to the applicability of certain techniques is a reflection of this variation. Such schedules as are listed give mean values for concentration and time of application of reagents but these may require considerable modification in order to accommodate this variation. This applies particularly to the genera of the Florideophyceae although in the Bangiophyceae the variation between different parts of the same plant is much less marked.

FIXATION

1 *Formalin/alcohol*

The standard fixative used by most older authors. The proportions recommended vary somewhat, that used by Drew being

70% alcohol	100 ml.
40% formaldehyde	6 ml.

Decolourisation may be speeded up by exposing the fixed material to strong daylight. Although suitable for use when it is proposed to use Haematoxylin or Brazilin in general this fixative has been found to be of little value for subsequent staining with Feulgen or acetocarmine. Nevertheless, Cole (1963) appears to have used this fixative successfully as a preliminary to the latter. Although extremely useful for morphological investigations this fixative suffers from the major defect that material is apt to become very hard and brittle after storage for more than a few days.

2 *Formalin/acetic/alcohol*

Various formulae have been proposed, that used by Westbrook (1935) being the most popular.

Glacial acetic acid	2·5 ml.
40% formaldehyde	6·5 ml.
50% alcohol	100·0 ml.

As has been pointed out by Magne (1964a), this fixative is apt to cause a certain amount of contraction of the nucleus. Very clear results may be obtained through its use so that it is advantageous for chromosome counting although the consequent shrinkage precludes its use for comparative cytology. For the best results immediate use is recommended. Material *can* be stored in it for some time although softening may ensue. If this softening, which may even be advantageous under certain circumstances, is so excessive that it results in disintegration, transfer to 70% alcohol after 24 hr. is a useful control. With material which is calcified the fixative should be changed at half-hourly intervals until decalcification is complete.

3 *Chromic acid/acetic acid mixtures*

Innumerable variations and modifications have been proposed (cf. Johansen 1940; Magne 1964a), the Papenfuss (1946) modification of Karpechenko being one of the most popular.

Solution A:

Chromic acid	1 gm.
Glacial acetic acid	5 ml.
Sea-water	65 ml.

Solution B:

40% formaldehyde	40 ml.
Sea-water	35 ml.

The two solutions are kept separate, equal volumes being mixed immediately before use. The need to transport two distinct solutions and the speed with which deterioration sets in once the two solutions have been mixed are the major objections to the use of this fixative. For these reasons other workers have adapted the simpler mixtures of chromic and acetic acids, without the formaldehyde content which is the cause of the need for the separation of the fixative into two fractions. The dilute mixtures are particularly suitable for the more delicate filamentous genera such as *Spermothamnion*, the cells of which may be distorted considerably by the stronger solutions. For calcareous genera the fixative should be changed at half-hour intervals until no further evolution of CO_2 is visible. One advantage of the chromic acid/acetic acid fixatives is that decolourisation is rapid, the major snag being that for cytological investigations prolonged washing is necessary otherwise various staining artefacts may be produced. For marine material, it is often suggested that sea-water should be used rather than distilled water, as in the formula given above, but this does not appear to be absolutely necessary.

4 *Alcohol/acetic acid mixtures*

The mixture of 95% ethyl alcohol and glacial acetic acid in the ratio 3:1 has been used extensively in recent years, although personal investigations in the Rhodophyta suggest that ratios of 2:1 or even 1 : 1 may give better results. These mixtures are not good for large-celled delicate forms as they cause excessive cellular shrinkage, although the nuclei are perfectly fixed even when such distortion has occurred. For calcified material the mixtures should be avoided completely if cellular identification is required. The acid content of the mixture is so high that the reaction between the mixture and the encrusting material is violent, the rapid formation of bubbles of CO_2 shattering the tissues completely. Fixation and decolouration are extremely rapid, so that only a few minutes' exposure is necessary for the smaller thalli, and if these are left in the mixture for more than half an hour disintegration may result (cf. Austin 1959). For more cartilaginous thalli, from one to six hours' immersion in the fixative may be required, the softening effects of the strong acid being advantageous in that no further softening is usually necessary. In addition to the rapid destruction of pigments the alcohol/acetic acid mixtures may also remove storage products, which often obscure cytological detail particularly in sporangia. The best results are obtained if the material is processed immediately after fixation, and this is often a serious handicap if marine material has to be collected a long way from laboratory facilities. Austin (1959) has claimed that material can be left from three to six weeks without harm but personal experience suggests that this should be avoided whenever possible, whilst the other alternative, to take the material down through the alcohol series and store it in 70% or 50% ethyl alcohol is not particularly satisfactory for red algal material. The removal of the fixative by washing may be critical in certain genera as has been discussed in detail by Austin (1959).

PREPARATIONS

1 *Whole mounts*

For the uniseriate filamentous thalli, whole mounts are often possible, although even here a certain amount of squashing is advantageous.

2 *Serial sections*

Although now falling into disfavour, serial sections of material embedded in paraffin wax are nevertheless of considerable value in cytological investigations under certain circumstances, particularly where cellular identification is of critical importance. The techniques required are standard (cf. Johansen 1940), although for the Rhodophyta the use of chloroform as the wax solvent rather than the more usual xylene can be recommended. Material may require a certain amount of softening prior to embedding; the appropriate methods for this are listed in the following section.

3 *Squash preparations*

The use of squash preparations has increased considerably in recent years. For many of the genera the fixed material is sufficiently soft to permit direct squashing. It is often necessary to use either an albuminised or gelatinised slide, if the staining procedure adopted is at all lengthy, as the natural adhesion between the material and the slide or coverslip is very weak and the bulk of the preparation will be lost in processing.

The hardness of red algal material varies considerably, particularly after fixation. Where acidic fixatives have been employed the material is often more soft than in the natural state, but even here additional softening may well be necessary, whilst in more cartilaginous thalli prolonged treatment is needed. For softening, most investigators have used dilute solutions of either hydrochloric acid or sodium hydroxide. The concentrations recommended have varied considerably; Kylin (1923) used 1% aqueous solution of either whilst Drew (1945) developed the use of 10% hydrochloric acid in 70% alcohol. Papenfuss (1937), Norris (1957) and Cole (1963) have used hydrochloric acid in concentrations up to 50% and Norris (1957) recommends the use of 10% solutions of sodium hydroxide. There are disadvantages to the use of these substances in cytological investigations although for morphological studies they are all reasonably satisfactory. The use of N hydrochloric acid is part of the technique of Feulgen staining and preliminary application should be avoided when this stain is used. For material which requires softening for cytological purposes, the best procedure appears to be that developed by Magne (1964a) in which dilute solutions of sodium carbonate are used. The considerable variation observed in the applicability or lack of effect of different softening agents after the use of particular fixatives is in agreement with the opinion of Norris (1957) 'that the fixative influences the chemical nature of the substance holding the cells together'. The need for albuminised or gelatinised slides is particularly critical after the use of softening agents as these appear to have a very deleterious effect on the natural adhesion between material and slide or coverslip.

The normal effect of the squashing process is to spread out and flatten the cells. Except with large cells, such as those of *Griffithsia* or *Corynospora*, or large sporangia it is very difficult to break the cell wall so that the contents can be removed, and when this is achieved the problem then arises as to the identity of the cell from which the nucleus was obtained.

One major difficulty with investigations of the carposporophyte in the Rhodophyta is that the structure being studied is encased by a large amount of unwanted tissue, so that when a squash preparation is made the carpogonium or young carposporophyte is lost in a mass of cortical cells. One simple method of overcoming this difficulty is to make squash preparations of sections. The fertile axis is first softened and then sectioned on a freezing microtome using dilute gelatine as the supporting medium. With a modern freezing microtome it is possible to prepare sections 50–100 μ in thickness in a matter of minutes and these can then be squashed and stained.

STAINING

1 *Heidenheim's Haematoxylin*

Once the standard cytological stain for algal material, Heidenheim's Haematoxylin is now largely superseded, although Magne (1964a) made considerable use of this stain in his recent survey of the cytology of the Florideophyceae. No detailed discussion of its use is necessary in view of the long treatment by Johansen (1940). One disadvantage is that the use of mordant and stain in aqueous solution subjects the material to water for a period of up to 24 hr. and this often results in swelling of the cell wall, particularly in sporangia. Also, a counterstain is usually necessary to permit identification of the cell.

Other workers have used various Haematoxylin stains. Johansen (1940) recommends Harris's Haematoxylin whilst Norris (1957) preferred Mayer's acid haemalum. Cytologically these stains are of little consequence.

There has been some debate as to whether Haematoxylin should be used on the material in bulk, before squashing, or after the squash preparation has been made. The main objection to the latter is that much material tends to be lost in processing. The advantages of staining the preparation after squashing are obvious and the use of gelatinised or albuminised slides will prevent the loss of material.

2 *Brazilin*

The application of Brazilin to the study of red algal cytology is due to Drew (1934 *et seq.*). Spectacular results were achieved by her but the stain was never adopted widely outside her research school. Other workers who attempted to use it have commented unfavourably on the results obtained (cf. Magne 1964a). Details of the schedule used by Drew were never published and it is probable that the difficulties encountered by other workers are a result of this. Ignorance of the procedure adopted by Drew presumably led to the use of solutions in an 'unripened' state. Certainly, the use of stain and mordant in a raw state gives very crude preparations. It would seem profitable therefore to discuss the Drew technique in some detail.

The stock solution of Brazilin is made up as a 5% solution in 70% alcohol and then left for at least six months to ripen, preferably in a darkened cupboard. The stock solution remains in good condition for several years although it needs to be decanted or filtered from time to time. For use, the stock solution is diluted with 70% alcohol to give an 0·5% solution. A 2% solution of iron alum (ferric ammonium sulphate) in 70% alcohol is used as the mordant and this also requires to 'ripen' for several months before use. The changes involved in the ripening process are very complicated and by no means understood, but the speed with which a solution becomes ready for use appears to depend most on the type of glass bottle used.

The procedure is to transfer sections or squash preparations to the mordant in 70% alcohol for a period of one hour. They are then washed several times in 70% alcohol (to remove the excess mordant) and transferred to the Brazilin, usually for 12–16 hr. The number and frequency of the washings in 70% alcohol is the critical stage in the procedure as these determine the amount of stain taken up. Unlike the procedure for Heidenheim's Haematoxylin, where the excess stain taken up is reduced by secondary destaining, the procedure for Brazilin depends on getting the precise amount of mordant into the material before staining so that subsequent destaining is unnecessary. After removal from the Brazilin the preparation is washed twice in 70% alcohol and then taken up through the alcohol series for mounting.

The advantages of using Brazilin over Haematoxylin are threefold. First, both stain and mordant are applied in 70% alcohol so that the swelling effects of aqueous solutions are eliminated; secondly, both cytoplasm and cell wall are lightly stained, to give a pinkish colour, which is an adequate countereffect to the blackish-red reaction of nuclei and chromosomes; and thirdly, much less time is required for the process.

3 *Acetocarmine*

The acetocarmine schedule for algae given by Godward (1948) has been modified slightly to make it applicable to red algal material by various workers (Rao 1953; Austin 1959; Cole 1963; Chiu 1965). There is considerable variation between different species and between different parts of the same thallus in relation to the strength of mordant and time of application and these functions have to be worked out for each entity. As Magne (1964a) has indicated, the technique is valuable for obtaining chromosome counts although it is of limited application in the study of fine cytoplasmic detail, particularly in the resting nucleus.

4 *Feulgen*

Results of the application of the Feulgen technique to the Rhodophyta have been very confused. Westbrook (1935) in her early paper reported excellent results whilst Magne (1964a) has used the technique extensively. Westbrook commented that, having taken all precautions, the pit-connections and cell walls were sometimes stained and she suggested that this was a result of the release of reducing substances from extra-nuclear sources. Attempts by the late Dr. K. M. Drew and by the present author to apply the technique have not been particularly successful. Occasionally, magnificent results would be obtained in one or two cells, but with no constancy.

5 *Methyl green and pyronin*

The test for the histo-chemical detection of ribonucleoproteins has been applied to the Rhodophyta by Magne (1964a) without any real success. The chromatin stains only very feebly and the preparations were obscured by the cell wall taking up the stain.

CULTURE

Culture methods are of limited application in purely cytological studies of the Rhodophyta. For most red algae, fresh material is readily obtainable, although the ability to 'hold' material in the living state for a few days in the laboratory is often of considerable value. For this purpose, lightly aerated sea-water, or water from the habitat in which the organism was growing in the case of fresh-water representatives, is an adequate medium, providing that the quantity of liquid is sufficient for the amount of material and that the liquid medium is changed at intervals. Natural daylight is the best source of illumination and providing that the temperature is not excessive, i.e. more than 15–20°C, it is often possible to keep material in a perfectly healthy state on a laboratory bench near north light for periods of up to a week or more. For long-term work, the use of a controlled temperature room or tank running at a temperature of 10–15°C with artificial illumination up to 1,000 lux may be necessary. Most Rhodophyta are heavily epiphytised with diatoms or members of other algal divisions and these may prove troublesome over a long period. In the case of firm material the diatoms can simply be brushed away with a soft camel hair brush and the nuisance diminished in this way. For long-term cultures it is usually necessary to adjust the nutritive status of the medium. Provasoli, McLaughlan and Droop (1957) have given a detailed account of the development of artificial media for marine algae but the use of the complex media recommended by these authors is often not necessary for crude cultures of the type mentioned above. For Rhodophyta, natural sea-water is often sufficient as the medium although addition of small quantities of nitrate, phosphate or iodide may have beneficial results. One advantage in using plain sea-water for crude cultures of the Rhodophyta is that this medium is sufficiently minimal to reduce the growth of the epiphytes and experience has shown that over a long period (9–14 months) the contaminants may be even exterminated completely. The latter has been found to be the only way of obtaining growing material of the encrusting non-calcified Rhodophyta as their natural growth rate is so low that within a matter of weeks they became swamped by epiphytes in anything other than plain sea-water. Material brought into the laboratory may frequently form new attachment structures and this is particularly helpful as damage from handling is reduced when the material has become attached to a new solid substrate.

The nuclear behaviour in sporangia may often be deduced from the cytological examination of the germlings derived from the spores released by these sporangia. Although the spores will often germinate in plain sea-water or the natural fresh-water the addition of small quantities of soil extract, trace element or vitamin mixtures is essential if the germlings are to grow to any appreciable size.

The growth of contaminants may often be reduced by diminution of light intensity as the brushing technique is too violent to permit the removal of diatoms from the germling cultures. A major problem to be guarded against in any spore germination experiments with red algal material is the possibility of small fragments of material being shed with the spores. The ease with which new attachment structures are formed, even from unicellular fragments, and the similarities in appearance between such reattached fragments and older germlings mean that unless such vegetative propagation is detected at an early stage in development it could be the cause of major errors in interpretation.

Various members of the Rhodophyta have now been grown in axenic culture (cf. Fries 1963), but the effort necessary for the purification of the material, normally heavily epiphytised by bacteria or other algae, is simply not justified if the aim of the investigation is purely cytological. Furthermore, such Rhodophyta as have been obtained in axenic culture frequently exhibit morphological aberrations or gross abnormalities, and usually fail to form reproductive structures so that the value of such axenic cultures is limited.

THE INTERPHASE NUCLEUS

The number of nuclei in each cell, their shape, size and arrangement in the cell vary considerably in the Rhodophyta. In the Bangiophyceae, the cells are always uninucleate both in young and old tissues, even in the most elaborate thalli. The position in the Florideophyceae is more complex, the apical cells are either uninucleate or multinucleate, the segments formed by their division having at the moment of formation the same nuclear characteristics as the apical cell from which they have been produced. In some genera where the apical cell is uninucleate the cells of the mature thallus remain uninucleate throughout the life of the plant whereas in other genera there is an increase in the number of nuclei as a consequence of nuclear division without any corresponding cell division. It should be noted also that in those genera where secondary pit connections are formed, nuclei are transferred between cells during the formation of these structures. Where the apical cells are multinucleate, these may contain a considerable number of nuclei and the number may continue to increase still further with age. The segments formed by the division of multinucleate apical cells are also multinucleate at the time of formation and the number of nuclei may increase as the cells mature. The largest numbers of nuclei are found in cells of various species of *Griffithsia*. Lewis (1909), for instance, estimated that the apical cells of *Griffithsia globulifera* (referred to *G. bornetiana* by him) contain from 12 to 50 or even 75 nuclei, recently formed segments from 100 to 500 nuclei, whilst the oldest cells were estimated to contain from 3,000 to 4,000 nuclei. These cells are among the largest found anywhere in the Florideophyceae; in other genera with multinucleate cells the numbers are still impressive, though much fewer than those recorded in *Griffithsia globulifera*. In *Pleonosporium borreri*, for instance, the apical cell may contain some 4 or 5 nuclei, with 20 to 30 in the older cells.

The position of the interphase nucleus or nuclei in the cell is related to the number of nuclei present and the state of the cell. In the Bangiophyceae, the single nucleus is placed centrally in young, non-vacuolate cells and parietally in older vacuolate cells. Similarly in the Florideophyceae where a single nucleus is present in an apical cell or derivative cell this lies in a central position although after enlargement and the associated vacuolation the nucleus moves to the periphery of the cell. Occasionally, after vacuolation the single nucleus may be held in the centre of the cell by strands of cytoplasm but this is relatively rare. In genera where the thallus is obviously filamentous the single nucleus migrates to the basal pole of the cell where it lies in close proximity to the primary pit connection, as in *Ceramium*. Where the apical cell and its derivatives contain many nuclei, these lie at the periphery of the cell whether this is vacuolate or not.

According to Magne (1964a) the shape of the interphase nucleus is determined by its position in the cell and this hypothesis appears to be correct. Those nuclei lying in a central position are spherical whilst the parietal nuclei are somewhat flattened, with a lenticular shape. It has been claimed that nuclei with an irregular outline occur in certain genera and it is not clear to what extent these are simply fixation artefacts. Magne (1964a) has dismissed for this reason the statements of Svedelius (1911) that amoeboid nuclei occur in *Delesseria sanguinea* and this would appear to be justified in view of the fixative employed by the latter. On the other hand Magne also records nuclei with an irregular outline in the apical cells of *Gracilaria verrucosa* and in the apical cells of the filaments of limited growth in *Furcellaria fastigiata* and claims that these can not be ascribed to bad fixation. There are also reports of the occurrence of elongate fusiform nuclei in certain tissues which may or may not be regarded as fixation artefacts. In old tissues where division of nuclei and cells has ceased the nuclei often exhibit curious changes in shape and appearance which appear to be a consequence of the disintegration of the nucleus. Clearly, further investigation of these phenomena are necessary before any adequate interpretation is possible.

The size of the nucleus shows considerable variation between species and also in different tissues of the same species, with further variation according to the time of year at which the material is examined and the conditions under which the plant is growing. The average size of the nuclei in the Rhodophyta is of the order of 3 μ. In general, the smallest nuclei are found in some genera of the Cryptonemiales and Gigartinales where the diameter may be less than 1 μ, whilst the largest occur in some members of the Ceramiales. The variation in size of the nuclei in a given plant is very complex as is shown by the detailed discussion of this given by Magne (1964a). The nuclei of apical cells, whether these are of filaments of limited or unlimited growth, tend to be larger than the nuclei of their derivative cells. The complications arise with older maturing cells where both cell division and nuclear division have ceased. Figures have been published showing nuclei of considerable size in such cells, as for instance in *Plocamium coccineum* where Kylin (1923, Fig. 34d) figured a nucleus in face view with a diameter of 30 μ The difficulty is that with vacuolation, the nuclei move to the periphery of the cell, becoming markedly flattened, so that accurate measurement of their dimensions is not easy, except in face view. However, if nuclear volume is calculated the increase in volume of the nucleus as the cell matures is considerable, far greater than could be accounted for by errors in measurement.

The early observations on the structure of the interphase nucleus are somewhat contradictory. The presence of one nucleolus, and occasionally more than one, was agreed by most investigators, although the presence or absence of a so-called 'chromatic reticulum' in the interphase nucleus was disputed. These differences of opinion were largely a result of inadequate technique and with the increased use of Feulgen staining the presence of fine strands in the interphase nucleus has been demonstrated.

MITOSIS

From various studies of mitosis, in members of both Bangiophyceae and Florideophyceae, it is agreed that the process is essentially similar to that found in higher plants. However, in recent studies, Magne (1964a, b) has claimed that in certain genera of the Gigartinales and Cryptonemiales there are certain important differences in both mitotic and meiotic nuclear division from that found in the majority of the Florideophyceae. The organization in the former, which has been termed the 'calliblepharidian' nuclei by Magne, will be considered after a discussion of the more general type of mitosis found in the Florideophyceae.

The first indication of the commencement of mitosis is that the nuclei increase in size slightly. The subsequent changes are most easy to follow in those nuclei where fine 'chromatic' strands are readily observable in interphase. The chromocentres increase both in size and number and become more heavily stained. By the middle of prophase the fine strands representing the chromonemata have contracted so that the chromocentres have coalesced into chains of granules of varied length. In nuclei such as those of primary apical cells, where the interphase chromonemata are not readily observable as a result of the surface of the nucleus reacting as a homogeneous Feulgen-positive region, the process is more difficult to follow but it appears to follow the same course. During late prophase the chains of chromocentres contract further to produce the chromosomes which lie at the periphery of the nucleus, the membrane of which disappears. The chromosomes at the end of prophase are of various shapes, some being elongate, others sausage-shaped, whilst the smallest are spherical. The shape of the chromosomes varies from species to species. Drew (1939) reported that the chromosomes of *Plumaria elegans* are of the three types listed above although she commented that this degree of variation is not found in other species that she examined. In *Rhodochorton floridulum*, Magne (1964a) has shown that the chromosomes are all of the elongate type whilst in many other species, such as *Rhodymenia palmata*, the chromosomes are much smaller, being spherical or only slightly elongate.

The one or more nucleoli also disintegrate towards the end of prophase although occasionally these may persist well into metaphase. Many of the early authors considered that some or all of the chromosomes were formed directly from the nucleolus. Westbrook (1935) reviewed these early observations and concluded that there was no real evidence to justify this opinion. Most recent work has supported the interpretation of chromosome formation given above. The nucleolus, at the time of disappearance, often fragments into a number of small diffusely staining structures and it may well be that as a result of the staining technique used these fragments were misinterpreted by the early workers.

During metaphase the chromosomes are usually contracted to the greatest extent. They move to the equator of the cell where they are very closely packed together. The aggregation of the chromosomes on the metaphase plate is so great that it is impossible to count the number of chromosomes present, even in polar view. The longitudinal partition of the chromosomes into chromatids is almost impossible to observe and only rarely has the occurrence of chromatids in metaphase been reported. This is not merely a result of their small size and close packing because they are still not visible when the cell is squashed so hard as to shatter the wall and spread the contents.

Critical observations on the spindle and polar bodies in the Rhodophyta are very few. Magne (1964a) has given a brief résumé of the previous observations and from a consideration of these and of his own investigation he concludes that in the 'normal' mitosis the mitotic figures are too small to permit any adequate analysis of the origin of the spindle. The outline of the spindle shows considerable variation in that the ends may be either pointed, truncated or round and it is peculiar that different types of spindle occur in different nuclei in the one plant. Polar bodies were described by all the earlier workers on red algal cytology but more recently the observations have been more critical. Westbrook (1935) was able to observe polar bodies in only two of the genera which she investigated and then only rarely, whilst more recently Magne (1964a) has commented that occasionally polar bodies could be observed but that there is considerable variation in appearance. For this reason, Magne argues that these polar bodies should not be regarded as centrosomes and this would appear to be a justifiable conclusion in view of the present inadequate knowledge. Until the reasons for their irregular appearance and ephermal nature are understood it would be best simply to refer to these structures as 'polar bodies'.

The stages of anaphase and telophase proceed rapidly in all Rhodophyta. The two sets of chromosomes each tend to separate as a mass and little detail can be observed. Because of the close packing it is not possible to obtain any information on the centromeric attachment although, as will be seen later, some data on this feature can be obtained during meiosis.

As has been mentioned previously, Magne (1964a, b) has drawn attention to the occurrence in certain members of the Cryptonemiales and Gigartinales of differences in the process of mitosis. In these genera the chromosomes are formed in the normal way but the nucleus is markedly fusiform and in metaphase the polar bodies are very large and deeply staining. With the disappearance of the nuclear membrane, the outline of the elongate nucleus remains, sharply circumscribed from the remainder of the cytoplasm. The polar bodies become more prominent during late metaphase and anaphase, becoming irregularly saucer-shaped.

There appears to be considerable variation in the time at which mitosis occurs. Some investigators have claimed that mitotic figures could be obtained only at particular times or states of the tide in marine species, whilst other workers have found that mitosis occurred at all times. Even the same species may behave in different ways, in *Lemanea fluviatilis*, for instance, mitotic figures were obtained at one site by day or night with no marked increase in frequency at any time, whereas at a second site, only a few miles from the first, mitoses could be observed only in material fixed between 10.00 p.m. and midnight.

MEIOSIS

As with mitosis, the process of meiosis in the Rhodophyta is similar in most respects to that found in higher plants, although, as will be seen, there are some slight points of difference. As has been indicated by Magne (1964a, p. 586), many of the early reports are incorrect in certain details. The various disagreements, particularly with regard to the relationship of the nucleolus to chromosome formation, are largely a consequence of faulty technique. The position in the life-history at which meiosis takes place, and, in particular, the structures in which this type of division occurs, will be discussed at the end of the present section.

The early stages of the first prophase differ from the equivalent stages in mitosis in that the fine 'chromatic' strands (so-called 'reticulum') appear to be much more diffuse. Subsequently, a typical leptotene stage appears. Magne (1964a) has rightly drawn attention to the curious use of the term 'spireme' by both Drew (1934) and Westbrook (1935) to describe this highly filamentous state of the 'chromatin' in the Rhodophyta. The data on leptotene and zygotene stages are particularly sparse in the Rhodophyta. The pairing of the chromosomes is often very difficult to interpret and it would appear that many of the observations on the phenomena described under the terms 'synapsis' or 'synizesis' are the result of aberrant fixation, as claimed by Austin (1960b). Magne (1964a), on the other hand, has figured various stages of zygotene which are very clear and he has shown also that in pachytene the chromosomes may not be fully paired along their whole length. The chromosomes, which up to this stage have the appearance of chains of granules become thicker, shorter and more uniform in appearance. In the most favourable Feulgen preparations it is sometimes, but not always, possible to observe coiling, as indicated by Austin (1960b). During zygotene the chromosomes are frequently gathered to one side of the nucleus in such a way as to appear as a radiating mass. Further contraction occurs towards the end of pachytene and the paired chromosomes migrate again to occupy the whole of the nuclear area. In higher plants, as the diplotene stage proceeds, the paired chromosomes of the bivalent part and each chromosome is then seen to be composed of two chromatids. There is no real evidence for the occurrence of chromatids at this stage of meiosis in the nuclei of the Rhodophyta. This may be partly a consequence of the small size of the chromosomes but even in the larger nuclei, such as occur in the Ceramiales, chromatids cannot be seen. The crossed and looped arrangements of diplotene indicate the presence of one or more chiasmata. There is some variation in the number of chiasmata per bivalent, Austin (1960b) showing that on average there are two chiasmata per bivalent in *Furcellaria* whereas in some other genera there are fewer chiasmata. In favourable preparations it is usually possible to determine the position of the centromeres at this stage, whether lying in terminal, subterminal or median positions. One of the most characteristic features of meiosis in the Rhodophyta is that there is a marked interruption in the process towards the end of diplotene. The intensity of the staining reaction of the chromosomes falls off considerably so that they become much less obvious. This 'diffuse stage' which has been reported in various plants and animals (cf. Darlington 1937) as well as in members of the Phaeophyta (Magne 1964a) represents a partial reversion to the interphase condition. Throughout these stages of meiotic prophase the size of the nucleus has been increasing steadily and it reaches a maximum at the end of diplotene. During late diplotene the paired chromosomes shorten even more until at diakenesis they are represented by almost globular bivalents, although occasionally these may often have an angular appearance.

The nucleolus persists to the end of diakinesis. At this time it begins to disintegrate although occasionally the nucleolus may not disappear until well into metaphase. During metaphase the chromosomes become arranged on the equatorial plate, the nuclear membrane disappears and the volume occupied by the nucleus diminishes considerably. The arrangement of the spindle fibres is often clearer in the first meiotic metaphase than in mitosis, the fibres lying clearly between the polar body and the chromosome. In some nuclei the chromosomes have been described as consisting of numerous granules (Westbrook 1928; Suneson 1950) although in other nuclei massive hemispherical structures have been reported (Davis 1898; Lewis 1909; Svedelius 1911, 1914a; Westbrook 1935; Magne 1964a). These structures appear during the diffuse stage of diplotene and have been identified as 'centrospheres' or 'centrosomes'. As Magne (1964a, p. 612) has commented, until more knowledge is available on the fine structure of these objects it would be better simply to call them 'polar bodies'. Separation of the metaphase chromosomes takes place rapidly once the orientation of the chromosome pairs on the equatorial plate has occurred. The anaphase and telophase stages of the first meiotic division do not exhibit any special features, the two sets of chromosomes each separating as a mass to the poles although occasionally an odd chromosome may lag behind its associates. The clusters of chromosomes which form cup-shaped masses, despiralise and the individual chromosomes increase in length. The nucleoli and the nuclear membrane are reconstituted whilst the staining reaction of the chromosomes diminishes and an interphase intervenes. Yamanouchi (1906b) alone has claimed that there is no interphase between the first and second divisions in the meiosis in *Polysiphonia violacea* (= *P. flexicaulis*), the two sets of chromosomes from the first division passing directly from telophase to the second division. Even in other species of the genus (Iyengar and Balakrishnan 1950; Magne 1964a) no evidence to support this view has been obtained. The second meiotic division does not appear to differ in any way from a normal mitosis except that the nucleolus and the nuclear membrane tend to disappear at a relatively early stage.

The only calculation of the duration of meiosis appears to be the rough estimate given by Austin (1960b), who has stated that in *Furcellaria fastigiata* 'meiosis . . . takes a number of hours to reach completion, perhaps twelve or more'.

Interpretation of the life-histories in the Rhodophyta has been a popular topic for discussion among phycologists for many years. In such studies, knowledge of the position in the life-history at which meiosis takes place and, in particular, of the structures in which it occurs is obviously of vital importance, but unfortunately much of the data which have been widely accepted are of doubtful validity. Unverified assumptions have been regarded as definite proof, so that a critical reappraisal is necessary if any valid conclusions are to be drawn. The places at which meiosis occurs will be discussed, first, for the Florideophyceae and secondly, for the Bangiophyceae.

In the Florideophyceae, Yamanouchi (1906a, b) first demonstrated the occurrence of meiosis in tetrasporangia of *Polysiphonia flexicaulis*, incorrectly referred by him to *P. violacea*. There have been numerous subsequent investigations which have confirmed the occurrence of meiosis in these sporangia and it is now clear that there is enough evidence, both cytological and cultural, to justify the acceptance of the occurrence in numerous Florideophyceae of what might be termed the '*Polysiphonia*' type of life-history, with a succession of haploid sexual, diploid carposporic and diploid tetrasporic phases, the first and last of which are morphologically identical. On the other hand the converse deduction, that the presence of tetrasporangia is proof of the occurrence of meiosis, is not always justified. The evidence for apomeiotic phenomena in tetrasporangia is discussed in a later section. Also, the numerous members of the Florideophyceae in which tetrasporangia are unknown must also be considered. The first cytological investigations of such algae was undertaken by Svedelius (1915), who claimed that in *Scinaia furcellata* meiosis occurred immediately after fertilisation. On the basis of these observations it appeared that both sexual and carposporic plants were haploid. Further investigations in related genera supported the conclusions of Svedelius (Kylin 1916a, b, 1917) and it became accepted that this '*Nemalion*' type of life-history was of widespread occurrence particularly in the Nemalionales. Observations not in agreement with this conclusion were ignored, whilst the very real inadequacy of the 'evidence' which had been accepted was overlooked. The need for a critical reappraisal of this classical interpretation has only recently been appreciated. Investigation of the Bonnemaisoniaceae has disclosed the occurrence of tetrasporic phases which are so different from the sexual plant that they were referred to other genera (and even Orders), whilst the more critical cytological studies of Magne (1961a, b, 1964c) have shown that the old concepts must be abandoned completely. A full discussion of the old and new evidence has been given by Magne (1964a, pp. 624–632), who has rightly concluded that there is no evidence at all to justify the original conclusion of the occurrence of meiosis in the carpogonium or in a closely related cell. The life-history of such algae as *Bonnemaisonia* consists of the sequence of haploid sexual, diploid carposporic and diploid tetrasporic phases as occurs in *Polysiphonia*, the major point of difference from the latter being that the sexual and tetrasporic phases are morphologically dissimilar. In relation to the present discussion, the most important conclusion is that the idea of the occurrence of meiosis in the carpogonium (or a closely related cell) of *Nemalion* and the other so-called 'haplobiontic' Florideophyceae is no longer tenable.

Considering next the tetrasporangia of the Florideophyceae, the primordia of these are relatively small when first formed and usually uninucleate, even in thalli where the vegetative cells are multinucleate. The only real exceptions to the latter generalization are provided by Svedelius (1908, 1914a) in *Martensia* and *Nitophyllum* where he has shown that the primordia are initially multinucleate, all but one of the nuclei eventually degenerating although more than one may show the first indications of the commencement of the meiotic prophase. The observations of Heydrich (1901, 1902), who described a pseudo-sexual fusion of nuclei in a multinucleate tetrasporangium initial before division, are so peculiar and so badly documented that they must be ignored. The first meiotic division occurs whilst the primordium is relatively small, but a rapid increase in volume occurs at the same time as the formation of plastids and the deposition of reserve storage products, the so-called 'Floridean starch'. Except in zonate tetrasporangia, where the four spores are formed in a line, the cleavage of the cytoplasm does not occur until after both divisions have been completed. The orientation of the two divisions has been the subject of some controversy. In general, it would appear that the four derivative nuclei are arranged tetrahedrally immediately after their formation, irrespective of the ultimate pattern of cellular cleavage. The comments made by Austin (1960b, p. 304), suggest that the arrangement may even be found in the zonate tetrasporangia of *Furcellaria* where the cytoplasm has divided before the second nuclear division has been completed. The time which elapses between the first indications of the imitation of tetrasporangia and the release of mature spores varies enormously. In some members of the Ceramiaceae, the whole process may be completed within a period of 12 to 14 days, whereas Austin (1960b) has shown that in *Furcellaria* the tetrasporangium initials are formed in late April or early May, with meiosis occurring in early November and tetraspores being released in mid-December. Furthermore, in *Furcellaria*, the maturation of the tetrasporangia and the release of the spores each occur more or less simultaneously, within a few days, throughout the whole population. On the other hand, in most other members of the Florideophyceae, the sporangia are initiated, they mature and then discharge, in strict acropetal sequence over a long period. In *Gelidium*, where all the tetrasporangia are initiated in the fertile axes at about the same time in June or July, meiosis and spore release occur over a long period and it may be six months or more before all the spores are shed (Dixon 1959). Following the release of spores from a sporangium, the mother cell of the tetrasporangium, lying beneath or to one side, may proliferate a new sporangium into the empty wall of the old sporangium. Aberrant forms of tetrasporangia, where more or fewer than the normal complement of spores are formed, have been reported in various genera. The production of more than four spores in a tetrasporangium, as in *Gelidium* (Dixon 1959) is rare and nothing is known of the cytology of such sporanga. A reduction in numbers is more frequent (Bauch 1937). Such cytological studies as have been undertaken will be considered later.

Sporangia containing more than four spores, occurring as the normal method of reproduction of a phase, have been reported in various genera throughout the Florideophyceae. The terms 'polysporangium' or 'parasporangium' have been applied to these structures somewhat indiscriminately and the situation is extremely confused. Schiller (1913) attempted to differentiate between the two types of sporangium but, in *Ceramium*, the system suggested by him proved to be inapplicable (cf. Rosenvinge 1924, p. 399). As a result of her detailed cytological and morphological studies of selected genera, Drew has suggested that in the Florideophyceae, the sporangia containing more than four spores are of two categories:

(a) Those which are homologous with tetrasporangia, in that meiosis takes place in the course of spore formation and that the structures occur in the organism in place of tetrasporangia.
(b) Those which are not homologous with tetrasporangia, in that meiosis does not take place during spore formation and that the structures are purely accessory reproductive organs.

She has proposed that the name 'polysporangium' should be retained for the first type of sporangium and that 'parasporangium' should be applied to the latter. Unfortunately there is still not sufficient information available to permit the complete application of this scheme and it is most usually applied on the basis of the secondary characteristic, whether the sporangia are accessory structures or whether they replace tetrasporangia. Furthermore, there are numerous reports of 'parasporangia' or 'polysporangia' which are nothing more than incorrect interpretations of gall-like proliferations, as in *Ceramium* (Dixon 1960). The only detailed cytological investigation of polysporangia is by Drew (1937) who showed that in *Spermothamnion snyderi* the primordia are initially multinucleate, containing from two to nine nuclei. None of these disintegrates, all the nuclei undergoing meiosis to produce from 8 to 32 daughter-nuclei. These nuclei become arranged around the periphery of the sporangium which then divides up by invagination furrows. The latter are not arranged in any geometrical pattern, but are sometimes so irregular that spores of different size are formed. The spores are usually uninucleate although binucleate spores are formed occasionally, whilst in one case a spore in a very irregularly divided sporangium contained four nuclei. Sporangia containing more than four spores also occur in place of tetrasporangia in other genera of Ceramiales, such as *Pleonosporium*, so that it is probable that these sporangia are of similar type to those investigated by Drew. The structures found in the Rhodymeniales are much more difficult to interpret. Occasional sporangia with from 15 to 20 spores occur, mixed with tetrasporangia, in *Gastroclonium coulteri* (Smith 1955) whilst in *Coeloseira compressa* and *C. parva* Hollenberg (1940) has reported that only multiple-spored sporangia were found, with no evidence of normal tetrasporangia. In the two latter species, the primordium is said to be initially multinucleate although one nucleus enlarges, becoming much more prominent than the remainder. The cytological data are extremely scanty but Hollenberg claims that the remaining small nuclei take no further part in the development of the sporangium and that the single large nucleus divides to give four daughter-nuclei which *then* undergo meiosis to give a total of 16 nuclei, from 12 to 16 spores being produced in each sporangium. The evidence for the occurrence of meiosis is extremely slender and for this reason it would seem best to await the results of a full cytological investigation before accepting Hollenberg's interpretation. Absolutely no cytological information is available in those genera such as *Compsothamnion* or *Callithamnion* or in the example of *G. coulteri* mentioned above, where sporangia containing more than four spores occur mixed with tetrasporangia.

Cytological proof of the nuclear behaviour in those sporangia containing more than four spores where the divisions are entirely mitotic, so that the structures are merely accessory reproductive organs, has been obtained only in *Plumaria elegans* (Drew 1939). These sporangia are therefore 'parasporangia' on the basis of Drew's definition. In *Plumaria* these parasporangia originate from a single uninucleate cell and Drew has shown that repeated nuclear and cell divisions take place in an entirely fortuitous manner to give a sporangium of very irregular outline containing a variable number of spores, the nuclear divisions being entirely mitotic. Drew has also shown that the parasporangia are restricted to the triploid plants. Oltmanns (1922) and Kylin (1937) both regarded the parasporangia of *Plumaria* as being homologous with tetrasporangia whereas Drew, on the basis of her investigations, concluded that they were asexual sporangia of a special type and she was very doubtful as to their homology with tetrasporangia.

The occurrence of sporangia containing only two spores has been reported widely in the Florideophyceae. As Bauch (1937) has shown, these bisporangia are most frequent in Corallinaceae and Ceramiales although they have been reported also in a few representatives of the Nemalionales and Gigartinales. Bisporangia occur either exclusively on a plant or mixed with tetrasporangia but they have never been reported as occurring on sexual plants. The general impression therefore (cf. Fritsch 1945) is that they are homologous with tetrasporangia. Bauch (1937) in his survey of bisporangia showed that there were in fact two distinct types, the mature spores being either uninucleate or binucleate, but his speculations as to the relationship between these two types had little factual basis. Subsequently, Suneson (1950) in a cytological investigation of *Lithophyllum litorale* and *L. corallinae* showed that in the former, for which only plants bearing bisporangia are known, meiosis did not occur in the bisporangia. Instead, two nuclei were produced by mitotic division and these passed into the two spores each of which is therefore uninucleate at maturity. In *L. corallinae*, on the other hand, only sexual and bisporic plants had been found on the Swedish coast prior to Suneson's investigation, although tetrasporic plants had been reported from the Mediterranean. Suneson showed that within the one species in Swedish waters there occurred, quadrinucleate tetrasporangia, quadrinucleate bisporangia and binucleate bisporangia, with meiosis occurring in the first two types of sporangium but not in the last. On the basis of these observations, the bisporangia of the Corallinaceae are homologous with tetrasporangia. However, in view of the somewhat confused reports of the occurrence of these sporangia in different ways in various species from different geographical areas (cf. Bauch 1937; Suneson 1950) there may well be considerable variation in cytological behaviour and life-history over the range of a species.

The occurrence of meiosis has been discussed, in the present section, in tetrasporangia, in certain bisporangia and sporangia producing more than four spores. In view of the large number of species of Rhodophyta for which tetraspores are the only known means of reproduction, one important question relates to the possibility that the production of tetrasporangia does not necessarily imply the occurrence of meiosis. The information obtained by Suneson (1950) which has been discussed previously indicates that in *Lithophyllum corallinae* certain sporangia may function to produce four spores, others to form only two, but with meiosis occurring in both of these types whereas in other sporangia only two spores are produced as a result of a mitotic nuclear division. This is the only clear-cut instance of facultative apomeiosis in the Rhodophyta for which the supporting data are sufficiently sound. One previous, and much-quoted example, relates to *Lomentaria orcadensis*, for which tetrasporic plants alone occur in northwest Europe. Svedelius (1935, 1937) in a detailed investigation of this species, under the name *L. rosea*, claimed that the nuclear division in the tetrasporangia was of a very special type. The data presented are extremely curious in that it is claimed that after formation the chromosomes migrate into the nucleolus where mitotic division takes place. Magne (1964a) has recently reinvestigated the species and shown that the nuclear division in the sporangia is perfectly normal and that the observations by Svedelius are probably based on the misinterpretation of granules within the nucleolus which may be very prominent on occasions. Chromosome counts during diakinesis have been obtained, the only problem being that these are not consistent, counts of $n = 10$ and $n = 20$ have been obtained in material from Brest and the Baie de Morlaix (Finistère, France) respectively. Unfortunately it has not been possible to obtain counts from mitotic divisions so that further interpretation of these new data is not possible. Finally, Magne (1959) has produced some evidence to suggest that apomeiosis may well occur in the tetrasporangia of *Rhodymenia palmata*. Tetrasporangia are the only known form of reproduction in this species and Magne obtained counts of 14 chromosomes in all cells of the thallus and observed 14 bivalents in the sporangia, the nuclei of which appear to undergo normal meiosis. A full explanation of this data is still not possible and it should be remembered that in the same species Austin (1956) reported the occurrence of 21 chromosomes. In conclusion, therefore, although there is some suggestive of apomeiosis, no absolute proof of its occurrence has been obtained. Furthermore, in view of the many unsolved taxonomic problems and the increasing number of instances where one 'species' in which only sexual reproduction had been reported is shown to be part of the same life-history as another species, often from a different genus or even family, in which only tetrasporangia has been reported, arguments that the presence of tetrasporangia as the only known form of reproduction *must* be proof of apomeiosis should be treated with extreme caution.

There are, in addition to the sporangial types which have been considered, others such as monosporangia and seirosporangia for which little or no cytological data are available. Monosporangia occur in various Florideophyceae, being particularly frequent in genera of the *Rhodochorton*/*Acrochaetium* complex. Here the uninucleate sporangium liberates a spore which in at least two instances, according to unpublished observations by Feldmann (cited by Magne) and Cleland, repeats the phase on which it is borne. The monosporangia of *Corynospora* (= *Monospora*) are mutlinucleate structures which appear to be formed by the direct modification of the apical cell of a two-celled branchlet. This situation led Schiller (1913) to conclude that the arrangement of monosporangium and stalk cell represented a modified bisporangium. This interpretation would seem improbable, as has been indicated by Feldmann-Mazoyer (1941), because the terminal cell is released as a whole, a situation rare in the Florideophyceae, where an empty sporangial wall normally remains after the spore is shed. Multinucleate monosporangia have also been recorded in *Nitophyllum* by Svedelius (1941b) but even less is known of these structures, whilst the monosporangia of *Falkenbergia* described by Thomas (1955) are probably nothing more than cells infected with *Olpidiopsis feldmannii* (Dixon 1963a). Seirosporangia, which occur in the genus *Seirospora* and *Dohrniella neapolitana*, may well represent chains of monosporangia. They have been reported by Chemin (1937) as occurring on the same plant as bisporangia and tetrasporangia in *S. seirosperma* (= *S. griffithsiana*) whilst Feldmann-Mazoyer (1941) reports their occurrence on sexual plants with Funk (1927) recording the presence of seirosporangia on the same plant as aborted procarps in an unidentified species. The general impression is that both monosporangia and seirosporangia are organs of vegetative reproduction. Although very probable, this conclusion may require modification once adequate cultural and cytological data are available.

In the Bangiophyceae the situation with regard to cytological observations and the interpretation of life-histories is even more confused than in the Florideophyceae. Drew (1956) in her review of reproduction in this group rightly commented on the scanty data available and made some order out of prevailing chaos by providing a basis for the classification of the spore types in the Bangiophyceae, although more recent studies have shown that some of her conclusions must be revised (see Dixon 1963b).

Despite innumerable investigations of *Porphyra* and *Bangia*, there is still no adequate cytological explanation of their life-histories. Dangeard (1927) and Tseng and Chang (1954, 1955) both consider that meiosis occurs prior to the formation of the carpospores, although the evidence presented, particularly by the former, is not very convincing. Conversely, Magne (1952) has claimed that in *Porphyra linearis* the divisions in the carpospore mother cells are exclusively mitotic. These investigators all believe that somatic and nuclear fusion precedes the formation of carpospores so that Dangeard, Tseng and Chang regard the latter as haploid whilst Magne claims that they are diploid. The position is complicated by the more recent work of Krishnamurthy (1959) who was unable to find any indication of fertilisation. Furthermore, the latter obtained the same chromosome count in the vegetative cells of the *Porphyra* plant, the spermatium-forming cells, the spore mother cells, subsequent generations during spore formation, liberated spores, germinating spores and the vegetative *Conchocelis* phase. The same sequence of somatic phases appears to occur in all species but the discrepancies between the various studies on fertilisation and cytology are such that a considerable amount of additional information will be necessary before any explanation is possible.

In the remaining members of the Bangiophyceae the site of meiosis is still not known. In *Rhodochaete*, Magne (1960b, c) showed that the 'monospore' described briefly by Thuret (in Bornet 1892) is a post-fertilisation spore and that its formation was preceded by the fusion of a hitherto unknown smaller spore-like gamete with the vegetative cell which ultimately gave rise to the monosporangium. Magne also showed that nuclear fusion follows gametic fusion and that the division by which the monosporangium is formed is mitotic. The location of meiosis is thus the outstanding problem and it would appear probable that there is an alternative phase, as yet undetected, in the life history. Sexual reproduction has also been described for *Compsopogon* (Flint 1947) and *Kyliniella* (Flint 1953) but the accounts are very unsatisfactory. In the latter, cells which 'appeared to have two or four segments' were described and these might possibly represent the site of meiosis, but the observations are so inadequate and the illustrations so poor that further detailed study is obviously necessary before any conclusions can be made.

CHROMOSOME COUNTS IN THE RHODOPHYTA

There have been no previous catalogues of chromosome numbers in the Rhodophyta as a whole. Magne (1964a) has given an almost complete list of the chromosome numbers in the Florideophyceae but there are a few omissions and the Bangiophyceae is excluded completely from his treatment.

For many years it was thought that there was considerable uniformity in the chromosome numbers in the Florideophyceae, with basic numbers of 10 and 20 in the so-called haplobiontic and diplobiontic genera respectively. Even after a sufficient number of examples was available to show that this interpretation was untenable it was retained by many authors (Fritsch 1945; Feldmann 1952; Chapman 1962). As can be seen from the present list, there is considerable range in chromosome number and often major disagreement between the results of different investigations. Some of these disagreements are undoubtedly a consequence of purely taxonomic problems; many are the result either of inadequate technique or of the difficulties involved in counting large numbers of chromosomes in relatively small nuclei. The histogram given by Dixon (1963c) shows the sort of spread which occurred in the data obtained by Drew (1939) where three ranges of count were obtained; 30 to 32 with a very prominent peak at 31, 59 to 65 with a prominent peak at 62, and 87 to 98 with no prominent peak, but with 93 as the most frequent count. One further source of error is that with numbers of this order, metaphase counting is virtually impossible and the need to obtain counts in late prophase may well have resulted in the interpretation of either prochromosomes or chromocentres as chromosomes.

The occurrence of polyploidy in the Rhodophyta has been demonstrated beyond doubt by Drew (1934, 1939, 1943) in *Plumaria elegans* and *Spermothamnion repens* (as *S. turneri*). The criticism made by Svedelius (1937) of Drew's investigation of the latter has been refuted by Fritsch (1942), whilst Barber (1947) and Feldmann (1952), although accepting the occurrence of polyploidy, offer an alternative interpretation of Drew's data. Drew (1948) replied to the comments of Barber and her interpretation is accepted in the present contribution. The occurrence on one plant of both sexual and tetrasporic reproductive organs has been reported in many of the Florideophyceae, but there has been a cytological investigation only of one other species in which this phenomenon has been recorded in addition to Drew's work on *S. repens*. Hassinger-Huizinga (1952) has claimed that in *Callithamnion corymbosum* she obtained counts of 30 chromosomes in haploid sexual plants and 60 chromosomes in diploid plants bearing only tetrasporangia, with two or four additional chromosomes in plants bearing both tetrasporangia and sexual organs. These claims must be treated with caution. Neither figures nor photographs of cytological preparations are given. Also, the details listed by Hassinger-Huizinga admittedly show a statistical difference but this is based on very few observations and the 'spread' of these is not significantly different from that found in any other example where approximately 60 chromosomes occur.

In the present list (Table 6.1), the majority of species is marine. For this reason, the sequence of orders and families is based on that of Parke and

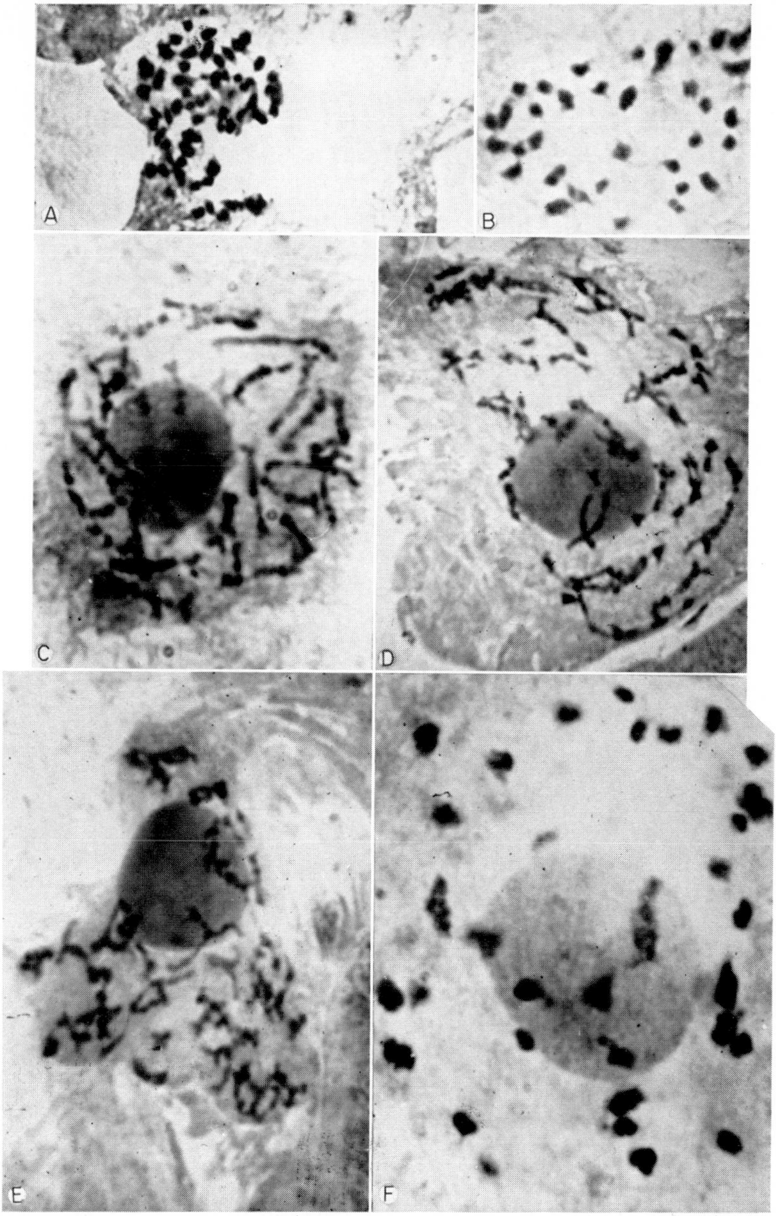

Fig. 6.1 *Furcellaria fastigiata.* **A** Late mitotic prophase in diploid ($2n = 68$) cortical cell of tetrasporophyte (x 850). **B** Late mitotic prophase in haploid ($n = 34$) cortical cell of sexual plant (x 1,600). **C** Zygotene stage of meiotic prophase in tetrasporangium (x 850). **D** Early diplotene stage in meiotic prophase in tetrasporangium (x 850). **E** Later diplotene stage (x 850). **F** Diakinesis in tetrasporangial nucleus (x 1,075)

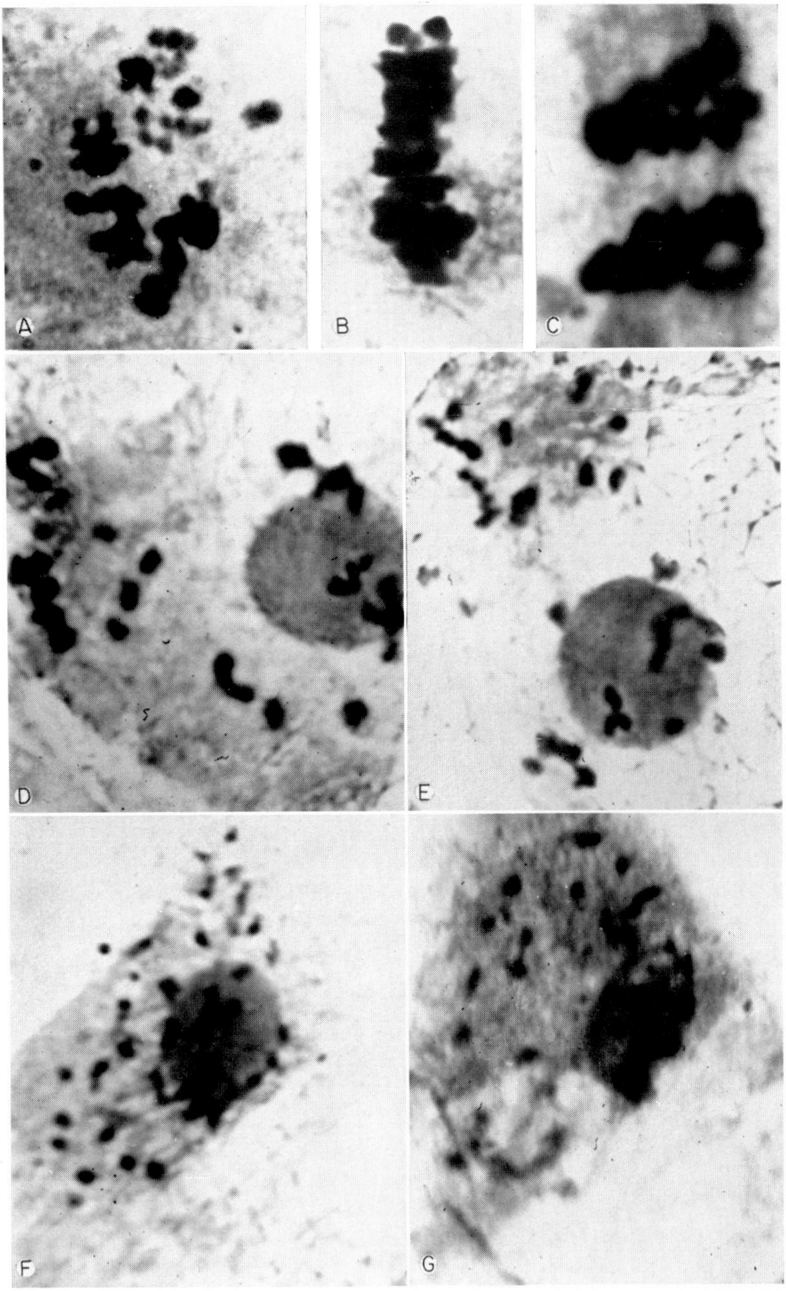

Fig. 6.2 *Furcellaria fastigiata.* **A** Early meiotic metaphase showing equatorial aggregation. **B** Early anaphase of first meiotic division showing aggregation at equator. **C** Later anaphase stage. **D** and **E** Two daughter-nuclei, formed during first meiotic division, in early prophase of the second division. **F** and **G** Re-organisation of telophase nuclei after second meiotic division. (x 1,000)

Dixon (1964), with modifications to accommodate freshwater and non-British taxa. In each family, genera and species are listed in alphabetical order. Where the original author used a name different from the correct binomial the former is given below in brackets with an equality sign to show synonymy, or cited in the form '(as . . .)' if a taxonomic misidentification in the original has been corrected. The original data show considerable variation in the degree of completeness and accuracy, so that some interpretation has been necessary. Exact counts are listed as a simple number, less precise data are cited either as a range or as a mean with standard error, depending on the manner in which the data were presented originally, whilst approximate counts are listed in the form 'c. 20', etc. In some cases, the investigation was so incomplete that counts are available only for sterile material. In these cases, it is impossible to interpret the nuclear state and the data are listed in the form '*n* or 2*n* = . . .' to avoid ambiguity.

Table 6.1 Chromosome counts in the Rhodophyta

Alga	Chromosome counts	Author
FLORIDEOPHYCEAE		
NEMALIONALES		
Acrochaetiaceae		
Rhodochorton floridulum	n or $2n$ = c. 20	Magne 1964
(= *Rhodothamniella floridula*)	$n = 10 \pm 1$; $2n = 20 \pm 2$	Knaggs 1964
Gelidiaceae		
Gelidium corneum	n = 4–5; $2n$ = 9–10	Dixon 1955
G. latifolium	n = 4–5; $2n$ = 9–10	,, ,,
G. latifolium var. *luxurians*	n or $2n$ = 25–30	Magne 1964a
Batrachospermaceae		
Batrachospermum moniliforme	n = c. 10	Kylin 1917
Batrachospermum sp.	n = c. 10	Yoshida 1959
Batrachospermum sp.	n = c. 22	Drew unpublished
Lemaneaceae		
Lemanea australis	n = 10	Mullahy 1952
L. rigida	n = 15–17; $2n$ = 31–34	Magne 1961a
Helminthocladiaceae		
Helminthora divaricata	n = 8–10	Kylin 1928
Nemalion helminthoides	n = 8; $2n$ = 16	Magne 1961b
N. multifidum	n = 8; $2n$ = 16	Wolfe 1904
	n = 8	Cleland 1919
	n = 10	Kylin 1916a

Table 6.1 (*cont.*)

Alga	Chromosome counts	Author
Chaetangiaceae		
Chaetangium erinaceum (= *C. saccatum*)	n = 8–10	Martin 1939
Galaxaura corymbifera	n = 9–10; $2n$ = 20	Svedelius 1942
G. diesingiana	n = 10–12; $2n$ = c. 17	„ „
G. tenera	n = c. 10; $2n$ = 16–19	„ „
Pseudogloiophloea capensis	n = > 12, c. 15–20	Svedelius 1956
Scinaia furcellata	n = c. 10	Svedelius 1915
	n = 7–9; $2n$ = 15–17	Magne 1961a
Bonnemaisoniaceae		
Asparagopsis armata	n = 10	Svedelius 1927, 1933
	n = c. 20; $2n$ = 30	Magne 1964a
Bonnemaisonia asparagoides	n = c. 20	Kylin 1916b
	n = c. 18	Svedelius 1933
	n = 18; $2n$ = 35–36	Magne 1960a
B. hamifera	n = 20–25; $2n$ = > 40	Magne 1964a
GIGARTINALES		
Furcellariaceae		
Furcellaria fastigiata	n = c. 16	Grubb 1925
	n = 34; $2n$ = 68	Austin 1955, 1957, 1960a, b
	n = c. 30	Magne 1964a
Rhodophyllidaceae		
Calliblepharis jubata (= *C. lanceolata*)	n or $2n$ = 35–40	„ „
Cystoclonium purpureum	n = c. 20	Kylin 1923
(= *C. purpurascens*)	$2n$ = 50	Austin 1956
Rhodophyllis divaricata (= *R. bifida*)	n = c. 20	Kylin 1923
Gracilariaceae		
Gracilaria foliifera (= *G. multipartita*)	n = 6–7	Greig-Smith 1955
G. verrucosa	n = 32	Magne 1964a
Phyllophoraceae		
Ahnfeltia plicata	n = 4; $2n$ = 8	Gregory 1930 [see note 1]
	n = 4	Rosenvinge 1931a, b
Gymnogongrus griffithsiae	n = 4; $2n$ = 8	Gregory 1930 [see note 1]
G. linearis	n = 6	Doubt 1935
G. platyphyllus	n = 8	„ „
Phyllophora brodiaei	n = 4; $2n$ = 8	Claussen 1929
Gigartinaceae		
Chondrus crispus	n = 30	Magne 1964a
Gigartina pistillata	n or $2n$ = 32	„ „
G. stellata	n or $2n$ = 15–20	Drew (*in* Marshall, Newton & Orr 1949)

Table 6.1 (*cont.*)

Alga	Chromosome counts	Author
CRYPTONEMIALES		
Squamariaceae		
Peyssonelia squamaria	n or $2n$ = 40–46	Magne 1964a
Corallinaceae		
Amphiroa abarrans	n = 24; $2n$ = 48	Segawa 1941
Corallina officinalis	n = 24	Suneson 1937
	$2n$ = 48	Magne 1964a
C. mediterranea (= *C. officinalis* var. *mediterranea*)	n = 24; $2n$ = 48	Yamanouchi 1913, 1921
Jania rubens	n = 24	Suneson 1937
Lithophyllum corallinae	n = 16; $2n$ = 32	Suneson 1950
L. litorale	$2n$ = c. 30	,, ,,
Mastophora lamourouxii	n = 24	Suneson 1945
Melobesia farinosa	n = 24; $2n$ = 48	Balakrishnan 1947
Dumontiaceae		
Dilsea carnosa	n = 26; $2n$ = c. 50	Magne 1964a
Dumontia incrassata	n = ?7	Dunn 1917
(= *D. filiformis*)	n or $2n$ = 22–24	Magne 1964a
Polyideaceae		
Polyides rotundus	n = c. 20	Kylin 1923
(= *P. caprinus*)	n = 68–72	Rao 1956
RHODYMENIALES		
Champiaceae		
Chylocladia verticillata (= *C. kaliformis*)	n = c. 20	Kylin 1923
Lomentaria articulata	n = 10	Magne 1964a
L. clavellosa	n = 10	Svedelius 1937
	n = 22–23	Magne 1964a
L. orcadensis	n = c. 20	Svedelius 1935, 1937
(= *L. rosea*)	n or $2n$ = 10, 20	Magne 1964a
Rhodymeniaceae		
Rhodymenia palmata	n = > 20	Westbrook 1928
	n = 21	Austin 1956
	n or $2n$ = 14	Magne 1959
R. palmata f. *mollis*	n or $2n$ = c. 14	Sparling 1961
CERAMIALES		
Ceramiaceae		
Antithamnion plumula	n = 23, $2n$ = 46	Magne 1964a
A. spirographidis	n = 32–34	Rao 1960
Callithamnion arbuscula (as *C. purpurascens*)	n = 28–33	Harris 1962
C. brodiaei	n = 28–33	,, ,,
C. byssoides	n = 28–33	,, ,,
C. corymbosum	n = 30; $2n$ = 60	Hassinger-Huizinga 1952
	n = 28–33	Harris 1962

Table 6.1 (*cont.*)

Alga	Chromosome counts	Author
C. hookeri	$n = 28–33$	Harris 1962
C. roseum	$n = 39$	" "
C. tetragonum (= *C. brachiatum*)	$n = 9–10$; $2n = 18–20$	Mathias 1927, 1928 [see note 2]
	$n = 28–33$	Harris 1962
C. tetricum	$n =$ c. 25; 2n = c. 50	Westbrook 1930
	?$n = 90–100$	Harris 1962
Ceramium deslongchampsii	$2n = 40$	Dammann 1930 [see note 3]
C. ruhrum	$n = 6–8$	Grubb 1925
	$n =$?8	Petersen 1928 [see note 4]
	$n = 34$	Austin 1956
	$2n =$ c. 64	Magne 1964a
Griffithsia corallinoides	$n = 20$; $2n = 40$	Kylin 1916c
(= *G. corallina*)	$n = > 10$, c. 13–14	Grubb 1925
G. globulifera (= *G. bornetiana*)	$n = 7$; $2n = 11–14$	Lewis 1909
Halurus equisetifolius	$n =$ c. 10	Grubb 1925
Plumaria elegans	$n = 31$; $2n = 62$	Drew 1939 [see note 5]
Spermothamnion repens (= *S. turneri*)	$n = 30$; $2n = 60$	Drew 1934, 1943 [see note 6]
S. snyderi	$n = 32$; $2n = 64$	Drew 1937
Wrangelia penicillata	$n = 28$	Magne 1964a
Delesseriaceae		
Apoglossum ruscifolium	$n =$ c. 20	Kylin 1923
Cryptopleura ramosa	$n =$ c. 8	Grubb 1925
(= *Nitophyllum laceratum*)	$n = 30$	Austin 1956
Delesseria sanguinea	$n = 20$; $2n = 40$	Svedelius 1911, 1914c
	$n = 31$	Austin 1956
	$n = 31$	Magne 1964a
Membranoptera alata	$n = 32$	Austin 1956
Nitophyllum punctatum	$2n = 40$	Svedelius 1914a, b
Phycodrys rubens (= *P. sinuosa*)	$n = 20$	Kylin 1923
Dasyaceae		
Dasya hutchinsiae (= *D. arbuscula*)	$2n =$ c. 40	Westbrook 1935
D. pedicellata (= *D. elegans*)	$n =$ c. 20; $2n =$ c. 40	Rosenberg 1933
Heterosiphonia plumosa	n or $2n = 44$	Magne 1964a
Rhodomelaceae		
Chondria crassicaulis	$n = 20$; $2n = 40$	Yabu & Kawamura 1959
C. dasyphylla	$n =$ c. 25; $2n =$ c. 50	Westbrook 1928, 1935

Table 6.1 (*cont.*)

Alga	Chromosome counts	Author
C. tenuissima	n = c. 25; $2n$ = c. 50	Westbrook 1935
Laurencia hybrida	n = c. 20; $2n$ = c. 40	,, ,,
L. obtusa var. *majuscula*	n = 20; $2n$ = 40	Yabu & Kawamura 1959
L. papillosa	n = 20; $2n$ = 40	,, ,,
L. pinnatifida	n = c. 20	Kylin 1923
	n = 15–16, ?c. 20	Grubb 1925
	n = c. 20; $2n$ = c. 40	Westbrook 1928, 1935
	n = 29; $2n$ = 58	Austin 1956
	n = 29	Magne 1964a
Polysiphonia brodiaei	n = 29–31	Magne 1964a
P. elongata	n = 37	Austin 1956
P. flexicaulis (*as P. violacea*)	n = 20; $2n$ = 40	Yamanouchi 1906a, b
P. japonica	n = 20; $2n$ = 40	Yabu & Kawamura 1959
P. lanosa	n = 27	Austin 1956
P. nigrescens	n = c. 20; $2n$ = c. 40	Kylin 1923
	n = 30; $2n$ = 60	Austin 1956
P. platycarpa	n = c. 26	Iyengar & Balakrishnan 1950
Rhodomela confervoides	n = c. 20	Westbrook 1935
(= *R. subfusca*)	n = 32	Austin 1956
	n = 32	Magne 1964a
R. virgata	n = 20; $2n$ = 40	Kylin 1914
BANGIOPHYCEAE		
BANGIALES		
Bangiaceae		
Bangia fuscopurpurea	n = 3	Dangeard 1927
Porphyra linearis	n = 2	,, ,,
(= *P. umbilicalis* f. *linearis*)	n = 4; $2n$ = 8	Magne 1952
P. onoi	n = 3	Yabu & Tokida 1963
P. purpurea (= *P. umbilicalis* var. *laciniata*)	n = 5	Krishnamurthy 1959
P. tenera	n = 3	Ishikawa 1921
	n = 5, $2n$ = 10	Tseng & Chang 1954, 1955
	n = 4; $2n$ = 8	Fujiyama *et al.* (cited by Yabu & Tokida 1963)
P. yezoensis	n = 3; $2n$ = 6	Yabu & Tokida 1963

Table 6.1 (*cont.*)

Alga	Chromosome counts	Author
Porphyra sp.	$n = 3$	Fujiyama *et al.* (cited by Yabu & Tokida 1963)
Boldiaceae		
Boldia erythrosiphon	$n = 8 \pm 1$	Nichols 1964a
COMPSOPOGONALES		
Compsopogonaceae		
Compsopogon coeruleus	$n = 7 \pm 1$	Nichols 1964b
RHODOCHAETALES		
Rhodochaetaceae		
Rhodochaete parvula	$n = 4$; $2n = 8$	Magne 1960a, b

Notes

1 These data must be regarded with suspicion. The chromosome counts presented by Gregory (1930) in the initial brief summary of results are not even mentioned by her in the later, more detailed, treatment (Gregory 1934).

2 Westbrook (1930) has shown that Mathias (1928), in this study, incorrectly identified the nucleolus as the nucleus. Following further work by Mathias (1931) this argument is presented again, in more detail (Westbrook 1935).

3 Westbrook (1935) has argued that Dammann (1935) misinterpreted nucleolar fragments as diakinetic phenomena.

4 Both Westbrook (1930) and Magne (1964a) suggest that Petersen (1928) interpreted nucleolar fragments as chromosomes.

5 Drew (1939) also obtained counts of 87–98 chromosomes in plants bearing parasporangia which she interpreted as triploid plants ($3n = 93$).

6 Drew (1934, 1943) obtained also counts of 45–50, 90 and 120 chromosomes, which she interpreted as representing $3n/2$, $3n$ and $4n$ respectively. Both Barber (1947) and Feldmann (1952) offer the alternative interpretation of $n = 15$, $2n = 30$, $3n = 45$, $4n = 60$, $6n = 90$, and $8n = 120$.

ACKNOWLEDGEMENTS

I am greatly indebted to Dr. Francis Magne for many arguments and discussions, over the years, on cytological problems in the red algae and for making available a proof copy of his thesis in advance of publication. I would also like to thank Dr. A. Austin for permission to use, and for supplying, the photographs used in this contribution.

REFERENCES

AUSTIN, A. P. (1955). Meiosis in *Furcellaria fastigiata* (L.) Lamour. *Nature, Lond.*, **175**, 905.

— (1956). Chromosome counts in the Rhodophyceae. *Nature, Lond.*, **178**, 370–371.

— (1957). Studies in the autecology and cytology of *Furcellaria fastigiata* (L.) Lamour. *Brit. phycol. Bull.*, **1** (5), 16–17.

— (1959). Iron-alum aceto-carmine staining for chromosomes and other anatomical features of Rhodophyceae. *Stain Tech.*, **34**, 69–75.

— (1960a). Life history and reproduction of *Furcellaria fastigiata* (L.) Lam. 1. The haploid plants and the development of the carposporophyte. *Ann. Bot., Lond.*, N.S., **24**, 257–274.

— (1960b). Life history and reproduction of *Furcellaria fastigiata* (L.) Lam. 2. The tetrasporophyte and reduction division in the tetrasporangium. *Ann. Bot., Lond.*, N.S., **24**, 296–310.

BALAKRISHNAN, M. S. (1946). The morphology and cytology of *Melobesia farinosa* Lamour. *J. Indian bot. Soc.* [Iyengar Comm. Vol.), 305–319.

BARBER, H. N. (1947). Genetics and algal life cycles. *Aust. J. Sci.*, **9**, 217–218.

BAUCH, R. (1937). Die Entwicklung der Bisporen der Corallinaceen. *Planta*, **26**, 365–391.

BORNET, E. (1892). Les algues de P.-K.-A. Schousboe récoltées au Maroc et dans la Méditerranée de 1815 à 1829. *Mém. Soc. nat. Sci. Cherbourg*, **28**, 165–376.

CELAN, M. (1941). Recherches cytologiques sur les algues rouges. *Rev. Cytol., Paris*, **5**, 1–168.

CHAPMAN, V. J. (1962). *The algae*, pp. viii + 472, Cambridge University Press, London.

CHEMIN, E. (1937). Le développement des spores chez les Rhodophycées. *Rev. gén. Bot.*, **49**, 205–234, 300–327, 353–374, 424–448, 478–536.

CLAUSSEN, H. (1929). Zur Entwicklungsgeschichte von *Phyllophora brodiaei*. *Ber. dtsch. bot. Ges.*, **47**, 544–547.

CLELAND, R. E. (1919). The cytology and life-history of *Nemalion multifidum*, Ag. *Ann. Bot., Lond.*, **33**, 323–351.

COLE, K. (1963). Aceto-carmine stain in the cytogenetical investigation of some marine algae of the Pacific coast. *Proc. IX Pacif. Sci. Congress*, **4**, 313–315.

DAMMANN, H. (1930). Entwicklungsgeschichtliche und zytologische Untersuchungen an Helgoländer Meeresalgen. *Wiss. Meeresuntersuch., Abt. Helgoland*, **18** (4), 1–36.

DANGEARD, P. (1927). Recherches sur les *Bangia* et les *Porphyra*. *Botaniste*, **18**, 183–244.

DARLINGTON, C. D. (1937). *Recent advances in cytology*, 2nd edn., pp. xvi + 671, J. & A. Churchill Ltd., London.

DAVIS, B. M. (1898). Kerntheilung in der Tetrasporenmutterzelle bei *Corallina officinalis* L. var. *mediterranea*. *Ber. dtsch. bot. Ges.*, **16**, 266–272.

DIXON, P. S. (1955). Nuclear observations of two British species of *Gelidium*. *Brit. phycol. Bull.*, **1** (2), 4.

— (1959). The structure and development of the reproductive organs and carposporophyte in two British species of *Gelidium*. *Ann. Bot., Lond.*, N.S., **23**, 397–407.

— (1960). Studies on marine algae of the British Isles: the genus *Ceramium*. *J. mar. biol. Ass. U.K.*, **39**, 331–374.

DIXON P. S. (1963a). Studies on marine fungi I: The occurrence of *Olpidiopsis feldmannii* in the British Isles. *Nova Hedwigia*, **5**, 341–345.

— (1963b). The Rhodophyta: some aspects of their biology. *Oceanogr. mar. Biol. ann. Rev.*, **1**, 177–196.

— (1963c). Variation and speciation in marine Rhodophyta. In *Speciation in the sea*, Harding, J. P. and Tebble, N., pp. 199, London.

DOUBT, D. G. (1935). Notes on two species of *Gymnogongrus*. *Amer. J. Bot.*, **22**, 294–310.

DREW, K. M. (1934). Contribution to the cytology of *Spermothamnion turneri* (Mert.) Aresch. I. The diploid generation. *Ann. Bot., Lond.*, **48**, 549–573.

— (1937). *Spermothamnion snyderi* Farlow, a Floridean alga bearing polysporangia. *Ann. Bot., Lond.*, N.S., **1**, 463–476.

— (1939). An investigation of *Plumaria elegans* (Bonnem.) Schmitz with special reference to triploid plants bearing parasporangia. *Ann. Bot., Lond.*, N.S., **3**, 347–367.

— (1943). Contributions to the cytology of *Spermothamnion turneri* (Mert.) Aresch. II. The haploid and triploid generations. *Ann. Bot., Lond.*, N.S., **7**, 23–30.

— (1944). Nuclear and somatic phases in the Florideae. *Biol. Rev.*, **19**, 105–120.

— (1945). Use of hydrochloric acid for softening algal tissues for microtome sections. *Nature, Lond.*, **156**, 479.

— (1948). Genetics and algal life histories. *Nature, Lond.*, **161**, 223.

— (1956). Reproduction in the Bangiophycidae. *Bot. Rev.*, **22**, 553–611.

DUNN, G. A. (1917). Development of *Dumontia filiformis*. II. Development of sexual plants and general discussion of results. *Bot. Gaz.*, **63**, 425–467.

FELDMANN, J. (1952). Les cycles de reproduction des algues et leurs rapports avec la phylogénie. *Rev. cytol., Paris*, **13**, 1–49.

FELDMANN-MAZOYER, G. (1941). *Recherches sur les Céramiacées de la Méditerranée occidentale*, pp. 510, Algiers.

FLINT, L. H. (1947). Studies of freshwater red algae. *Amer. J. Bot.*, **34**, 125–131.

— (1953). *Kyliniella* in America. *Phytomorphology*, **3**, 76–80.

FRIES, L. (1963). On the cultivation of axenic red algae. *Physiologia Pl.*, **16**, 695–708.

FRITSCH, F. E. (1945). *The Structure and Reproduction of the Algae*, Vol. 2, pp. xiv + 939, University Press, Cambridge.

FUNK, G. (1927). Die Algenvegetation des Golfes von Neapel. *Pubbl. Staz. zool. Napoli*, **7** (Suppl.), 1–507.

GODWARD, M. B. E. (1948). The iron alum acetocarmine method for algae. *Nature, Lond.*, **161**, 203.

GREGORY, B. D. (1930). New light on the so-called parasitism of *Actinococcus aggregatus*, Kütz., and *Sterrocolax decipiens*, Schmitz. *Ann. Bot., Lond.*, **44**, 767–769.

— (1934). On the life-history of *Gymnogongrus griffithsiae* Mart. and *Ahnfeltia plicata* Fries. *J. Linn. Soc. (Bot.)*, **49**, 531–551.

GRIEG-SMITH, E. (1955). Cytological observations on *Gracilaria multipartita*. *Brit. phycol. Bull.*, **1** (2), 4–5.

GRUBB, V. M. (1925). The male organs of the Florideae. *J. Linn. Soc. (Bot.)*, **47**, 177–255.

HARRIS, R. E. (1962). Contribution to the taxonomy of *Callithamnion Lyngbye* emend. Naegeli. *Bot. Notiser*, **115**, 18–28.

HASSINGER-HUIZINGA, H. (1952). Generationswechsel und Geschlechtsbestimmung bei *Callithamnion corymbosum* (Sm.) Lyngb. *Arch. Protistenk.*, **98**, 91–124.

HEYDRICH, F. (1901). Die Befruchtung des Tetrasporangium von *Polysiphonia* Greville. *Ber. dtsch. bot. Ges.*, **19**, 55–71.

— (1902). Das Tetrasporangium der Florideen, ein Vorläufer der sexuellen Fortpflanzung. *Bibl. bot., Stuttgart*, **57**, 1–9.

HOLLENBERG, G. J. (1940). New marine algae from Southern California, I. *Amer. J. Bot.*, **27**, 868–877.

ISHIKAWA, M. (1921). Cytological studies on *Porphyra tenera* Kjellm. I. *Bot. Mag., Tokyo*, **35**, 206–218.

IYENGAR, M. O. P. and BALAKRISHNAN, M. S. (1950). Morphology and cytology of *Polysiphonia platycarpa* Boerg. *Proc. Indian Acad. Sci.*, ser. B, **31**, 135–161.

KNAGGS, F. W. (1964). Cytological and life-history studies in the genus *Rhodochorton*. *Brit. phycol. Bull.*, **2**, 393.

KRISHNAMURTHY, V. (1959). Cytological investigations on *Porphyra umbilicalis* (L.) Kütz. var. *laciniata* (Lightf.) J. Ag. *Ann. Bot., Lond.*, **23**, 147–176.

KYLIN, H. (1914). Studien über die Entwicklungsgeschichte von *Rhodomela virgata* Kjellm. *Svensk bot. Tidskr.*, **8**, 33–69.

— (1916a) Über die Befruchtung und Reduktionsteilung bei *Nemalion multifidum*. *Ber. dtsch. bot. Ges.*, **34**, 257–271.

— (1916b). Die Entwicklungsgeschichte und die systematische Stellung von *Bonnemaisonia asparagoides* (Woodw.) Ag. nebst einigen Worten über den Generationswechsel der Algen. *Z. Bot.*, **8**, 545–586.

— (1916c). Die Entwicklungsgeschichte von *Griffithsia corallina* (Lightf.) Ag. *Z. Bot.*, **8**, 97–123.

— (1917). Über die Entwicklungsgeschichte von *Batrachospermum moniliforme*. *Ber. dtsch. bot. Ges.*, **35**, 155–164.

— (1923). Studien über die Entwicklungsgeschichte der Florideen. *K. svenska Vetensk Akad. Handl.*, **63** (11), 1–139.

— (1928). Entwicklungsgeschichtliche Florideenstudien. *Acta Univ. lund.*, N.F., Avd. 2, **24** (4), 1–127.

— (1937). Anatomie der Rhodophyceen. In *Handbuch der Pflanzenanatomie*, LINSBAUER, K. Abt. II, **6** (2), viii + 347, Gebruder Borntraeger, Berlin.

LEWIS, I. F. (1909). The life history of *Griffithsia bornetiana*. *Ann. Bot., Lond.*, **23**, 639–690.

MAGNE, F. (1952). La structure du noyau et le cycle nucléaire chez le *Porphyra linearis* Greville. *C.R. Acad. Sci., Paris*, 234, 986–988.

— (1959). Sur le cycle nucléaire du '*Rhodymenia palmata*' (L.) J. Agardh. *Bull. Soc. phycol. Fr.*, **5**, 12–14.

— (1960a). Sur le lieu de la méiose chez le *Bonnemaisonia asparagoides* (Woodw.) C. Ag. *C.R. Acad. Sci., Paris*, **250**, 2742–2744.

— (1960b). Sur l'existence d'une reproduction sexuée chez le *Rhodochaete parvula* Thuret. *C.R. Acad. Sci., Paris*, **251**, 1554–1555.

— (1960c). Le *Rhodochaete parvula* Thuret (Bangioidée) et sa reproduction sexuée. *Cah. Biol. mar.*, **1**, 407–420.

— (1961a). Sur la caryologie de deux Rhodophycées considérées jusqu'ici comme à cycle cytologique entièrement haplophasique. *C.R. Acad. Sci., Paris*, **252**, 4023–4024.

MAGNE, F. (1961b). Sur le cycle cytologique du *Nemalion helminthoides* (Velley) Batters. *C.R. Acad. Sci., Paris,* **252**, 157–159.

— (1964a). Recherches caryologiques chez les Floridées (Rhodophycées). *Cah. Biol. mar.,* **5**, 461–671.

— (1964b). La mitose calliblépharidienne de certaines Rhodophycées. *C.R. Acad. Sci., Paris,* **259**, 3811–3812.

— (1964c). Les Rhodophycées à cycle haplophasique existent-elles? *Proc. IV Seaweed Symp.,* 112–116.

MARSHALL, S. M., NEWTON, L. and ORR, A. P. (1949). *A study of certain British seaweeds and their utilisation in the preparation of Agar,* pp. viii + 184, London.

MARTIN, M. T. (1939). The structure and reproduction of *Chaetangium saccatum* (Lamour.) J. Ag.–II. Female plants. *J. Linn. Soc. (Bot.),* **52**, 115–144.

MATHIAS, W. T. (1927). The cytology of *Callithamnion. Rep. Brit. Ass.,* **1927**, 380.

— (1928). The cytology of *Callithamnion brachiatum* Bonnem. *Publ. Hartley bot. Labs., Liverpool Univ.,* **5**, 1–27.

— (1932). The cytology of *Callithamnion brachiatum* Bonnem. *Ann. Bot., Lond.,* **46**, 185–187.

MULLAHY, J. H. (1952). The morphology and cytology of *Lemanea australis* Atk. *Bull. Torrey bot. Cl.,* **79**, 393–406; 471–484.

NICHOLS, H. W. (1964a). Developmental morphology and cytology of *Boldia erythrosiphon. Amer. J. Bot.,* **51**, 653–659.

— (1964b). Culture and developmental morphology of *Compsopogon coeruleus. Amer. J. Bot.,* **51**, 180–188.

NORRIS, R. E. (1957). Morphological studies on the Kallymeniaceae. *Univ. Calif. Publ. Bot.,* **28**, 251–334.

OLTMANNS, F. (1922). *Morphologie und Biologie der Algen,* Ed. 2, Bd. **2**, pp. iv + 439, Jena.

PAPENFUSS, G. F. (1937). The structure and reproduction of *Claudea multifida, Vanvoorstia spectabilis* and *Vanvoorstia coccinea. Symb. bot. upsaliens.,* **2** (4), 1–66.

— (1946). Structure and reproduction of *Trichogloea requienii,* with a comparison of the genera of the Helminthocladiaceae. *Bull. Torrey bot. Cl.,* **73**, 419–437.

PARKE, M. and DIXON, P. S. (1964). A revised check-list of British marine algae. *J. mar. biol. Ass. U.K.,* **44**, 499–542.

PETERSEN, H. E. (1928). Nogle Iagttagelser over Cellekernerne hos *Ceramium* (Roth.) Lyngbye. *Dansk bot. Ark.,* **5** (10), 1–5.

PROVASOLI, L., MCLAUGHLAN, J. J. A. and DROOP, M. R. (1957). The development of artificial media for marine algae. *Arch. Mikrobiol.,* **25**, 392–428.

RAO, C. S. P. (1953). Acetocarmine as a nuclear stain for Rhodophyceae. *Nature, Lond.,* **172**, 1197.

— (1956). The life-history and reproduction of *Polyides caprinus* (Gunn.) Papenf. *Ann. Bot., Lond.,* N.S., **20**, 211–230.

— (1960). Cytology of red algae. In *Proceedings of the symposium on algology,* KACHROO, P. pp. vii + 406. New Delhi.

ROSENBERG, T. (1933). *Studien über Rhodomelaceen und Dasyaceen,* pp. 87. Akad. Abhandl. Lund.

ROSENVINGE, L. K. (1924). The marine algae of Denmark. Contributions to their natural history. Part III, Rhodophyceae III (Ceramiales). *K. danske vidensk. Selsk.,* 7 *Raekke,* **7** (3), 287–487.

— (1931a). *Ibid.* Part IV, Rhodophyceae IV (Gigartinales, Rhodymeniales, Nemastomatales). *K. danske vidensk. Selsk.*, 7 *Raekke*, **7** (4), 491–630.

— (1931b). The reproduction of *Ahnfeltia plicata*. *Biol. Medd., Kbh.*, **10** (2), 1–29.

SCHILLER, J. (1913). Über Bau, Entwicklung, Keimung und Bedeutung der Parasporen der Ceramiaceen. *Öst. bot. Z.*, **63**, 144–149, 203–210.

SEGAWA, S. (1941). Systematic anatomy of the articulated Corallines (III). [Japanese, English summary]. *J. Jap. Bot.*, **17**, 164–174.

SMITH, G. M. (1955). *Cryptogamic Botany*, Vol. **1**, *Algae and Fungi*, 2nd edn., pp. x + 546. McGraw Hill, New York.

SPARLING, S. R. (1961). A report on the culture of some species of *Halosaccion, Rhodymenia* and *Fauchea*. *Amer. J. Bot.*, **48**, 493–499.

SUNESON, S. (1937). Studien über die Entwicklungsgeschichte der Corallinaceen. *Acta Univ. lund.*, N.F., Avd. 2, **33** (2), 1–102.

— (1945). On the anatomy, cytology and reproduction of *Mastophora*. With a remark on the nuclear conditions in the spermatangia of the Corallinaceae. *K. fysiogr. Sällsk. Lund Förh.*, **15** (26), 1–14.

— (1950). The cytology of the bispore formation in two species of *Lithophyllum* and the significance of the bispores in the Corallinaceae. *Bot. Notiser*, **1950**, 429–450.

SVEDELIUS, N. (1908). Über den Bau und die Entwicklung der Florideengattung *Martensia*. *K. svenska Vetensk Akad. Handl.*, **43** (7), 1–101.

— (1911). Über den Generationswechsel bei *Delesseria sanguinea*. *Svensk bot. Tidskr.*, **5**, 260–324.

— (1914a). Über die Tetradenteilung in den vielkernigen Tetrasporangiumanlagen bei *Nitophyllum punctatum*. *Ber. dtsch. bot. Ges.*, **32**, 48–57.

— (1914b). Über Sporen an Geschlechtspflanzen von *Nitophyllum punctatum*; ein Beitrag zur Frage des Generationswechsel der Florideen. *Ber. dtsch. bot. Ges.*, **32**, 106–116.

— (1914c). Über die Zystokarpienbildung bei *Delesseria sanguinea*. *Svensk bot. Tidskr.*, **8**, 1–32.

— (1915). Zytologisch-entwicklungsgeschichtliche Studien über *Scinaia furcellata*. Ein Beitrag zur Frage der Reduktionsteilung der nicht Tetrasporenbildenen Florideen. *Nova Acta Soc. Sci. upsal.*, ser. IV, **4** (4), 1–55.

— (1927). The cytology and development of *Asparagopsis armata*. *Rep. Brit. Ass.*, **1927**, 380–381.

— (1933). On the development of *Asparagopsis armata* Harv. and *Bonnemaisonia asparagoides* (Woodw.) Ag. A contribution to the cytology of the haplobiontic Rhodophyceae. *Nova Acta Soc. Sci. upsal.*, ser. IV, **9** (1), 1–61.

— (1935). *Lomentaria rosea*, eine Floridee ohne Generationswechsel, nur mit Tetrasporenbildung ohne Reduktionsteilung. *Ber. dtsch. bot. Ges.*, **53**, 19–26.

— (1937). The apomeiotic tetrad division in *Lomentaria rosea* in comparison with the normal development in *Lomentaria clavellosa*. A new type of life-cycle among the Rhodophyceae. *Symb. bot. upsaliens.*, **2** (2), 1–54.

— (1942). Zytologisch-entwicklungsgeschichtliche Studien über *Galaxaura* eine diplobiontische Nemalionales-Gattung. *Nova Acta Soc. Sci. upsal.*, ser. IV, **13** (4), 1–154.

— (1956). Are the haplobiontic Florideae to be considered reduced types? *Svensk bot. Tidskr.*, **50**, 1–24.

THOMAS, L. (1955). Observaciones sobre la ecologiá de las formas *Asparagopsis armata—Falkenbergia rufolanosa* y un neuvo órgano de reproducción. *Coll. Bot., Barcinone*, **4**, 399–407.

TSENG, C. K. and CHANG, T. J. (1954). On the origin of spores in the artificial cultivation of *Porphyra* [Chinese]. *Sci. Bull.*, **12**, 50–52.

— (1955). Studies on the life history of *Porphyra tenera* Kjellm. *Sci. sinica*, **4**, 375–398.

WESTBROOK, M. A. (1928). Contributions to the cytology of tetrasporic plants of *Rhodymenia palmata* (L.) Grev., and some other Florideae. *Ann. Bot., Lond.*, **42**, 149–172.

— (1930). The structure of the nucleus in *Callithamnion* spp. *Ann. Bot., Lond.*, **44**, 1012–1015.

— (1935). Observations on nuclear structure in the Florideae. *Beih. bot. Zbl.*, A, **53**, 564–585.

WOLFE, J. J. (1904). Cytological studies on *Nemalion*. *Ann. Bot., Lond.*, **18**, 607–630.

YABU, H. and KAWAMURE, K. (1959). Cytological study of some Japanese species of Rhodomelaceae. *Mem. Fac. Fish., Hokkaido Univ.*, **7**, 61–72.

YABU, H. and TOKIDA, J. (1963). Mitosis in *Porphyra*. *Bul. Fac. Fish., Hokkaido Univ.*, **14**, 131–136.

YAMANOUCHI, S. (1906a). The life history of *Polysiphonia violacea*. *Bot. Gaz.*, **41**, 425–433.

— (1906b). The life history of *Polysiphonia violacea*. *Bot. Gaz.*, **42**, 401–449.

— (1913). Life history of *Corallina officinalis* var. *mediterranea* [Japanese]. *Bot. Mag., Tokyo*, **27**, 279–285.

— (1921). Life history of *Corallina officinalis* var. *mediterranea*. *Bot. Gaz.*, **72**, 90–96.

YOSHIDA, T. (1959). Life-cycle of a species of *Batrachospermum* found in northern Kyushu, Japan. *Jap. J. Bot.*, **17**, 29–42.

Index